IMAGES
*of America*

# LIGONIER

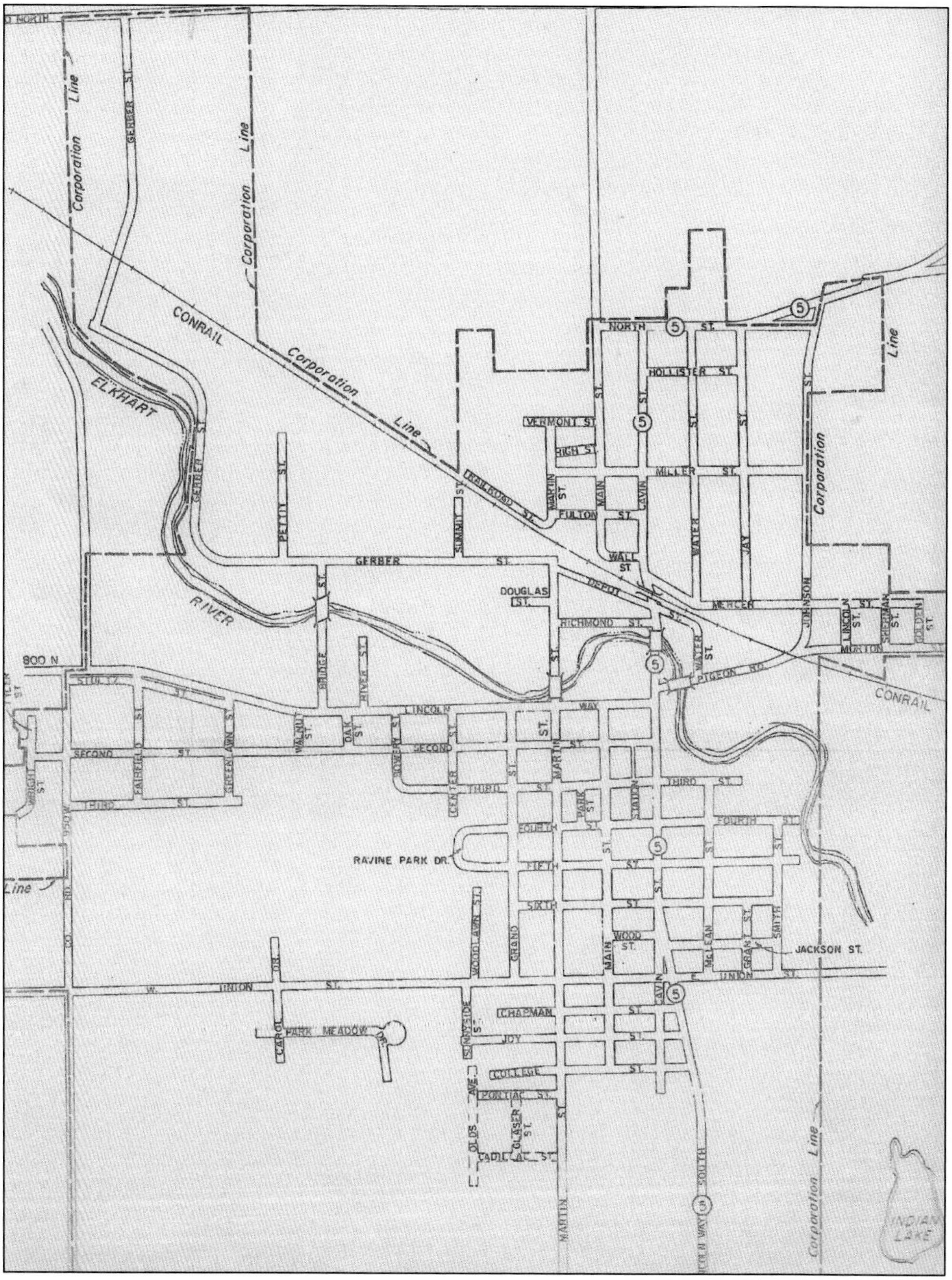


Pictured is a map of Ligonier, Indiana. (Courtesy of the Ligonier Historical Museum.)

**On the Cover:** The Ligonier Military Band is pictured. Begun as the Ligonier Cornet Band in 1875, it became the Ligonier Military Band in 1887, at its peak. During that year, it won three competitions and over $4,100 in prizes. The group disbanded around 1900. The last surviving band member died in 1946. (Courtesy of the Ligonier Historical Museum.)

IMAGES
*of America*

# LIGONIER

Daniel L. Replogle

ARCADIA
PUBLISHING

ISBN 978-1-4671-1692-3

Published by Arcadia Publishing
Charleston, South Carolina

Printed in the United States of America

Library of Congress Control Number: 2015960064

For all general information, please contact Arcadia Publishing:
Telephone 843-853-2070
Fax 843-853-0044
E-mail sales@arcadiapublishing.com
For customer service and orders:
Toll-Free 1-888-313-2665

Visit us on the Internet at www.arcadiapublishing.com

*This book is dedicated to my wife, Jean Ann Replogle,*
*and her tolerance of me needing time to compile it.*

# Contents

# Acknowledgments

I was assisted by the following friends, whom I acknowledge here: Members of the Ligonier Historical Society who assisted me were Ruth Hite; Cyndi Schlemmer; Jeana Leamon; Earle Franklin; Everett Newman; Anne Ringler; Floyd Warren, DVM; and Helen Wolfe. Wendy Soltz has assisted the organization of the museum contents. Other persons who contributed to this book's formation were Jerry Blanchard, Chris Fought, Sharon McNair, Amanda Smith, Steven Venuti, David Tranter, Marilyn Goldman, Rosemary Dickinson West, Susan Dickinson Tomblinson, and Tim Ringler. My wife, Jean Replogle, assisted with the photography in Ligonier. Terry Lewis, photographer and RAW to TIFF converter, gave hours to the project. Mark Biggerstaff and Mayor Patty Fisel allowed the scanning of their historical collections. Dot Foster and Mary Gaerte also related their memories of Ligonier. The Arcadia representative who assisted in the details for this book's formation is Sarah Gottlieb. I hope I have not forgotten anyone, but I probably have. If so, recognize that I am a fallible human and forgive me, please.

Unless otherwise noted, all images are courtesy of the Ligonier Historical Museum.

# INTRODUCTION

Isaac Cavin was the founder of Ligonier, Indiana. He was a native of Pennsylvania, born on October 22, 1807.

In 1830, at age 23, he made a prospecting trip by horseback to northeastern Indiana and stayed about six weeks before returning to his home in Ligonier, Pennsylvania. About six months later, he returned by horseback to Indiana and worked as a hired man for about a year. With his earnings for this time and the money he had brought with him ($400), he purchased from the government the south half of Section 2 in Perry Township, upon which he established a home and resided for the remainder of his life. He returned by horseback to Ligonier, Pennsylvania, where he married Elizabeth Marker in March 1834. She rode a horse with him from Pennsylvania to Indiana. Today, that trip would take eight hours by car on good roads. The days and weeks of sloughing through the mud may have made Elizabeth wonder what she had gotten herself into when she married Isaac. Using some Google estimates, it was calculated that it took Isaac and Elizabeth 16 to 40 days to make their journey.

Isaac cleared his own land in 1835 and recorded the east half of the southwest quarter of Section 27 in what is now Perry Township, Noble County. He platted it as the village of Ligonier, named after his native town in Pennsylvania, which was situated on similar land in Indiana. However, Isaac never lived in the town of Ligonier. His homestead was a few miles to the north. His son, John L. Cavin, did live in Ligonier.

A city clock at the corner of Cavin and Fifth Streets, erected in 1924, was a gift from John L. Cavin (Isaac Cavin's son) and William A. Cavin (John's son and Isaac's grandson) in memory of Isaac. A photograph of this clock is shown on page 13.

Isaac Cavin died on May 3, 1884, at the age of 76 years. Elizabeth died in 1884 also. They are buried in Salem Cemetery, Perry Township.

Isaac and Elizabeth had a rough life, not unlike the lives of most of the early settlers. Half of their children died before reaching age 13: Julia A. Cavin (1837–1840), Celestia Cavin (1842–1849), and George M. Cavin (1849–1861). Their surviving children were William A. Cavin (1836–1892), Mary Cavin (1841–1879), and John L. Cavin (1849–1923).

Isaac Cavin platted a wide Main Street and intended businesses to grow here. The public square is on Main Street, as is the library. The very wealthy built homes on Main Street. But the merchants built their businesses on Cavin Street, because that was where the traffic was. The first business was Isaac Spencer's general merchandise. He was the owner for two years.

By 1840, two or three families lived in Ligonier. By 1847, Taylor Vail owned a foundry at Rochester, a small town one mile east of Ligonier. He moved the foundry to Ligonier later. The first post office opened in 1848. In 1852, a sawmill was built in Ligonier. A second was added in 1856. A third was added in 1865. A gristmill was built in 1858. Another mill was built by Albert Banta and A.C. Fisher, and others followed. In 1860, over 31,000 bushels of wheat were shipped out of Ligonier. In 1880, five hundred thousand bushels were shipped. The Michigan Southern & Northern Indiana Railroad passed through Ligonier in 1858.

In 1837, the first school was built out of logs. In 1851, a frame building replaced the log school. This was called the Red Schoolhouse and was built on Main Street. In 1857, a white frame schoolhouse was built on the north side of Ligonier. In 1865, the Red Schoolhouse was replaced with a three-story brick schoolhouse. In 1873, the white schoolhouse was replaced by the Northside Schoolhouse. In 1877, a high school was built on Grand Street. In 1899, the Northside Schoolhouse was replaced. In 1911, wings were added to either side of the high school and other additions to the structure were made in 1928.

In 1831, ministers of the Methodist Episcopal, Presbyterian, and Baptist denominations appeared around where Ligonier would be built, but of course, they did not know that then. Meetings were held in log cabins and in barns. In 1846, the first church in Ligonier was the Methodist Episcopal church.

In 1833, Frederick William Straus was born in Laufersweiler, Prussia (now Germany). Solomon Mier was born in 1833 in Kirchberg, Prussia. It is not known if these men emigrated from Prussia separately or as a duo. They immigrated to northeast Indiana and probably resided in Auburn or Butler. Straus's uncle Isaac Stiefel, who was Jewish, taught the two how to peddle merchandise. Stiefel and Straus and Mier were all from the same Prussian region, what is now Rhein-Hunsrück-Kreis, Germany. Later, these men decided to go out on their own and peddle. Uncle Isaac suggested they try Ligonier.

Advertisements in the 1854 newspaper declared that the Lake Shore & Michigan Southern Railroad would likely go thorough Ligonier, Indiana, and a station would be established in the town. That railroad did not go through Ligonier, but another one did. This speculation probably helped attract Straus and Mier to Ligonier, a village of 300 people. By 1900, Ligonier had grown to 2,200 residents, including 55 Jewish families, more than 200 people. The Jewish community had by then established a temple with a full-time resident rabbi. It also established a Sabbath school, a cemetery society, a ladies benefit society, a B'nai B'rith lodge, and a social club, and it was a force in the Ligonier community. From 1854 to 1928, the Jewish community was an integral part of Ligonier and was influential in its growth and success.

After settling in Ligonier, F.W. Straus opened a small general store, and by 1860, he had brought his brothers, Mathias and Jacob, from Prussia. Members of the Straus family branched out into other business ventures.

They purchased their first farm in 1860. One morning, two of the Strauses rode into the country in one of their factory-made buggies with the idea of selling buggies to local farmers. A trade was made: the farm and land for some buggies. In a short time, some timber was sold. This amount of money equaled the Strauses' initial investment. After repairs were made to the dilapidated farm buildings, a profit was made from the sale of the farm. The deed for 80 acres was recorded on January 28, 1861, and they sold the farm on April 2, 1861. From this beginning, the Straus Quality Farms developed into the largest farm brokerage firm in the United States.

In 1868, the Straus Brothers General Store was sold, and the brothers founded the Citizens Bank. In less than 15 years, the Straus brothers had replaced their backpacks with a clothing and general merchandising store and emerged as successful land brokers and bankers. In 1884, Frederick W. Straus and Mathias Straus retired and moved to Chicago. Jacob Straus remained in Ligonier until 1892 and, with his sons, Simon and Isaac, and son-in-law, Abe Goldsmith, carried on and expanded the businesses already established. The firm outgrew Ligonier and Indiana. Banks were founded in Ohio, Michigan, Illinois, Minnesota, North Dakota, and southern Ontario. Jacob returned to Ligonier in 1898 and built the beautiful white house that is be described later in the book. Jacob died in 1914, Mathias died in 1890, and Frederick died in 1898.

About 1854, Solomon Mier opened a general merchandising store in the pattern of F.W. Straus. Mier's businesses were in partnership with his sons. In 1862, he opened the Banking House of Solomon Mier. This continued until 1928, when it merged with the Citizens Bank, managed by Abe Mier. The merged bank was called American State Bank. Mier's carriage factory was formed from 1908 to 1909. His runabout model sold for $600 and had a two-cylinder, water-cooled engine, plus a friction wheel transmission with a chain drive. Solomon Mier and Company became one of the largest farmland dealers in the Midwest.

Jewish relatives—cousins, nieces, aunts, and uncles—came to Ligonier under the sponsorship of Straus or Mier. Some worked for them, some started their own businesses immediately, and others remained as clerks or workers. The Jewish merchants and their specialties were Jacobs (general merchandising), Loeser (horses), Schloss (dry goods), Selig (cattle), and Wertheimer (grain, seed, and wood).

The US Census for 1850 lists no Jews in Noble County. In 1860, there were 11,600 citizens and at least 17 Jews in the county.

Farmers from more than a 30-mile radius of Ligonier brought their crops and livestock to the Jewish merchants in Ligonier, because the merchants paid more money for the crops and livestock than the farmers could realize by shipping them to Chicago or Toledo. The Jewish merchant thus attracted the farmer to his store to purchase the farmer's other needs.

In 1878, the population of Ligonier was 1,800, and about 100 stores grossed $1 million in total sales. Approximately 10 Jewish-owned stores earned one-third of this sum. Straus Brothers and Mier & Sons accounted for the major part of all Jewish sales.

The Jewish community did a lot for Ligonier. In 1876, a public elementary school and high school were established. The driving forces behind this were F.W. Straus and John B Stahl, a Presbyterian. The Jews of Ligonier especially required their children's strict attention to their duties in school, as well as household chores, and together these took much of the children's time.

Solomon Mier was the prime mover for the installation of the first sewer. In 1889, he insisted that the waterworks should be publicly owned and not be subject to private control. Joel Selig was a town trustee in 1890 and was involved when the vote was taken to incorporate Ligonier as a city. Selig was elected one of the trustees of one of the three wards in the city. Simon J. Straus was the president of the city council from 1894 until 1898.

A.B. Mier was a councilman from 1896 to 1898. Will Baum was appointed to the library board in 1907. Sol Henoch was a councilman from 1912 to 1918 and was mayor from 1918 to 1921.

The Jewish community was not without its flaws. There were nervous breakdowns, suicides, mentally and emotionally disturbed children, and frustrated and disappointed adults. There was acute competition between the Straus and Mier families. No marriages occurred between these families in the first and second generations in Ligonier.

By 1865, the need for formal worship was fulfilled when 15 families formed the Congregation Ahavath Shalom (Lovers of Peace). Bar mitzvah was required for all 13-year-old boys. The men did not wear yarmulkes but did wear hats. During the High Holidays, the older men wore tallisim. Families observed the dietary laws and followed the custom of using two sets of dishes, milchich for dairy foods and flalshig for meats.

In 1871, the complexity and increasing needs of the congregation resulted in the building of a small frame synagogue on Main Street, where services, Hebrew school, and the necessary rituals were performed. Although it was an Orthodox congregation, several reforms were introduced to better meet the needs of the congregants. Family pews were established where the entire family sat together. In 1888, a larger and more elaborate temple was built, also on Main Street. D. Eppstein was the first rabbi. The dedication of the new temple was on September 6, 1889. Its 125th anniversary was celebrated in 2014.

In the next decade, the synagogue and Orthodox Judaism changed to the temple and Reform Judaism. The Hebrew school became the Sabbath school. The English language replaced the German language in the sermon. A Gentile choir and organist were hired to perform at services. Confirmation for boys and girls replaced bar mitzvah for boys only. The years approaching and including 1900 were the zenith of the Jewish community. The Jewish children had many Gentile friends. A period of waiting was necessary to see if a Gentile bride would fit comfortably and prove herself compatible with the Jewish group. If she was not an irritant but joined in the activities and became an active member of the Jewish community, then she was eventually accepted into Jewish society.

Temple membership began to decline in the 1920s. In the next 20 years, there was a sharp decline in the Jewish population in Ligonier. Why? Most immigrant Jews settled in the larger

American cities, which held a greater attraction for them, with more opportunities to make a living. Also, children of the Ligonier Jews attained their higher education in other cities and married and settled away from Ligonier. As the older Jews died, members of their families did not want to continue in the same business in Ligonier and left for other towns.

A section was provided for the Jewish dead at the Oak Park Cemetery. The area consisted of 187 graves. Impressive mausoleums of Meyer Jacobs and Jacob Straus sit in this section. With the Jewish population declining, there was concern for the continued existence of the cemetery, but this was solved in 1912, when $15,000 was raised by the sale of plots of land and by contributions that insured perpetual care of the cemetery section.

# One

# The Most Important Thing to a Community Is Its People

The start of this book is just like the start of any community. Without the people, there is nothing on which to build a community. The people come first.

This chapter introduces readers to four groups of people who are amazing in the stories they have to share.

Isaac Cavin founded Ligonier, Indiana, which he named after his hometown of Ligonier, Pennsylvania. The author feels the hardship of just getting to Indiana should have qualified him and Elizabeth, his wife, with an honor for perseverance.

Although his wife, Mabel, is not often mentioned, she may have been the influence that Dwight Green needed to make him a success. Dwight was born and grew up in Ligonier. He had a life of wealth and ease. His parents and family were wealthy. He turned left at the fork in the road. He was very involved in putting Al Capone in jail.

The Wilkinson sisters, Rosalie and Ona, did things that were almost unheard of in their time. They founded a company that is famous with quilters, the Wilkinson Quilt Company. Women could not start up a factory and did not usually meddle in business. Women born around 1870 were mostly channeled into raising children and making men comfortable. Women did not even need a high school diploma. They could not even vote until 1920.

Perhaps compared to the stars listed above, Paul and Hannah Beverforden really did not do much. But they focused their lives on helping their fellow man. Paul was a trooper with the Indiana State Police. Hannah was a teacher in the Ligonier school system. When they died, they passed on their story to the Ligonier Historical Museum. Thus their story lives on. Others might consider their treasures just old junk.

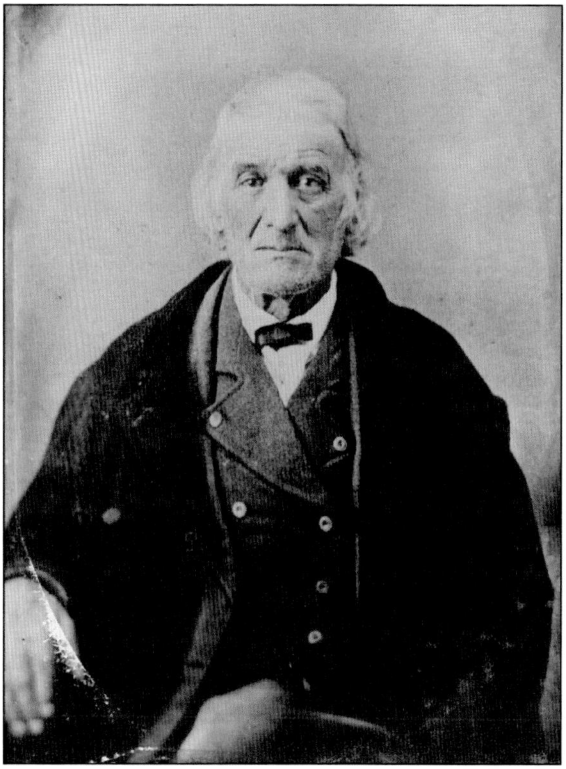

Isaac Cavin (1807–1884) founded Ligonier, Indiana, in 1835. He married Elizabeth Marker (1814–1884) in 1834 and rode with her on horseback from Ligonier, Pennsylvania, to the future site of Ligonier, Indiana. Elizabeth helped raise their six children and grieved for the 50 percent mortality rate of her children.

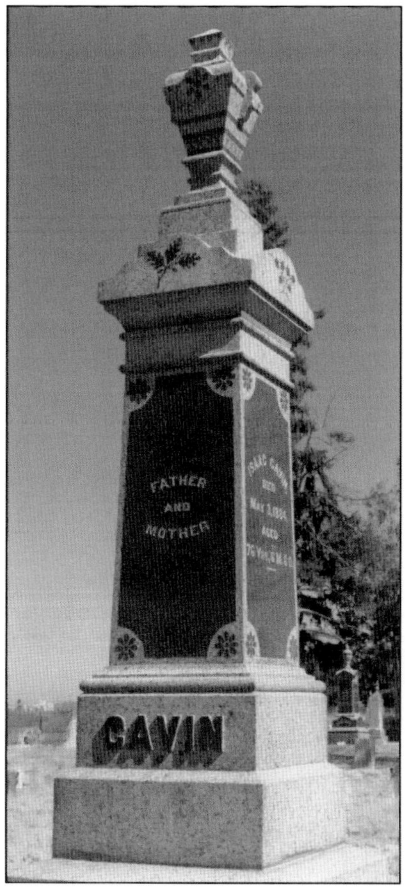


The tombstone of Isaac and Elizabeth Cavin at Salem Cemetery is about one mile north of Ligonier on State Road 5. Elizabeth died first in January 1884. Isaac followed her in May 1884.

The memorial clock for Isaac Cavin was donated to the City of Ligonier by John L. Cavin in 1924. The clock was manufactured by the Seth Thomas Clock Company in 1923. Pictured nearest the clock in 1945 are Ben Glaser (left) and Rev. Dr. David E. Culley. The clock was moved in 1968, when the bank was razed for a new building.

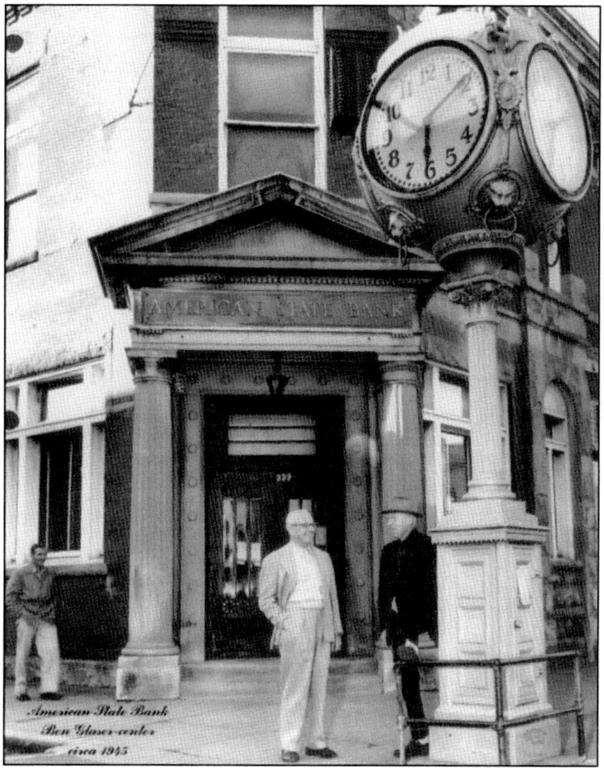


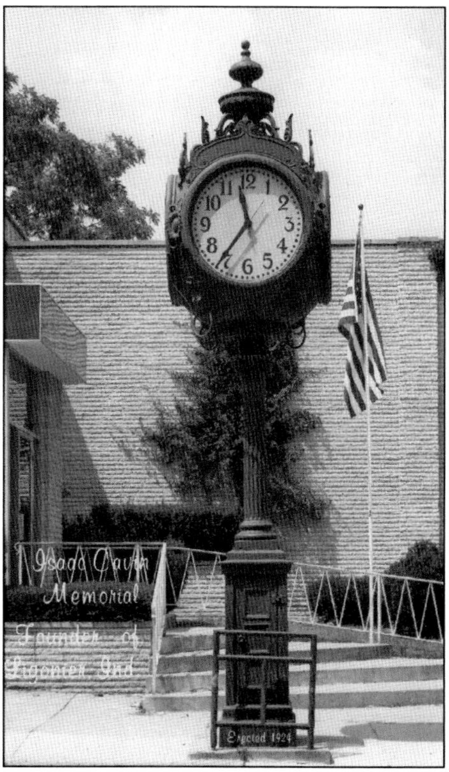


The memorial clock was moved to the Ligonier Telephone building in 1968. A semi hit the clock in 1981 and completely destroyed it. The company responsible did not have enough money to repair the clock, nor did the City of Ligonier, but a citizen donated $50,000 to have the clock repaired. In 1984, the restored and repainted memorial clock was moved to Wood Triangle Park at the south end of Cavin Street.

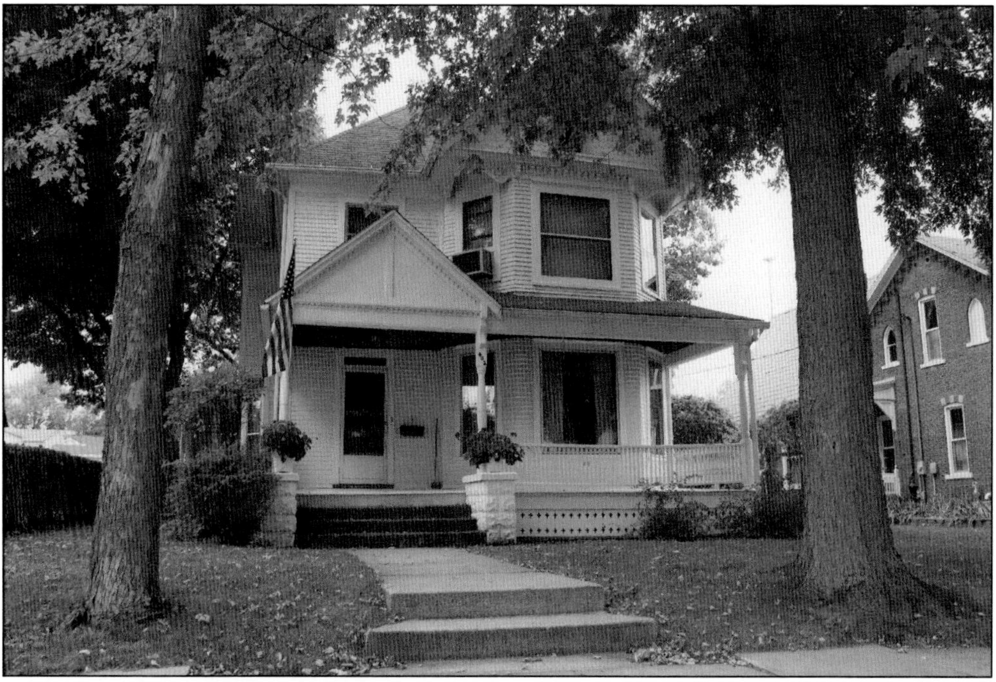

This is the home of Dwight H. Green (1897–1958), son of Harry and Minnie Gerber Green, at 402 South Main Street, almost directly west of the Ligonier Historical Museum. An application has been submitted to include the house in the National Register of Historic Places. Dwight was educated at Ligonier High School.

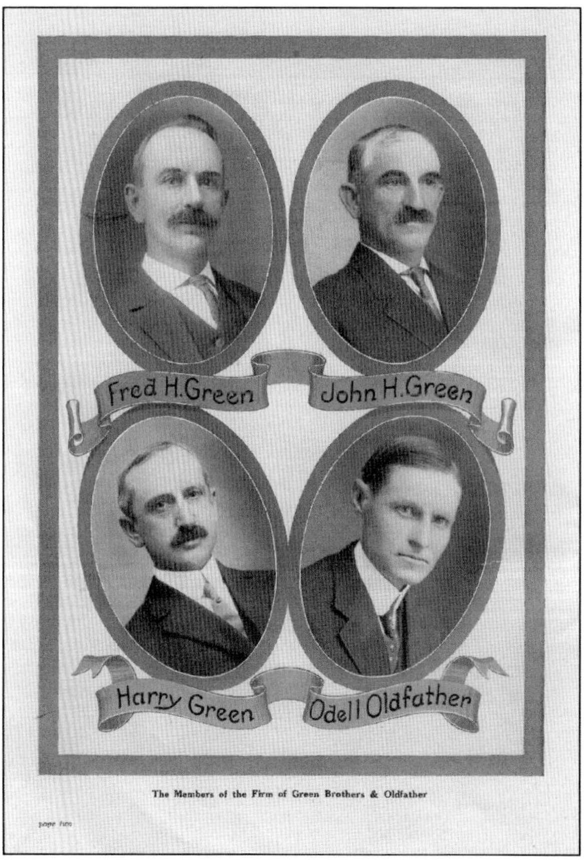


These are Dwight's uncles, Fred H. Green (1862–1924) and John H. Green (1864–1953). Fred was the president of the Merchants Bank. Dwight could have had a position in this bank if it had interested him. Instead, he attended Wabash College.

A cover of a catalog from Green Brothers & Oldfather offers farmland for sale around Ligonier. Dwight's father, Harry, worked at this business with his brothers, Fred and John.

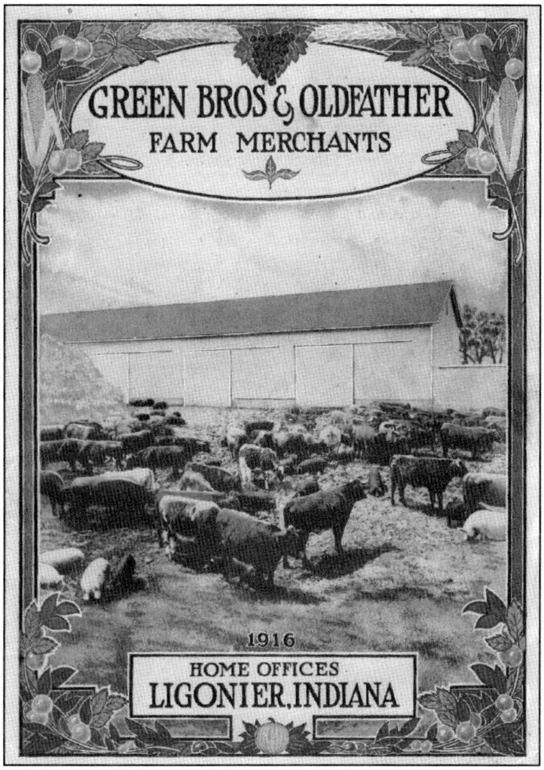


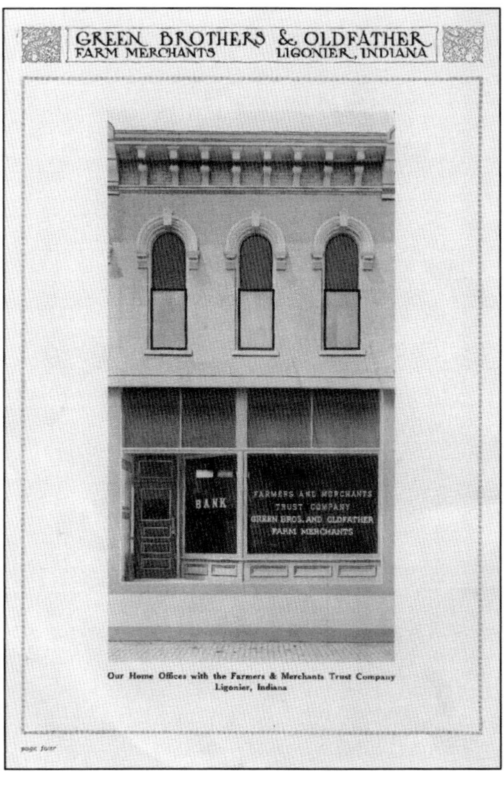


The Farmers and Merchant Trust Company bank stood at 203 South Cavin Street in Ligonier. Dwight entered World War I in the infantry. He was transferred to the Army Air Service. After four and a half hours of training, he soloed. Later, he was a trainer for other would-be pilots. Dwight graduated from Wabash College and moved to Chicago to work in the law office of Roy Keehn (also from Ligonier).

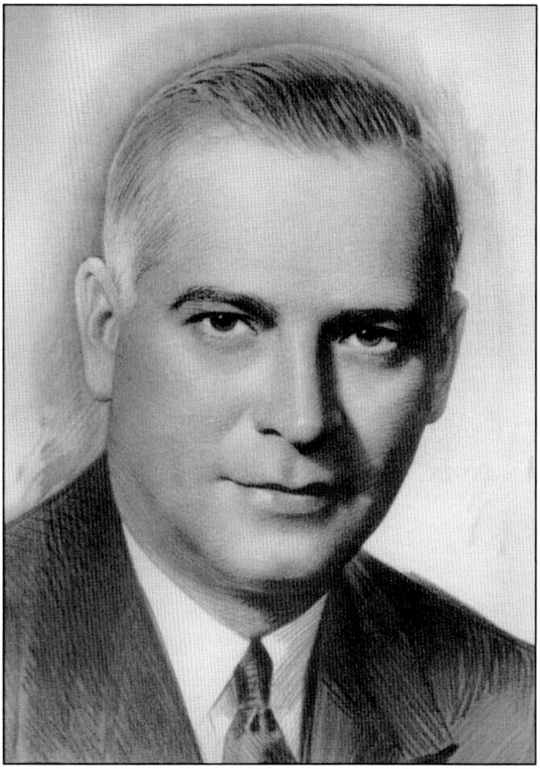

Dwight H. Green is sketched here. He attended the University of Chicago Law School and worked as a reporter for the *Chicago Examiner* before moving to Washington and joining the Bureau of Internal Revenue (later the Internal Revenue Service). He married Mabel Victoria Kingston in Washington. He returned to Chicago as an attorney for the Bureau of Internal Revenue.

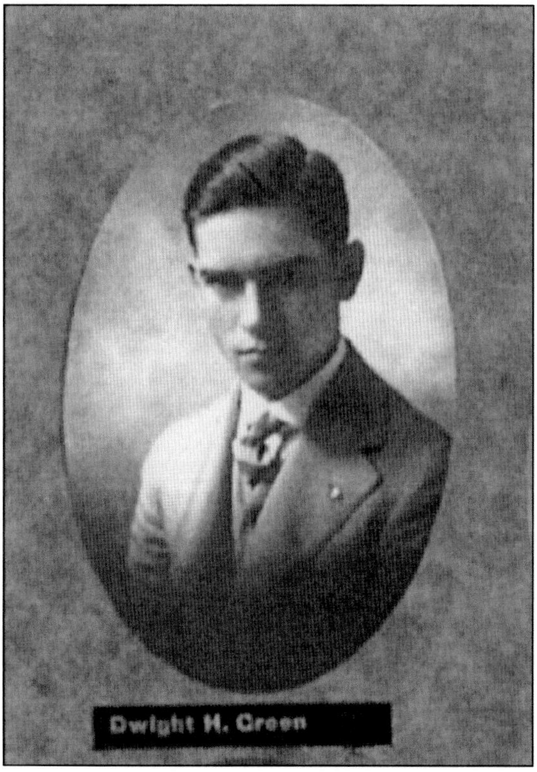


This is Dwight H. Green's Ligonier High School graduation picture. The young man shown here would grow up to become a principal player in convicting Al Capone in Chicago. Green was elected governor of Illinois in 1940 and reelected in 1944—serving two terms.

Ona Wilkinson was born in 1876 and Rosalie in 1892. In 1908, a Jewish woman approached Ona to make some quilts for her daughter's upcoming wedding. Ona was ill, so other family members helped her out with the two quilts that Ona agreed to make. When the quilts were shown at the wedding, the Jewish ladies got ideas. They wanted these beautiful quilts for their daughters. If Ona and Rosalie feared what they would do with their lives, that all was changing now. (Reprinted by permission, Marilyn K. Goldman.)

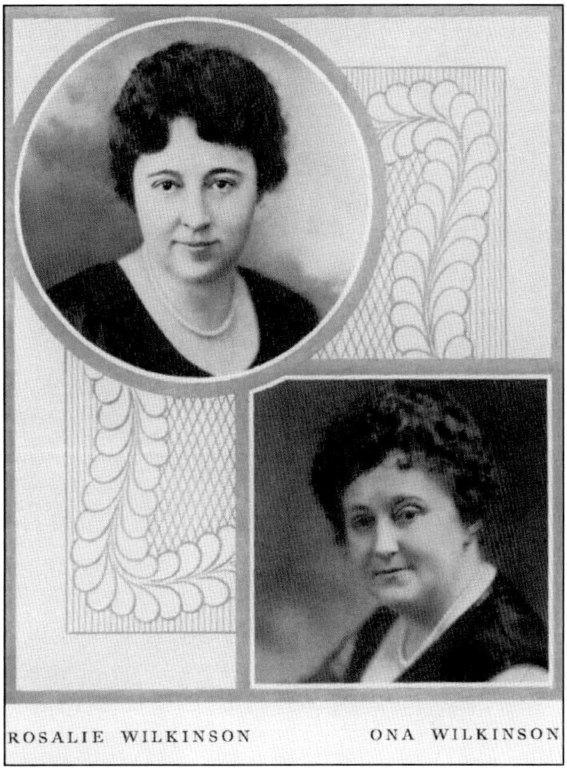


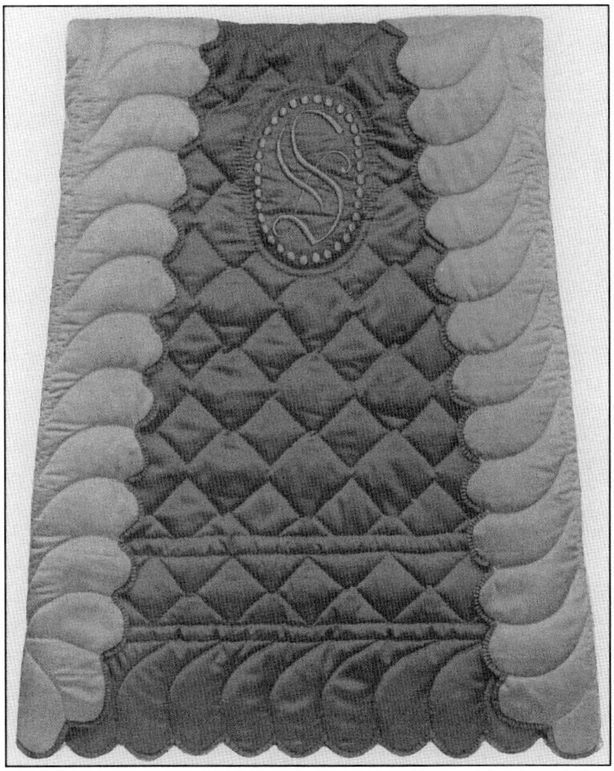

What women could do for a career in 1908 was limited by education and social mores. Women were not allowed to vote until 1920. Ona and Rosalie Wilkinson owned and ran a quilting business. This is a quilt shown in the Wilkinson Quilt Catalog. (Reprinted by permission, Marilyn K. Goldman.)

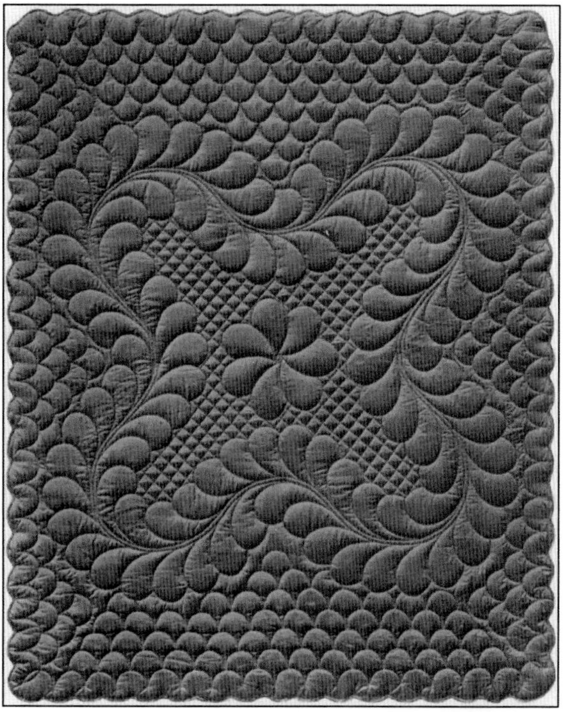

Many local Jewish people loved the quilts that Ona made. She had more orders than she could handle by herself. Her Jewish friends helped her get started in her own business with Rosalie as a partner. The Wilkinson Quilt Company was incorporated in 1914. Ads in local papers asked for help from other quilters as orders flowed in.

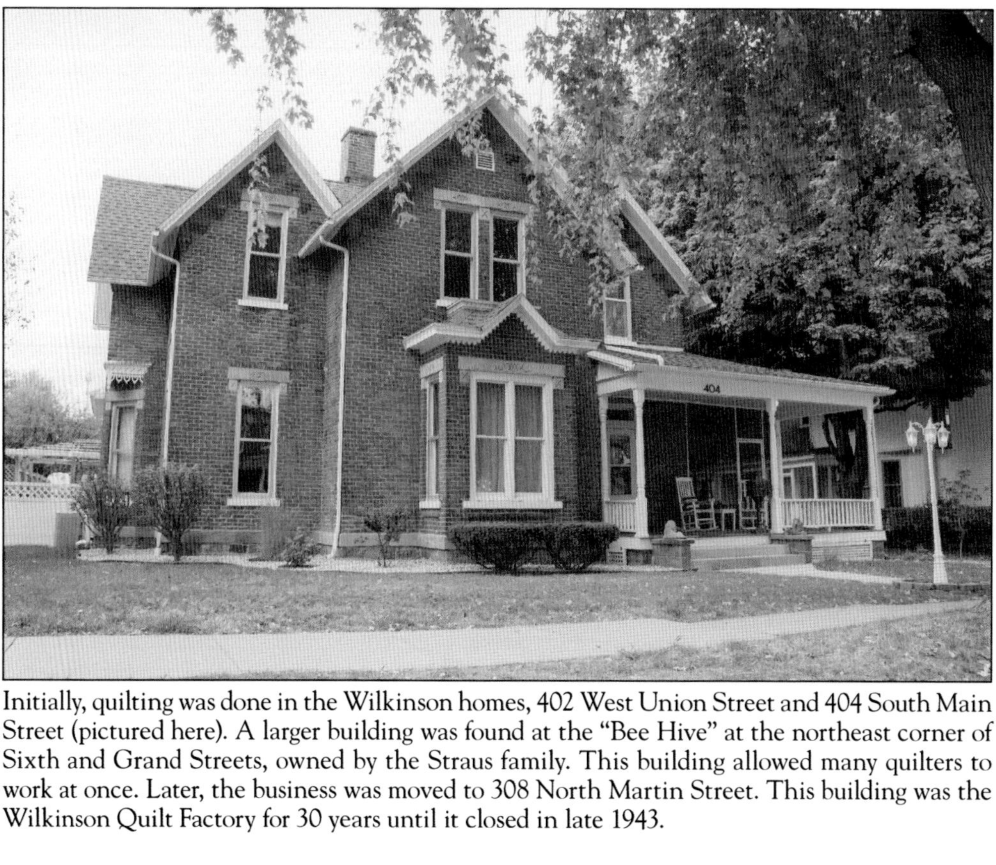


Initially, quilting was done in the Wilkinson homes, 402 West Union Street and 404 South Main Street (pictured here). A larger building was found at the "Bee Hive" at the northeast corner of Sixth and Grand Streets, owned by the Straus family. This building allowed many quilters to work at once. Later, the business was moved to 308 North Martin Street. This building was the Wilkinson Quilt Factory for 30 years until it closed in late 1943.

Ona was the traveler in the company. From 1908 through 1943, she traveled often by train to Chicago, but she also went to Cincinnati, Cleveland, Louisville, Memphis, St. Louis, Boston, Miami, the French Lick Springs Hotel in Indiana, and the Catskill Mountains in New York.

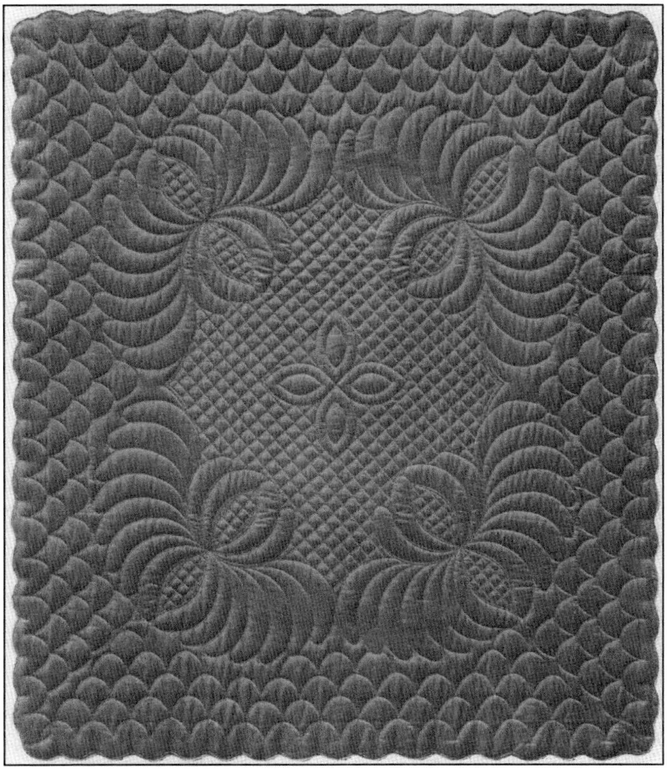

Rosalie worked the business and manufacturing end by staying in Ligonier. From 1908 through 1943, the company produced and sold over 10,000 quilts. It was known throughout the United States and in other countries as well. Few of the quilts remain today.

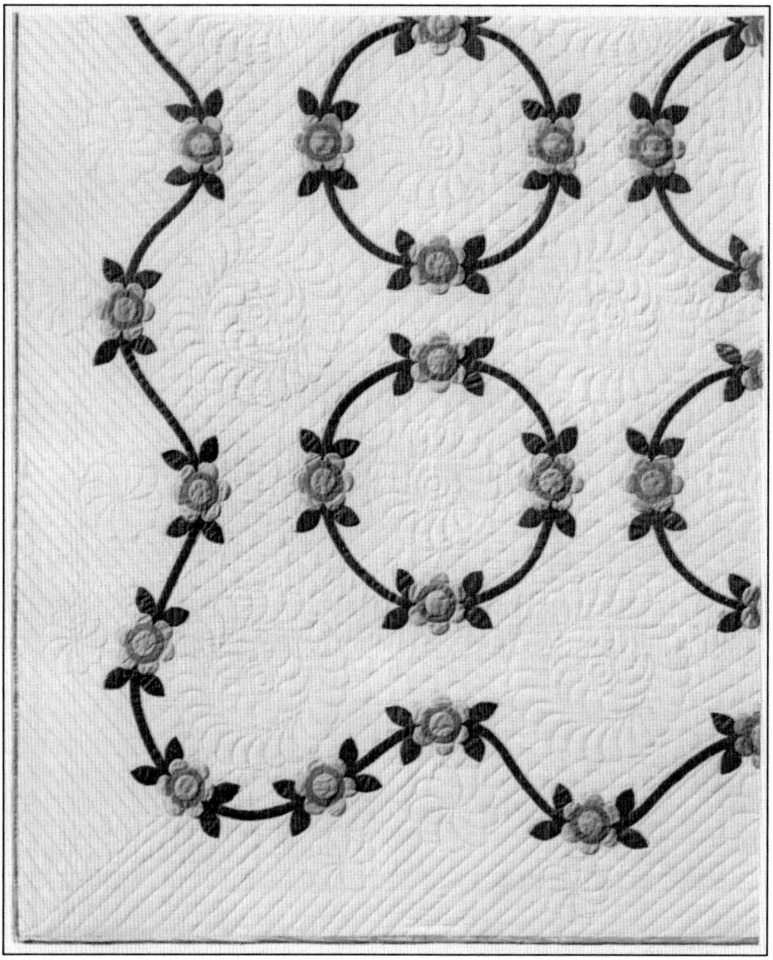

It is the author's belief that the Wilkinson sisters helped Ligonier develop and helped show women (and men) what women could accomplish. Ona married Ray Smalley in 1925. They did not have any children. Ona passed in 1949.

LIGONIER

—HOME OF

Wilkinson Hand Made Art Quilts

For Informaton Write

WILKINSON SISTERS

LIGONIER, - - - INDIANA

Rosalie married Harry Dickinson in 1917. They had only been married 11 years when Harry died, leaving a son and a daughter. Both children preceded Rosalie in death. Rosalie lived on alone until her passing in 1976. The ad shown here is from a Ligonier High School yearbook.

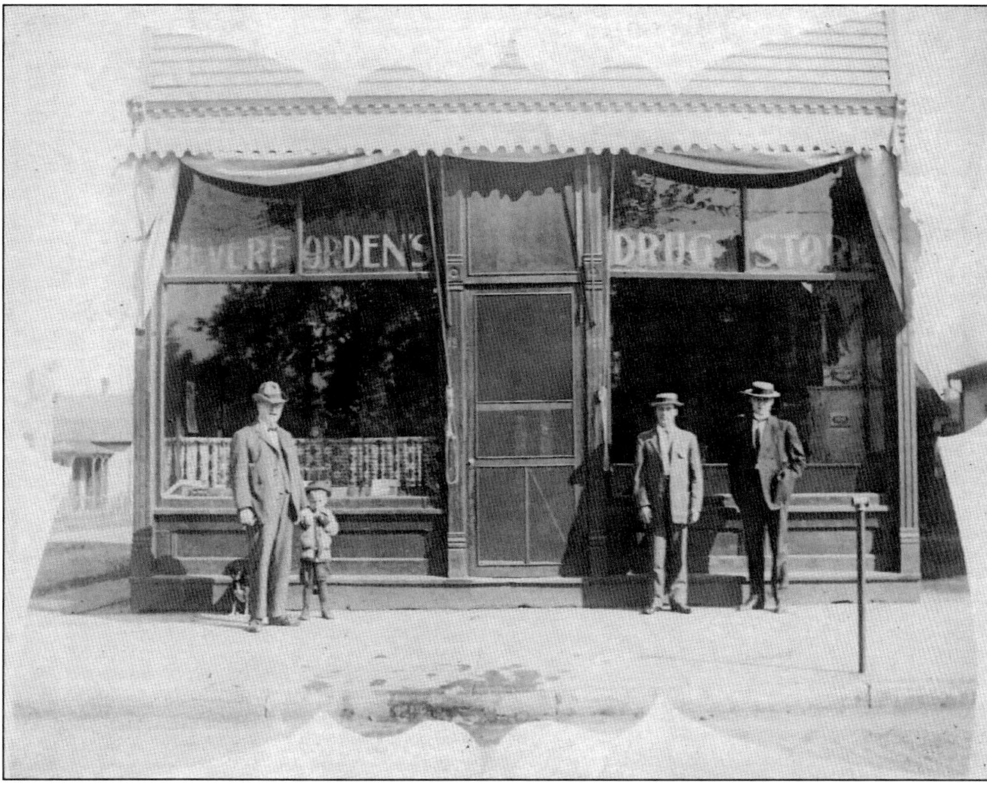

Hugo Beverforden and son Paul are standing (on the left) in front of Beverforden's Drug Store in Fort Wayne. Paul Beverforden was born in 1906. The men at right are unidentified.

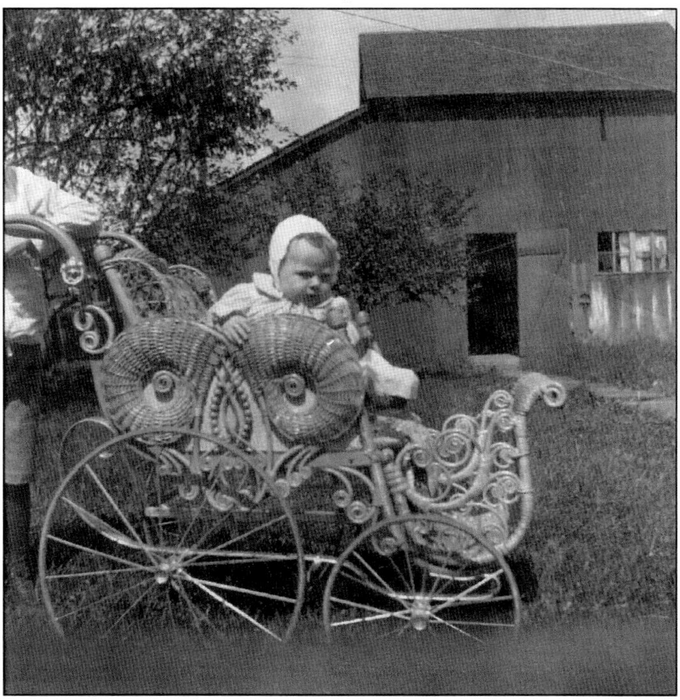

Ethel Beverforden (Paul's sister) is shown in very nice wicker baby carriage. It is surmised that the Beverfordens were well-off and hardworking.

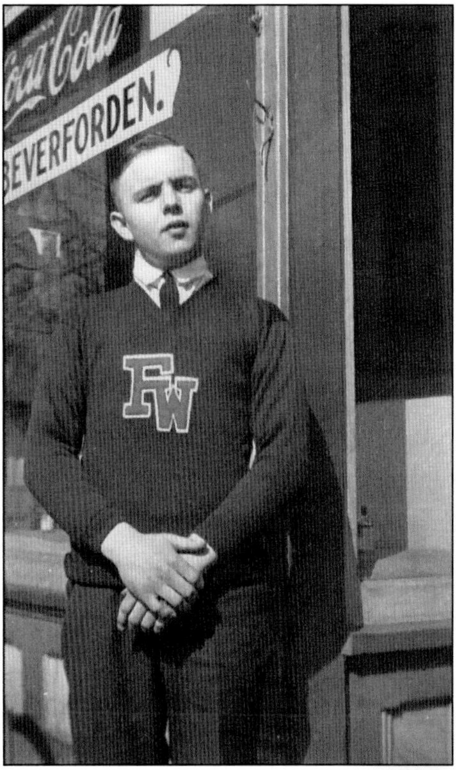


Paul is shown in front of the family pharmacy with his letterman sweater on. The *FW* stands for Fort Wayne, and at the time that Paul lived, there was a Fort Wayne High School.

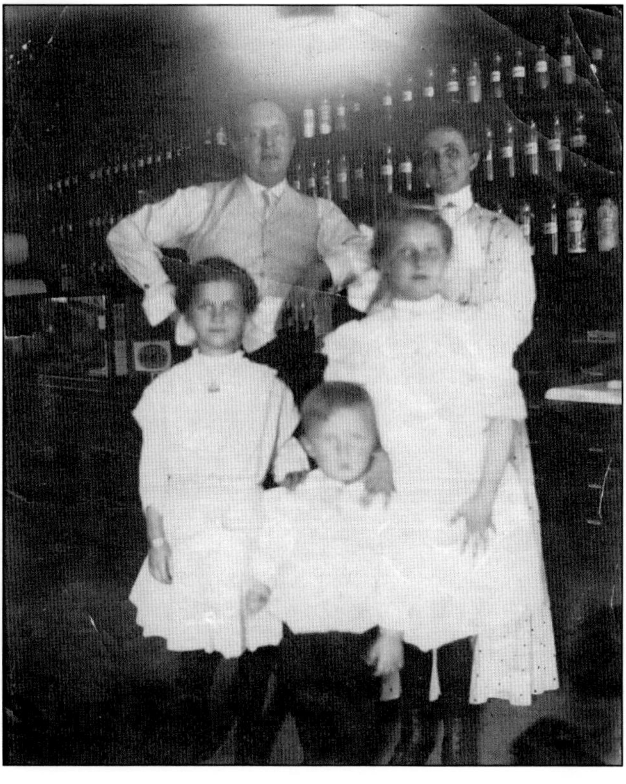

The Beverforden family is shown inside the drugstore in Fort Wayne. Pictured are (first row) Paul; (second row) unidentified girl (left) and Ethel; (third row) Hugo Friedrich and Charlotte.

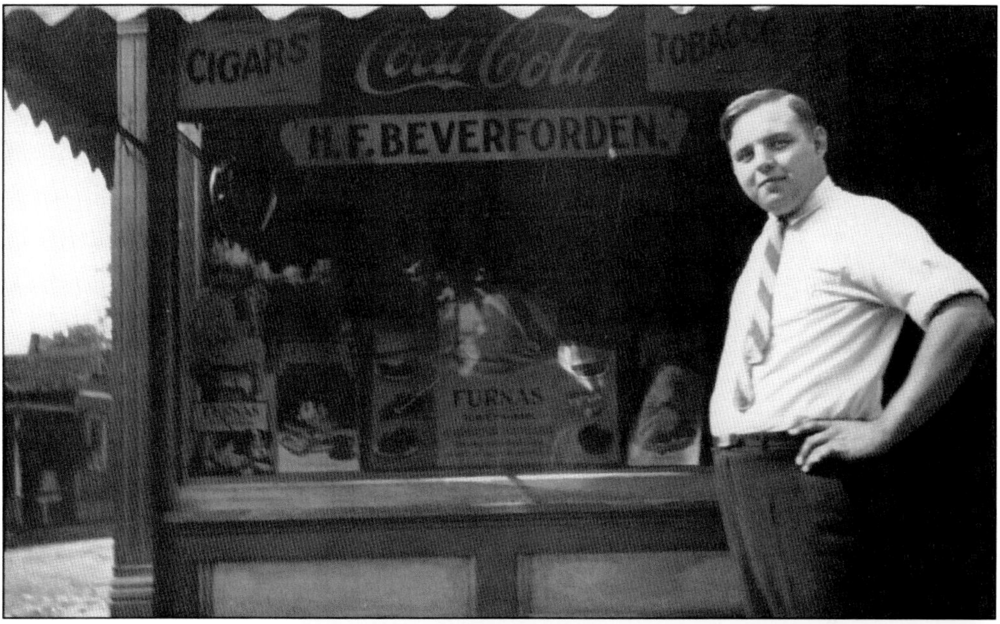


Paul Beverforden is pictured in front of Hugo Frederich Beverforden's drugstore in Fort Wayne. Hugo Frederich was born in 1878 in Bramsche, Prussia (now Germany).

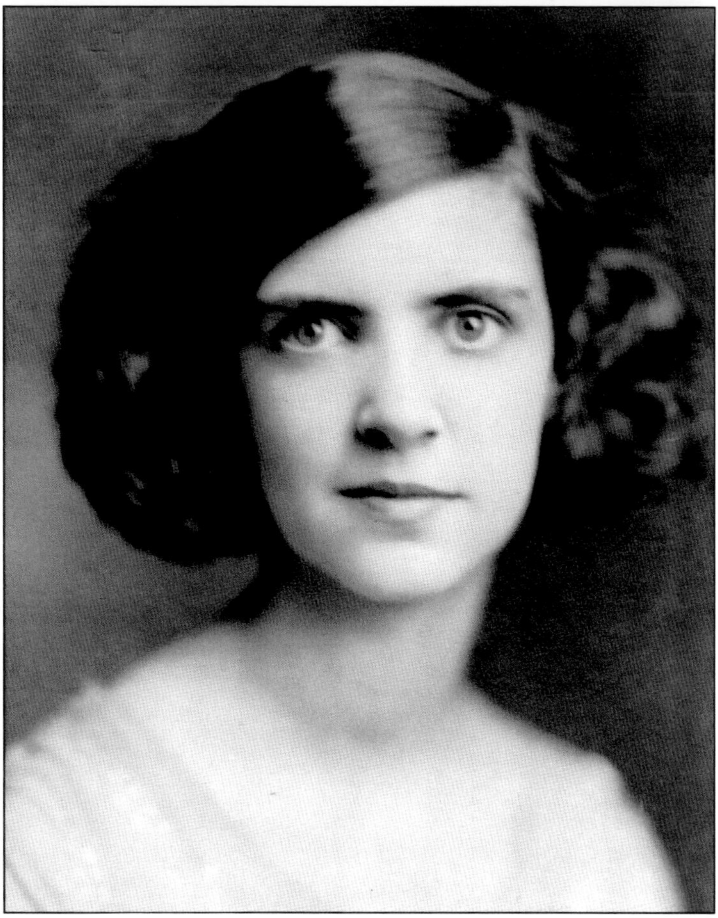

Hannah Kline Beverforden was born in 1905. She was the daughter of Edwin E. Kline, who owned and managed E.E. Kline Grocery Store in Cromwell, Indiana, for decades. Her mother was Minnie Hunt Kline. Her sister was Mary Kline. Hannah and Paul grew up in similar circumstances. Their parents owned their own stores and were their own bosses.

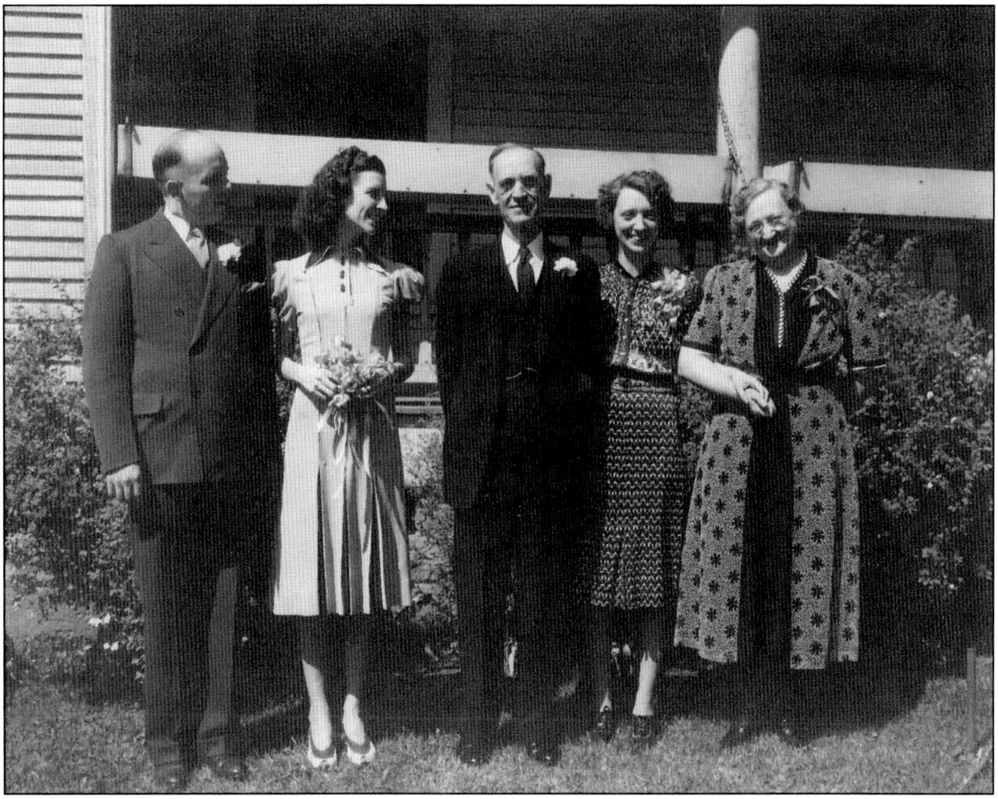

Paul Beverforden and Hannah Kline married on May 22, 1934. Pictured are, from left to right, Paul (groom), Hannah (bride), Edward E. Kline (father of the bride), Mary Kline (sister of the bride), and Minnie Kline (mother of the bride).

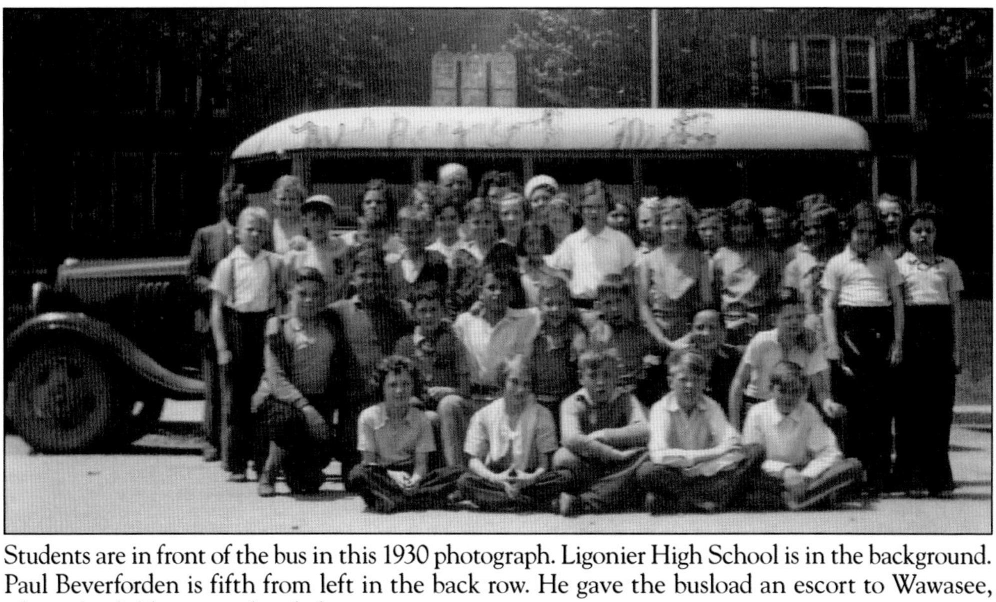

Students are in front of the bus in this 1930 photograph. Ligonier High School is in the background. Paul Beverforden is fifth from left in the back row. He gave the busload an escort to Wawasee, where the field trip was headed.

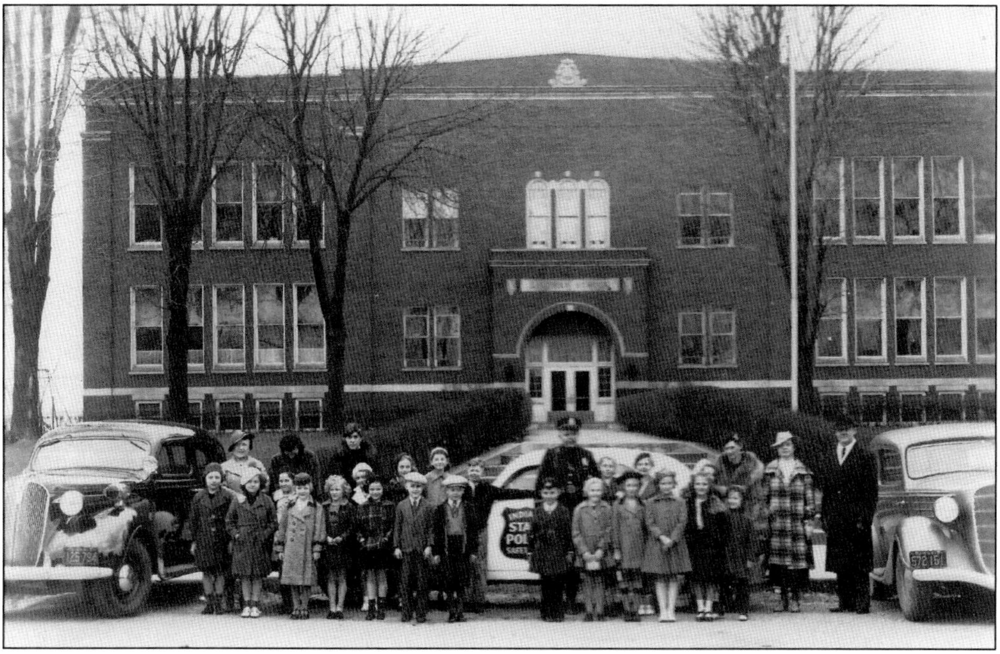

Paul Beverforden is in the center of this 1939 photograph in front of Ligonier High School. Paul's wife, Hannah Beverforden, taught school in Ligonier and helped get Paul involved with student groups talking about what he did. He was an Indiana State Police trooper. The cars have 1937 license plates.

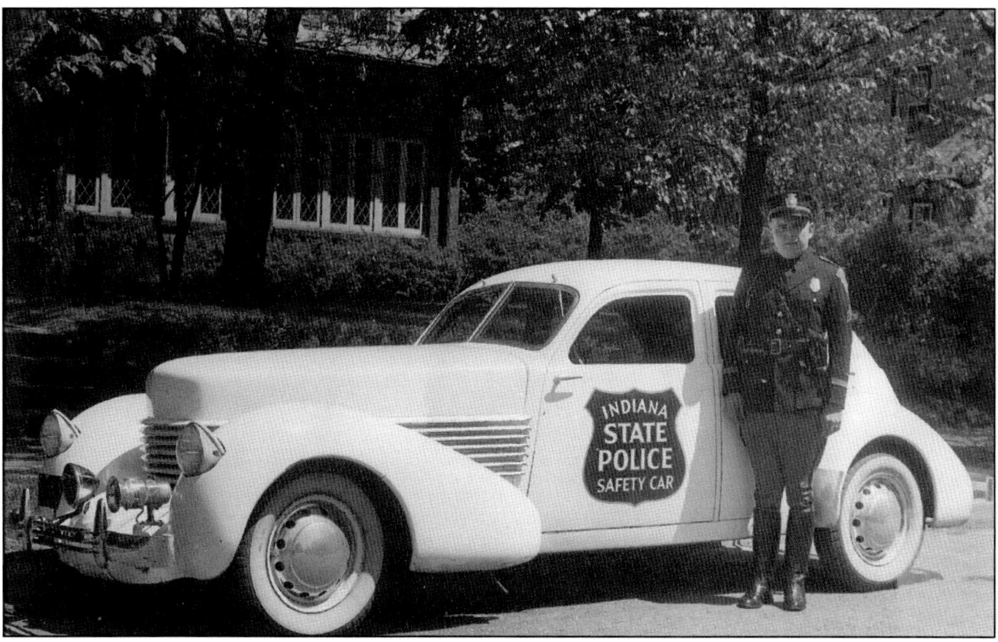


Paul Beverforden is with his Indiana State Police safety car. Paul was the superintendent of safety for Indiana. He was a major in the Indiana State Police from 1957 to 1960.

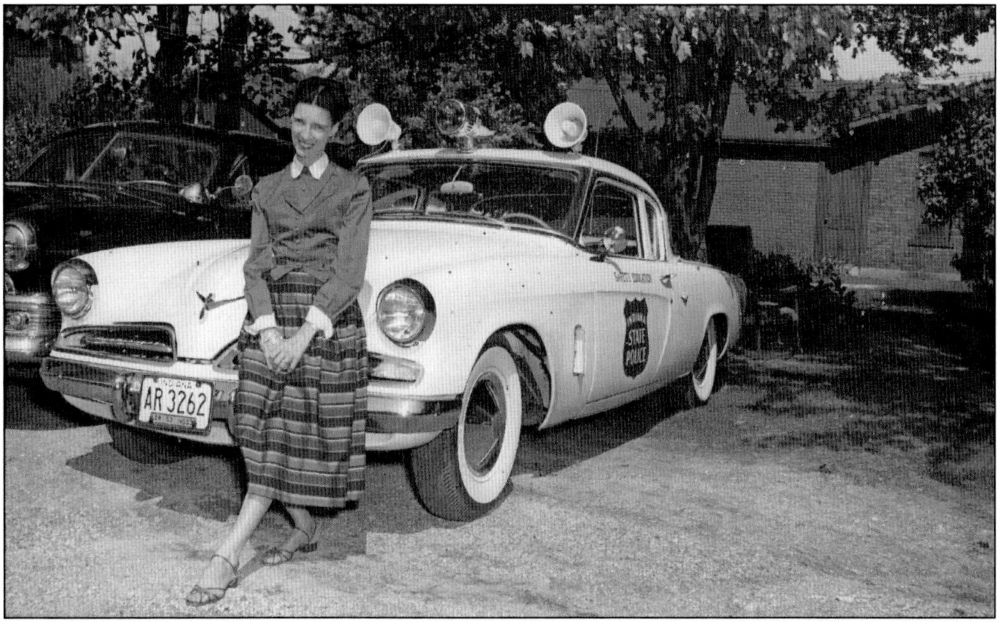


Hannah Kline Beverforden is in front of an Indiana State Police car driven by her husband, Paul Beverforden. This license plate on the car reads 1937.

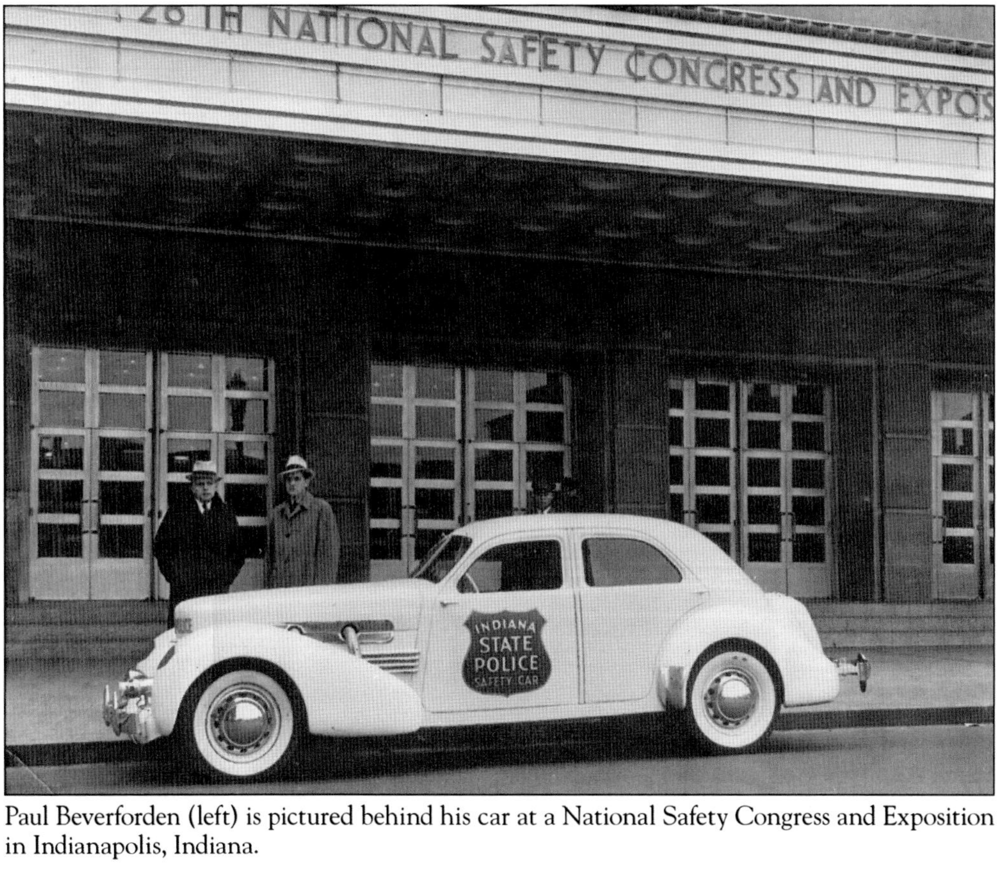


Paul Beverforden (left) is pictured behind his car at a National Safety Congress and Exposition in Indianapolis, Indiana.

# *Two*

# Money Makes the World Go Round

A community needs people. The people sell products or make products to sell or they provide services to sell. Money changes hands. The community grows because others want part of the money that is circulating in the community. Besides, the community has all of the nice things they want right at their fingertips.

Ligonier had all sorts of businesses that no longer exist in the town. But one is still here. That business was called the Ligonier Milling Company but is now called Star of the West Milling Company.

Soon after Ligonier started to have a population, the mills appeared to grind grain to make flour and meal. The mills got their power from the Elkhart River, which flowed by the town. Isaac Cavin knew his town would need this source of water.

A large mill started up in Waseon, Ohio, in 1861 (before the Civil War) and supplied troops with flour so they could eat. That mill moved to Ligonier in 1866 and became Ligonier Milling Company. In 1869, new mergers brought Lyon and Greenleaf's name to the business. In 1987, the name was changed to Star of the West Milling Company. It is still here in 2016.

The Ligonier Refrigerator Company was another big company in its day. It produced refrigerators that used ice to keep food cool, but the ice melted and no one needed them after electricity came to town.

Wirk Garment had its heyday around 1930 to 1959. It was a large employer in Ligonier in its time. The employment helped many people in the community, not just the management or the workers.

Kidd's Marshmallow Products had a real sticky, sweet mess in Ligonier. Founded in 1895 by Albert E. Kidd, the company moved to Ligonier from Chicago in 1946. In 1985, the factory employed over 200 people and was even featured in *Reader's Digest*. Now there is a Marshmallow Festival in town each fall, even though the company has closed.

Take a tour of Cavin Street's business district in the early days of Ligonier and visit Fashion Farm for some ice cream and pumpkin pie.

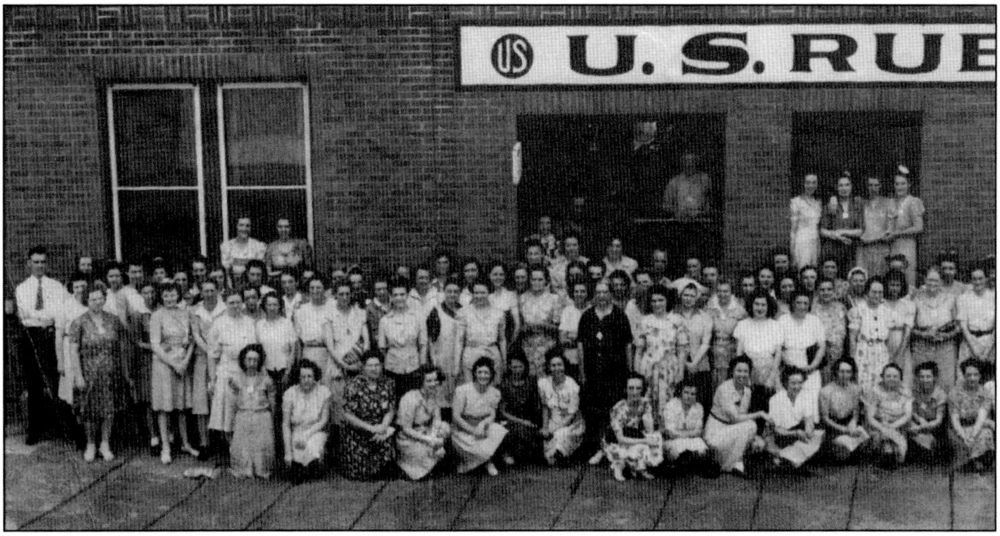

This is the left half of a group photograph of US Rubber Company. The company workers, shown near 1940, are gearing up in case war came. The company was in the former Ligonier Refrigerator Company building, just north of where the Lincoln Highway turned left off Cavin Street.

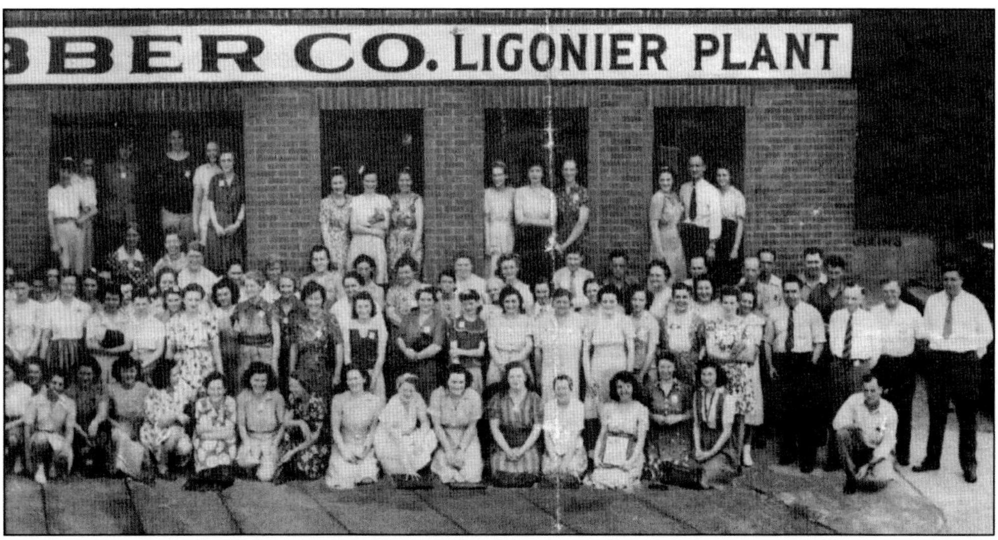

This is the right half of the group photograph. One can easily see that a lot of people worked for this company. Today, the Ligonier Rubber Company is just down the road on Cavin Street, on the left side past the viaduct under the railroad tracks.

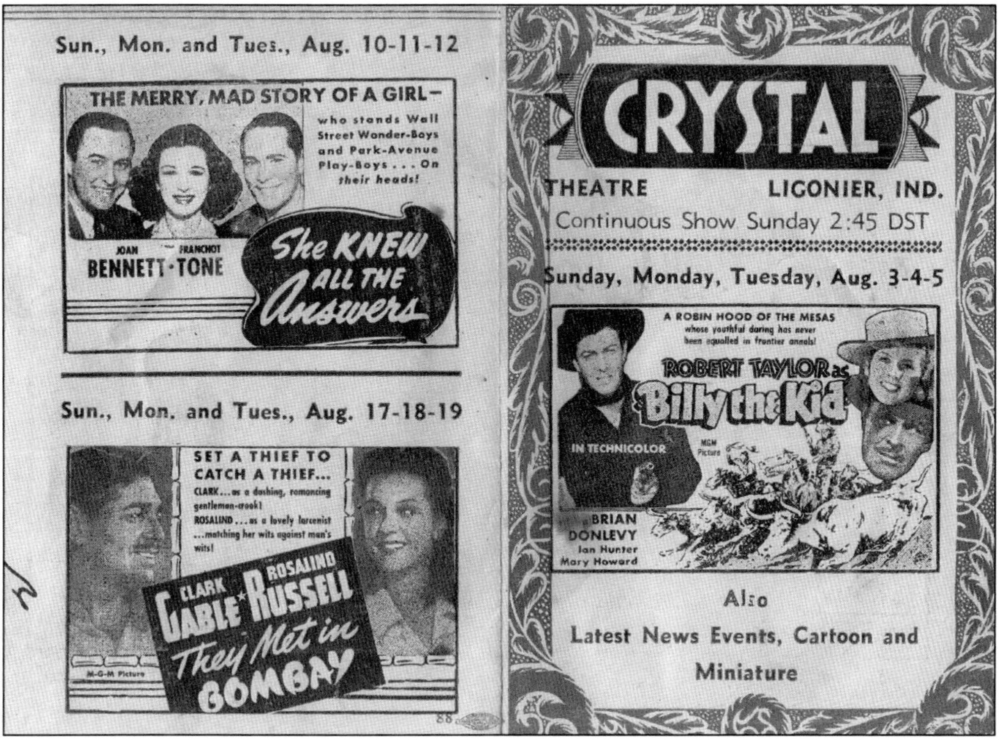

This business got several of the author's quarters (or whatever his parents paid for admission). But the author sure enjoyed every minute spent in the darkness of the Crystal Theatre. Each week, a brochure like the one shown was produced that told patrons what would be happening in the next week.

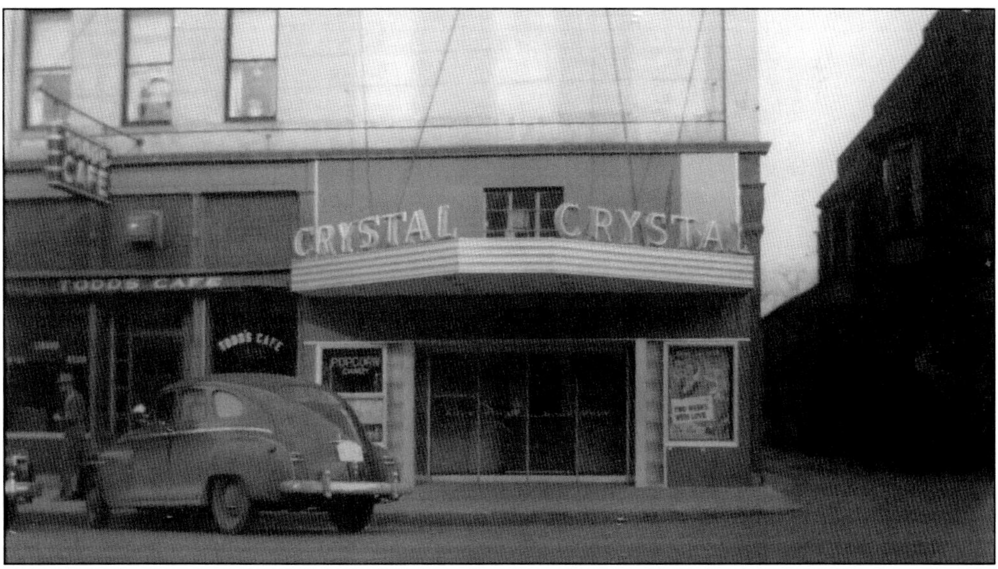

This is one of the author's treasured photographs. It is amazing how an important structure like a movie theater can latch onto a boy's brain. Whenever the author smells popcorn, he remembers the Crystal and the taste of Coca-Cola mixed with the sweet popcorn and a heavy dose of darkness. They made the floors sticky so one did not slip.

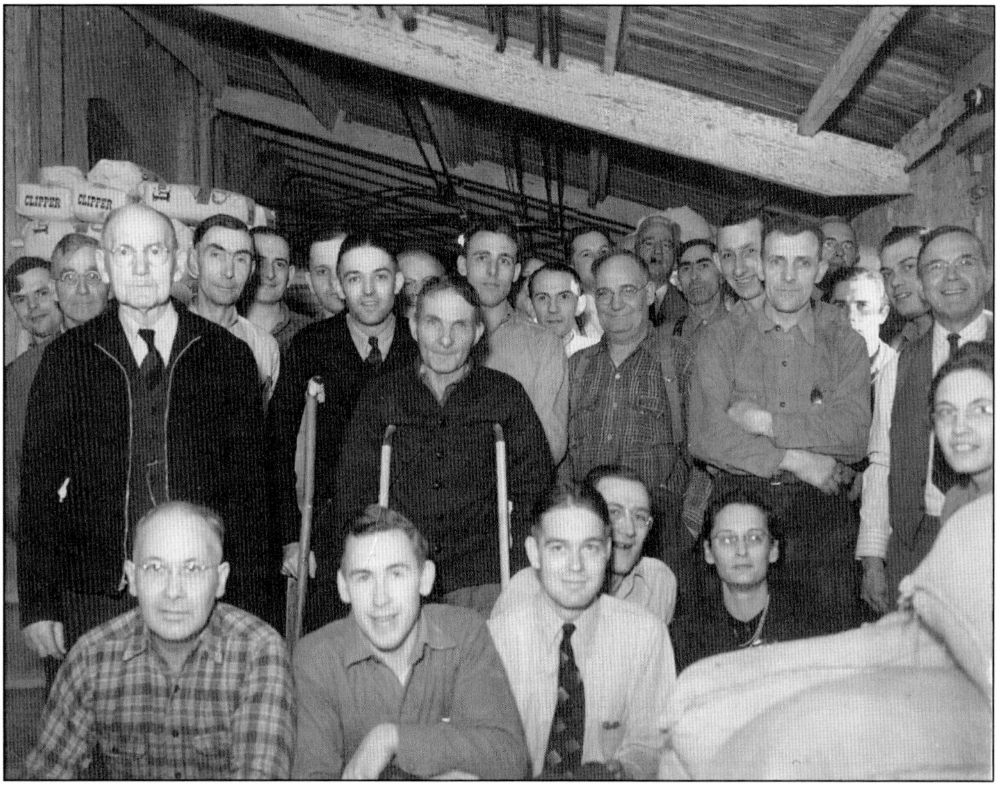


Employees at Lyon and Greenleaf in 1941 are, from left to right, (first row) Arthur Newman, unidentified, James Kelley, Harley Chrisman, Eunice Sack, and Helen Wolfe; (second row) Enos Golden, Charles Kline, four unidentified, Richard Botts, Chester Staton, three unidentified, Claude Mullins, two unidentified, Graham Lyon, Dewitt Burnheimer, Carl Shireman, Kelly Bowles, two unidentified, Chalmer Staton, and Arthur Kelley.

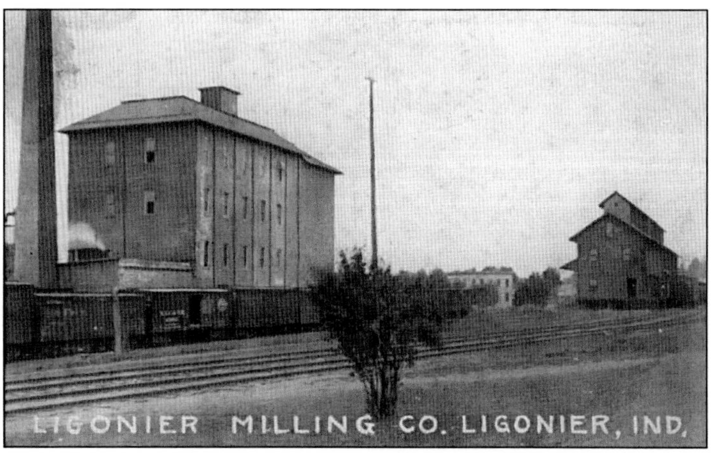


An earlier version of the mill is shown around 1900. Railroad service was critical to its success, and electrical power was also a requirement. Good roads and bridges added to the smooth operation of the mill, because semis transport much grain in to be processed.

This photograph shows improvements being made to the storage silos in 1954. The silos are located beside the railroad tracks for easy access to train service. The mill has operated in Ligonier from 1866 until today. In 1885, it could make 40,000 pounds of flour a day. Now, 800,000 pounds of flour is produced each day.

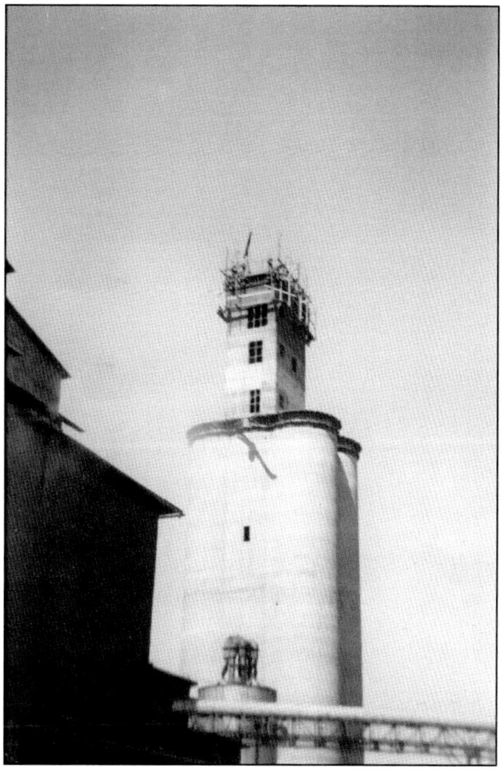

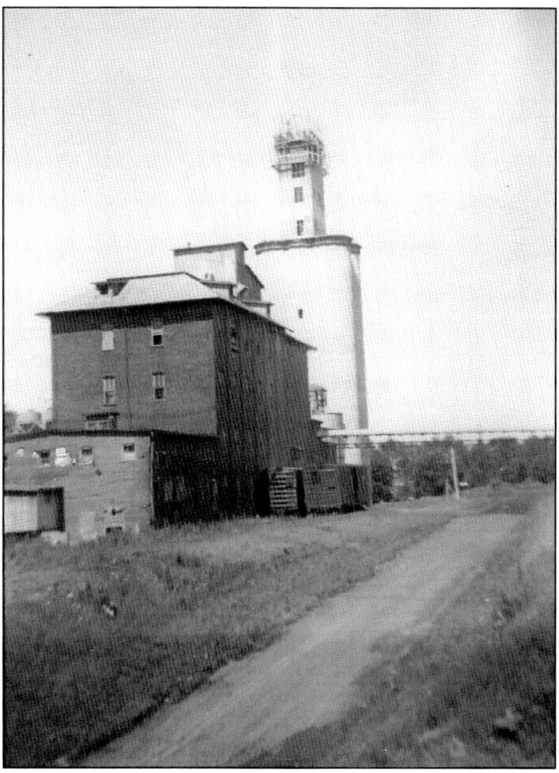

This is another view of the silos and the mill beside the railroad tracks. This improvement was made in 1954. The application to the National Register of Historic Places notes that this is the oldest continuously operated industry in Ligonier. That is a solid testimony to the tenacity of Ligonier's workers.

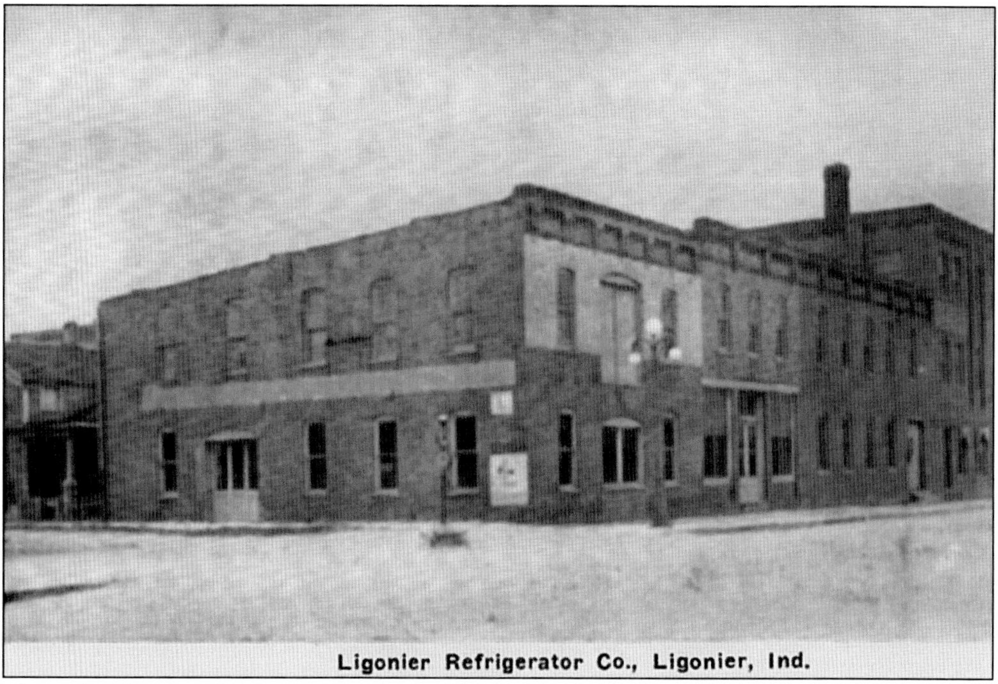


This is how Ligonier Refrigerator Company looked in the late 1890s. Compare this photograph to the next one, which shows the same building with a few modifications. This structure, by the way, is where the Straus family's Ligonier Carriage operated in Ligonier before the Ligonier Refrigerator Company utilized the building.

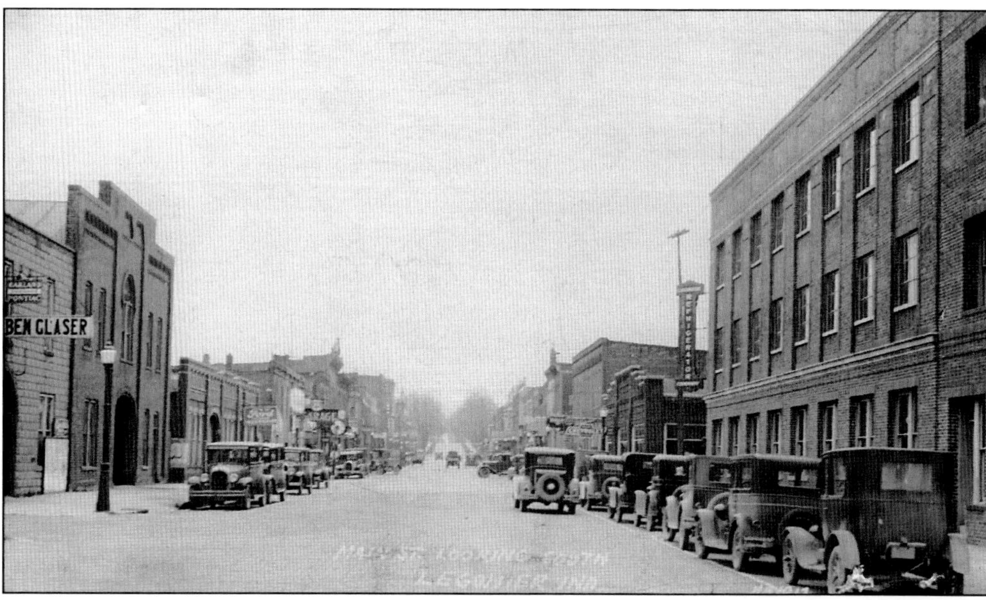


This early-1900 photograph shows the Ligonier Refrigerator Company on the right side. The large hanging sign on the right reads "Ligonier Refrigeration." This photograph has a view looking south. On the left is Ben Glaser Pontiac Garage. Ben was a fixture in Ligonier. He also was Jewish.

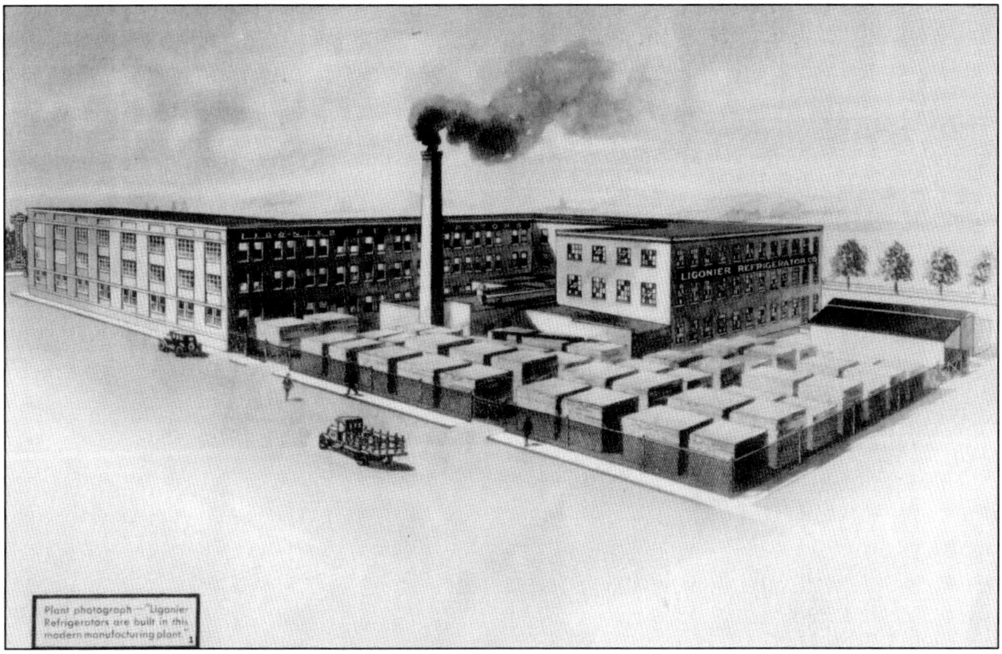


This sketch of the "Lig-O-Nier" Refrigerator Company may be exaggerated depiction of the facility. It was common then for a sketch like this to make the company look really impressive and have the smokestack belching all sorts of sooty black smoke. That is the sign of work being done, money being made, and power being generated.

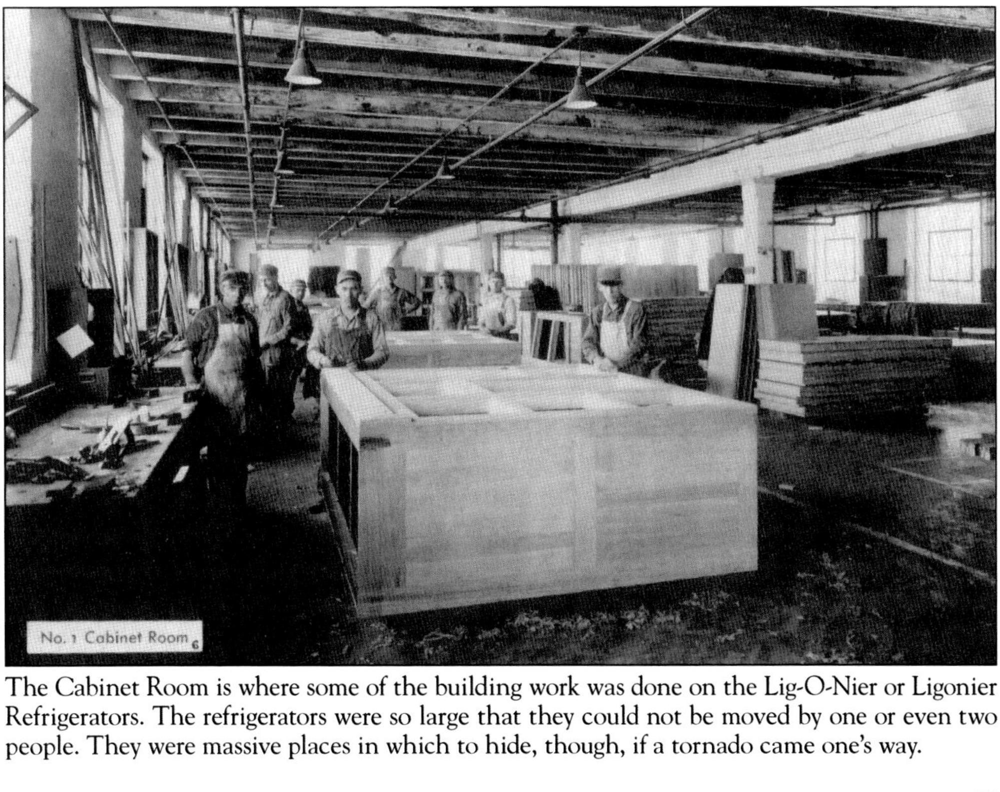


The Cabinet Room is where some of the building work was done on the Lig-O-Nier or Ligonier Refrigerators. The refrigerators were so large that they could not be moved by one or even two people. They were massive places in which to hide, though, if a tornado came one's way.

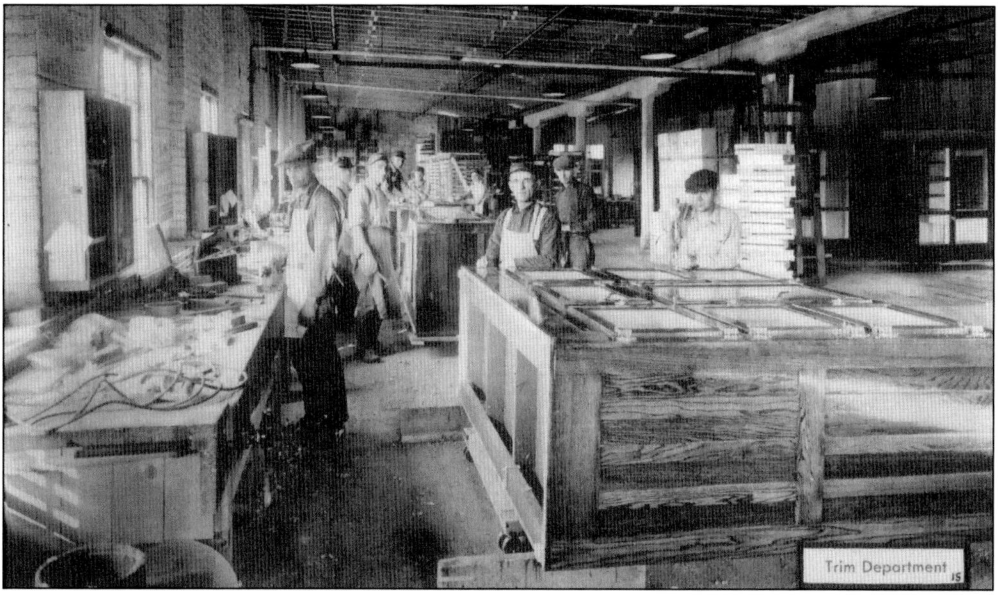


The Trim Department made the refrigerator look more like a refrigerator. See the glass doors on the refrigerator and the hinges. The wood looks stained and ready to work. The refrigerators were well insulated to keep the food cold and to keep the cost of ice as low as possible. These did not run on electricity but used ice instead. When electrically cooled refrigeration caught on, the company folded.

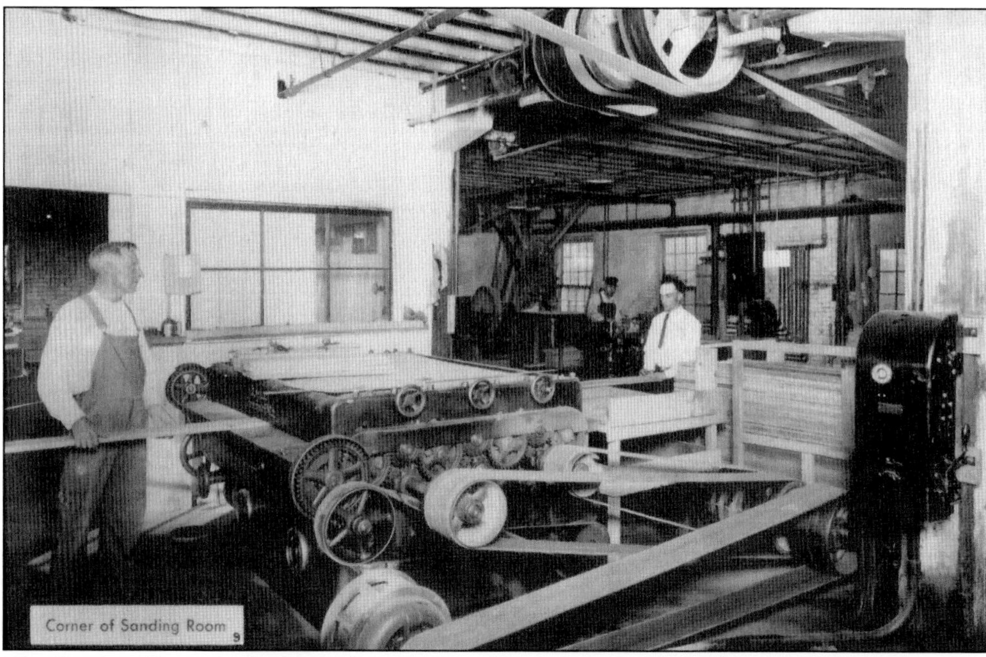


The Sanding Room looks like a dangerous and dusty place. All of those belts and pulleys and the power box to control the electricity to run these machines meant that this was not a quiet room to work in. No guards are on the gears or belts. The Occupational Safety and Health Administration would likely wear down pencils writing citations against what would now be considered an unsafe workplace.

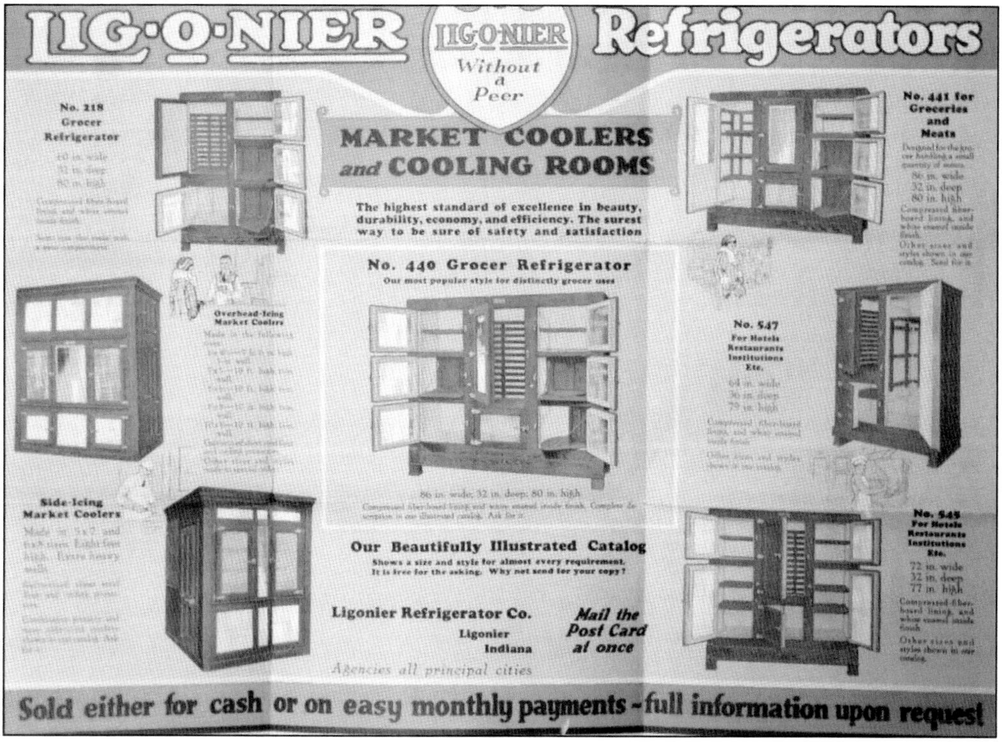


This color ad for the Ligonier Refrigerator shows the fine products made in Ligonier, Indiana. This company made over $1 million a year selling these refrigerators from around 1915 onward until it closed.

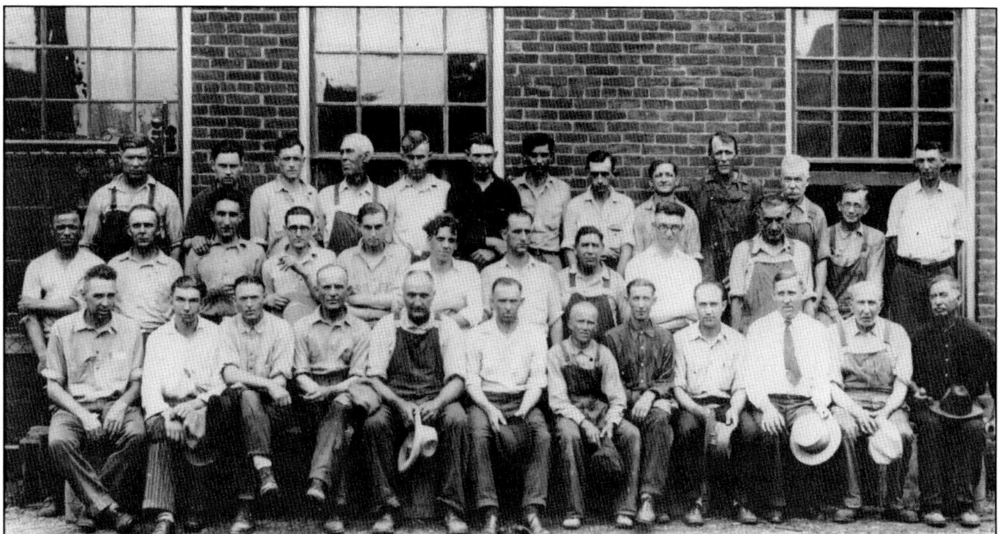

This group photograph shows Ligonier Refrigeration workers. Identified in the picture are (first row) ? Drake (second from left) and Mel Drain (eighth from left); (second row) Everett Vance (fifth from left), Harry Chiddister (sixth from left), Maynard Misner (ninth from left), and Vern Stage (twelfth from left); (third row) Sam Patton's grandfather (tenth from left) and Ozro Deardorff (twelfth from left).

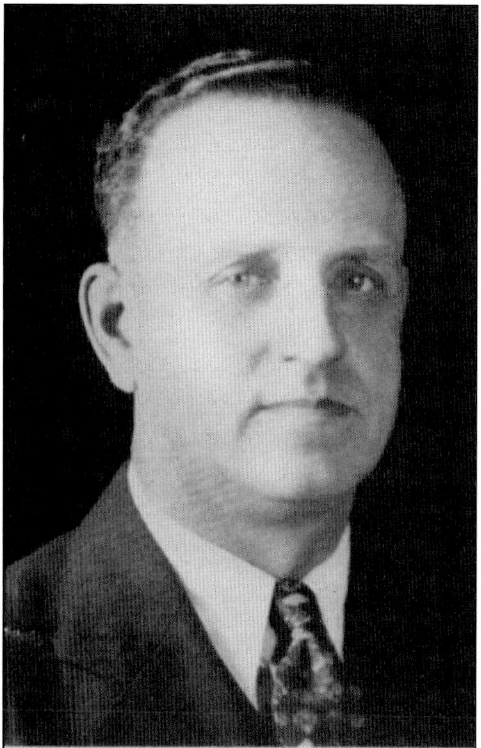

**CHARLES H. SIMMONS, Sales Mgr.**
**Ligonier Refrigerator Division**

Charles H. Simmons was the sales manager of the Ligonier Refrigerator Company. He had a vital job. If the refrigerators were not sold, there would be no need for the company. Then men who made the refrigerator would be out of work.

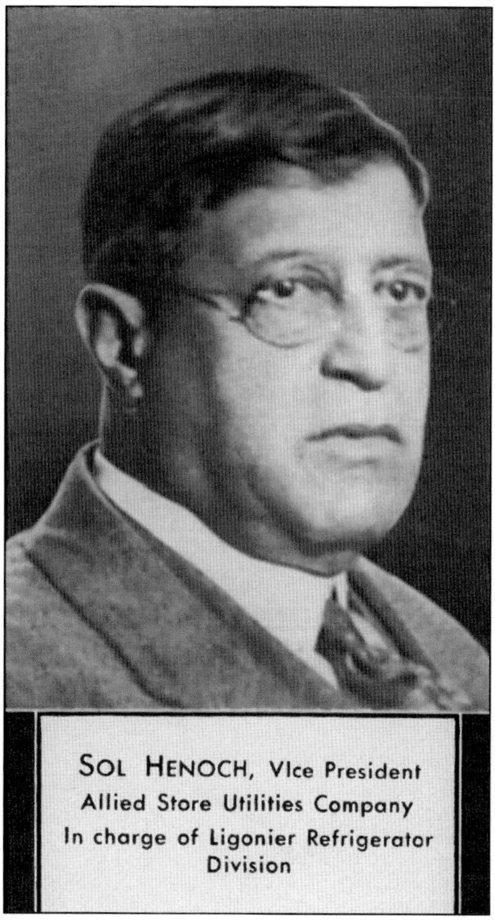

**SOL HENOCH, VIce President**
**Allied Store Utilities Company**
**In charge of Ligonier Refrigerator Division**

Sol Henoch was the vice president of Allied Store Utilities Company and was in charge of the Ligonier Refrigerator Division. He lived at 703 South Main Street, and he worshipped at the Jewish synagogue just down the street from his home.

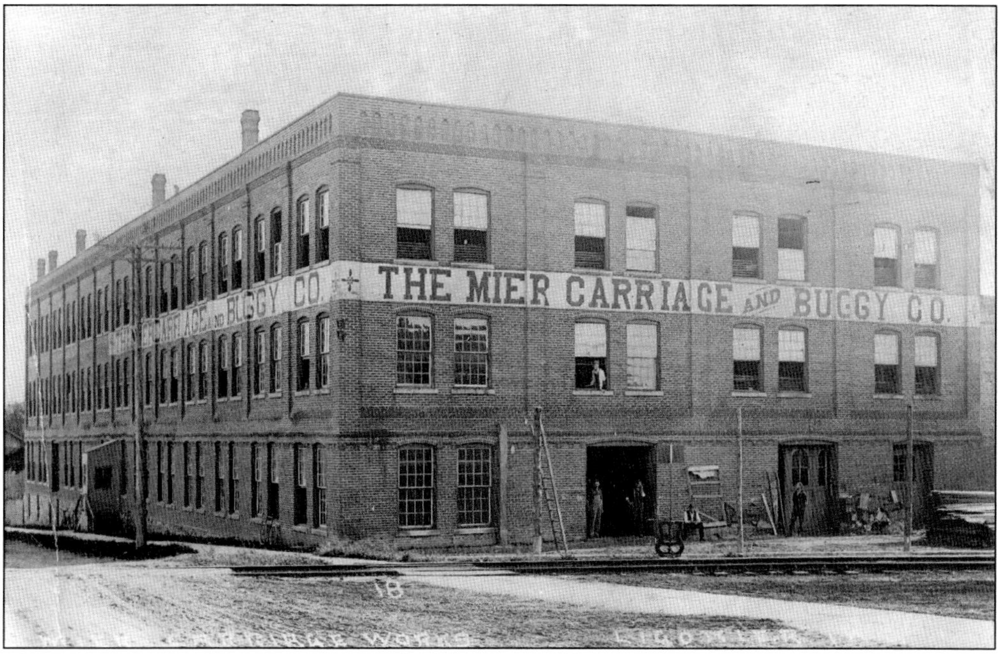


The Mier Buggy and Carriage Factory building was sold to Master Garment in 1932. The factory is shown here before "Master Garment" was painted on the side. Wirk Garment Industries was a manufacturer of work clothes for the George Master Garment Corporation, a direct sales corporation that moved to Ligonier from Chicago in 1930.

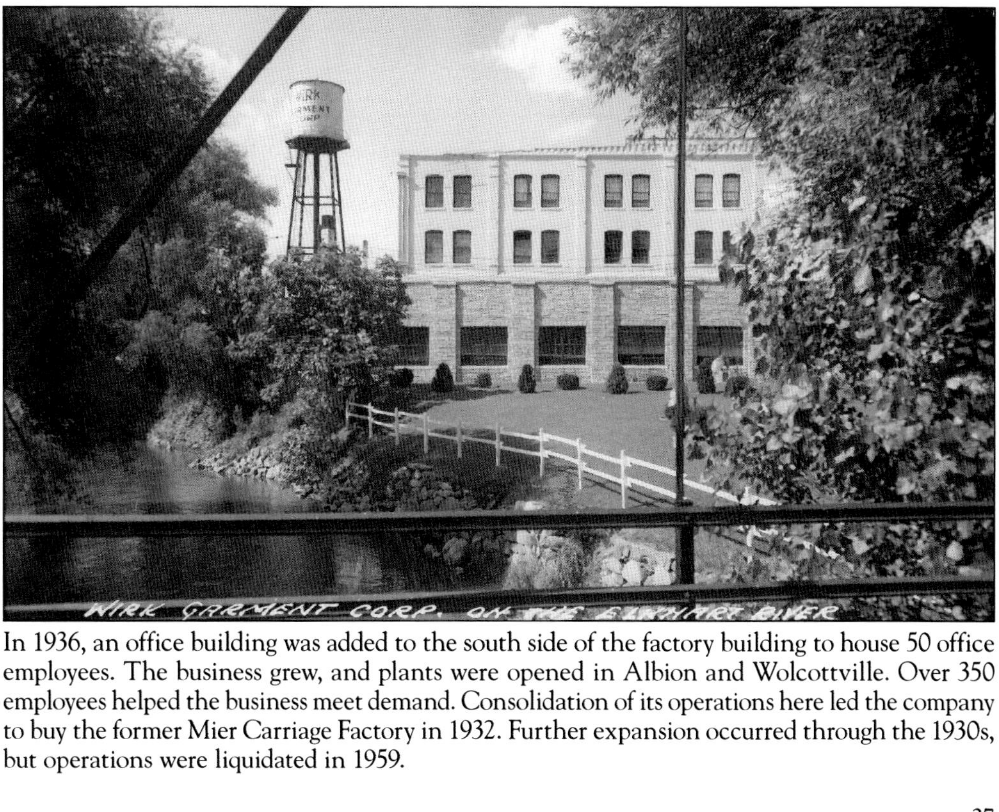


In 1936, an office building was added to the south side of the factory building to house 50 office employees. The business grew, and plants were opened in Albion and Wolcottville. Over 350 employees helped the business meet demand. Consolidation of its operations here led the company to buy the former Mier Carriage Factory in 1932. Further expansion occurred through the 1930s, but operations were liquidated in 1959.

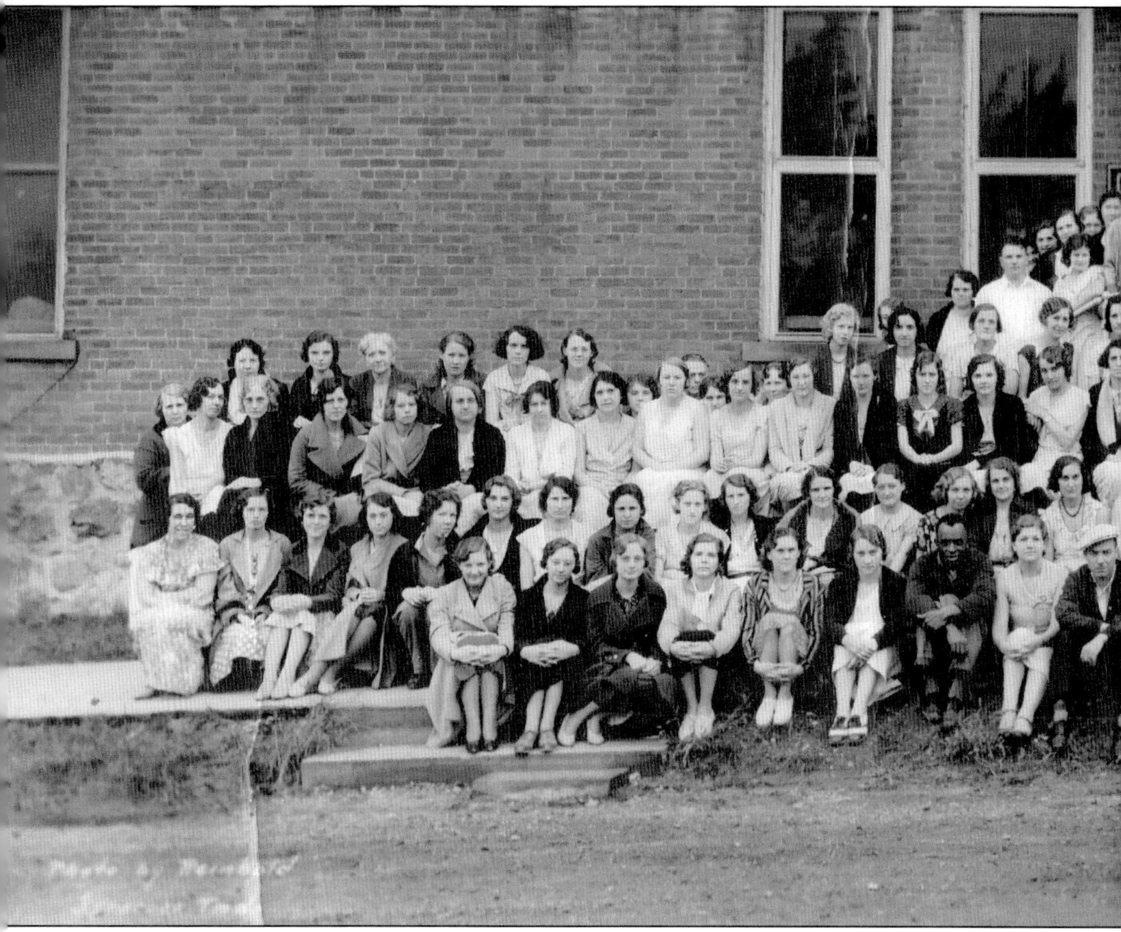

The 1933 employees are shown in this photograph. Most of the employees are women. In 1959, the management sold the Master and Wirk divisions and closed the plant. Like too many pictures at the Ligonier Historical Museum, there are no scribbles on the back or front to identify the

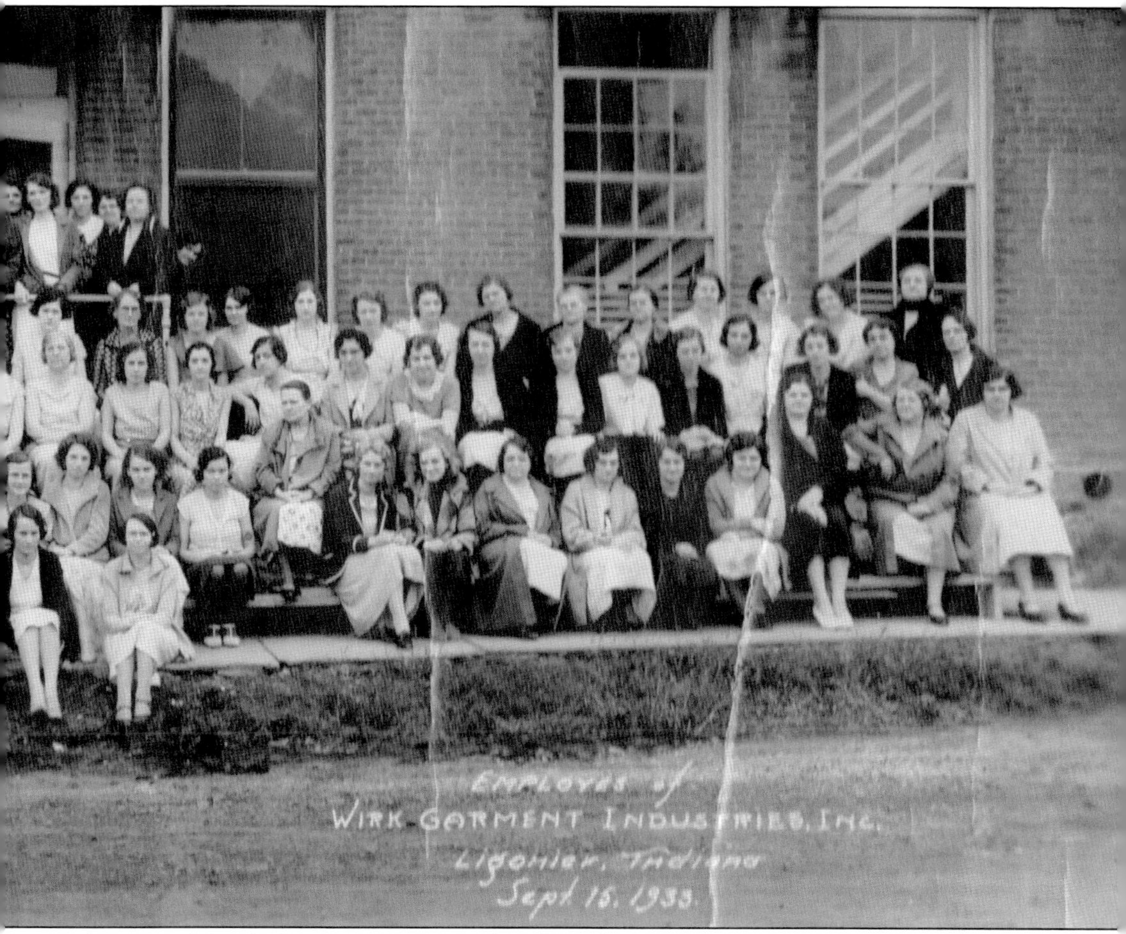


people pictured. Wirk Garment was a wonderful employer for Ligonier. There was said to be a family feeling. Christmas parties, dances, Valentine's Day parties, and more were held for Wirk employees and their families. See the photograph of a band playing at Wirk on page 89.

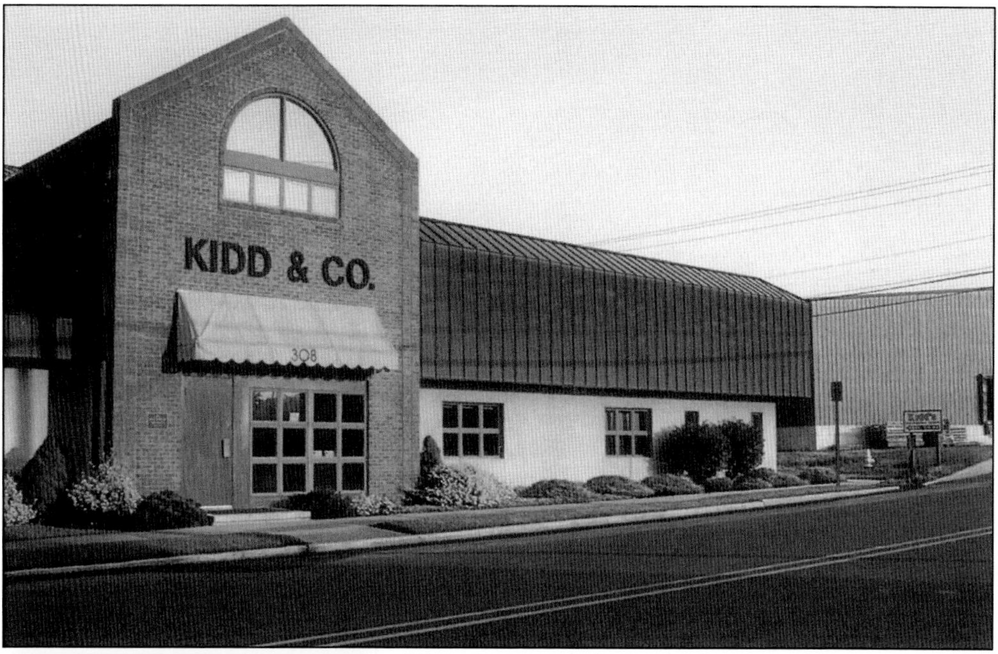


This photograph shows the former Kidd's Marshmallow factory in Ligonier. Located at 308 North Martin Street, it was very close to the railroad tracks, which aided in shipping out products or shipping in supplies. Ligonier is also on two major roads, US 33 and US 6, so semis can also help haul raw materials and products.

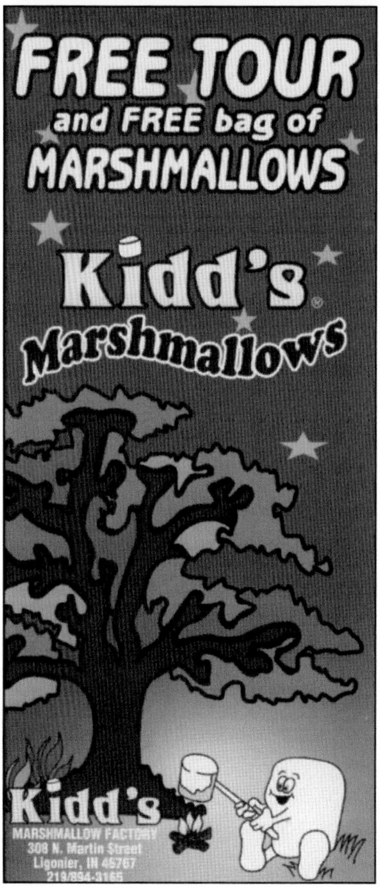


Kidd's helped introduce marshmallows to the public by offering free tours of its plant. At the end of the tour, visitors were given bags of marshmallows. The company is featured in a *Reader's Digest* story. Kidd's, which also helped with the Marshmallow Festival, had around 200 employees in 1985. At one time, Kidd's was among the largest producers of marshmallows in America.

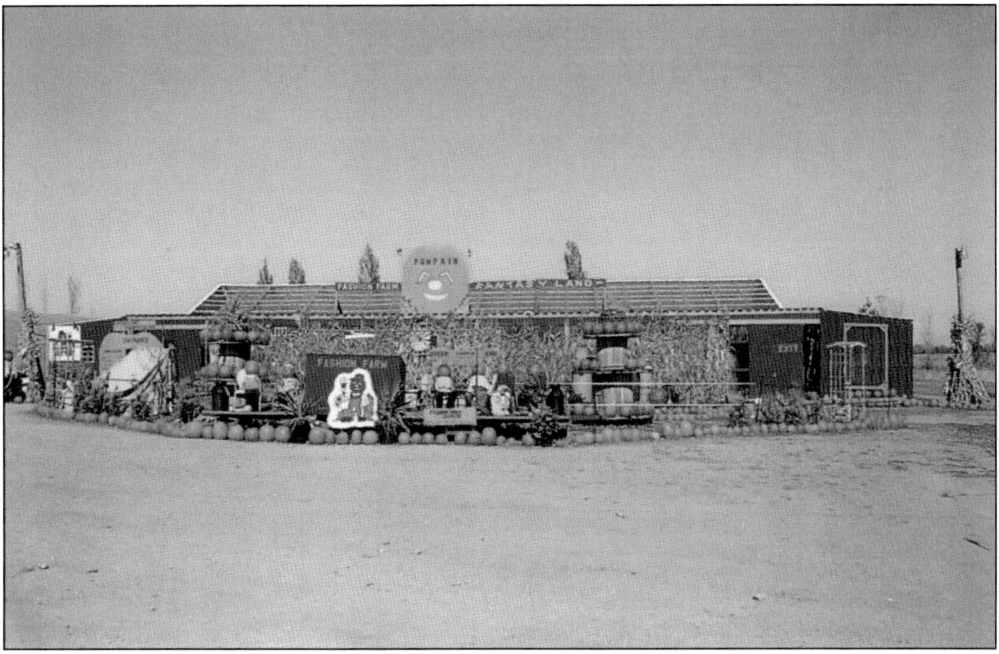


This photograph shows how the Fashion Farm looks in October each year for its Pumpkin Fantasyland. Charlie and June Williams purchased 200 acres of farmland from the Green family in 1959. The Fashion Farm grew out of that purchase. It is at 1680 Lincolnway West.

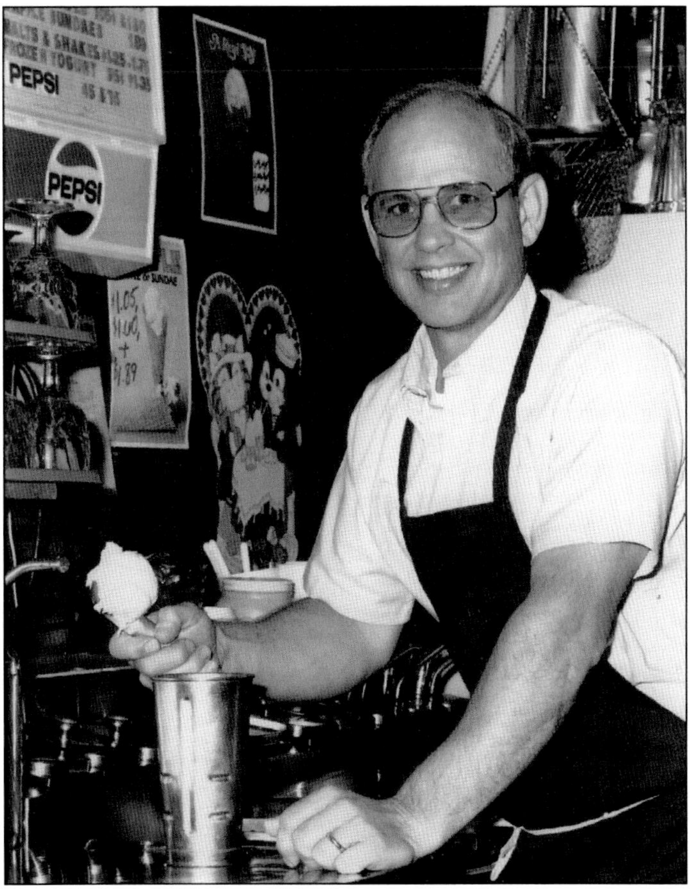


Rusty Becker serves ice cream at Fashion Farm. Lots of flavors and sizes and types are available. Save room for some pie with that. Rusty is in charge of the operations in the restaurant. His wife, Patti Williams Becker, is in charge of the floral department and the Pumpkin Fantasyland event. The restaurant is featured in the movie *Lonesome Jim*, written by James Strouse and starring Casey Affleck.

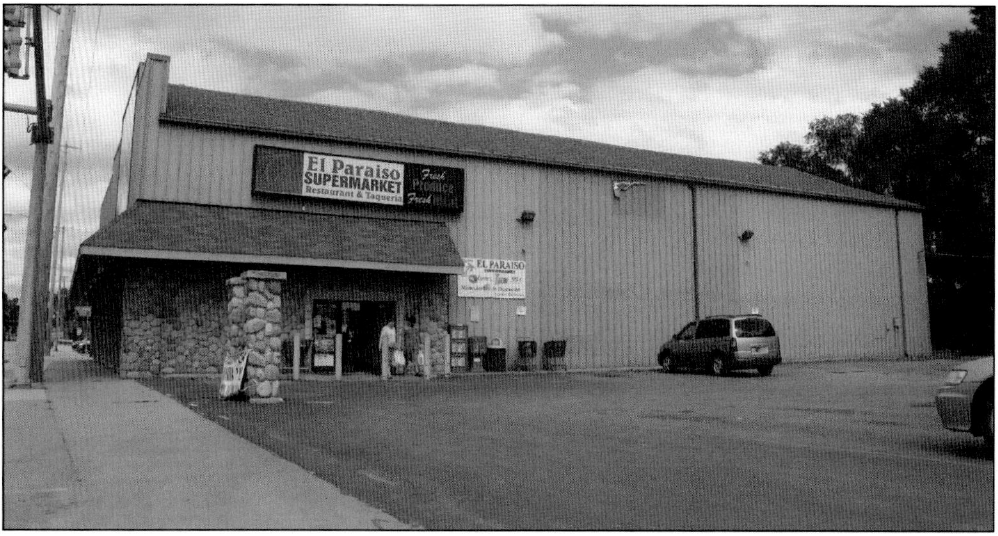


In this view facing north from the north end of Cavin Street, where Highway 33 turns west at the stoplight, the large building on the right at 103 North Cavin Street is El Paraiso Supermarket, the only business now in this block. The businesses that long ago filled this site from 101 North Cavin Street to 111 South Cavin Street were McHugh Auto Sales (101 North Cavin Street); Shobe Livery Barn, Ben Glaser Garage, and Bob Porter Garage (103); Lincoln Highway Garage, the Trading Post, and Highway Café (105); the Blazed Trail Garage (107); the Twentieth Century Lunch Car and the Lunch Car Café (109); and Candy Miller's Candy Shop, Hoffert's Tin Shop, Norman Biddle Plumbing and Heating, and Gingerich Plumbing Shop (111 South Cavin Street).

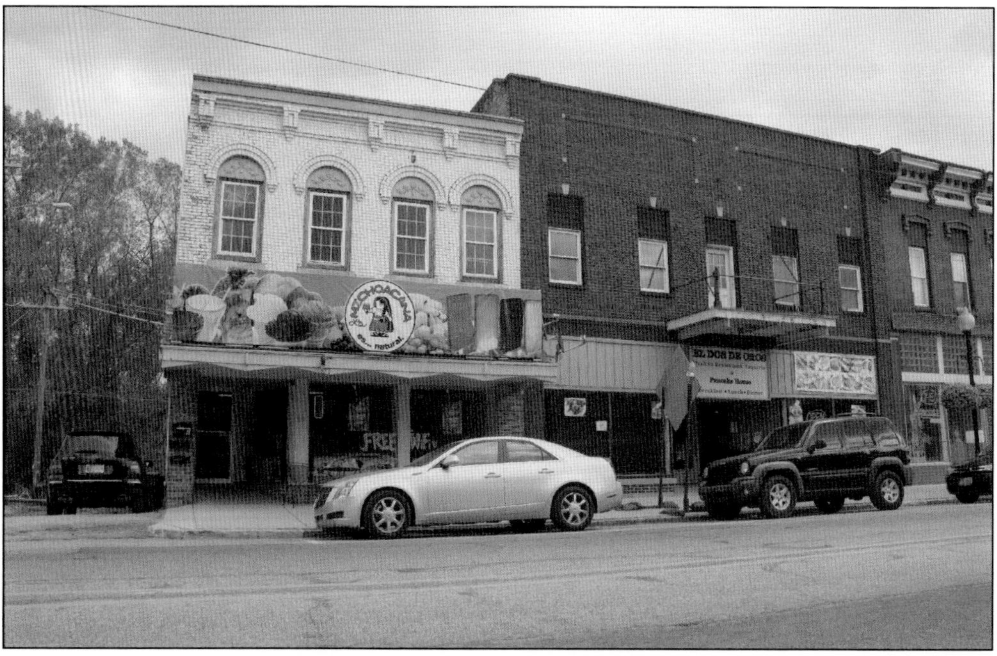

Michoacana is the name of this ice-cream shop at 113 South Cavin Street. Some local buildings have numbers, some building numbers are hidden, and some do have numbers posted at all. At 113, Clarence and Lena Wemple's Dry Goods Store, Grinnell Dime Store, Seeley Brown Variety Store, and the Bargain Center used to attract the crowds.

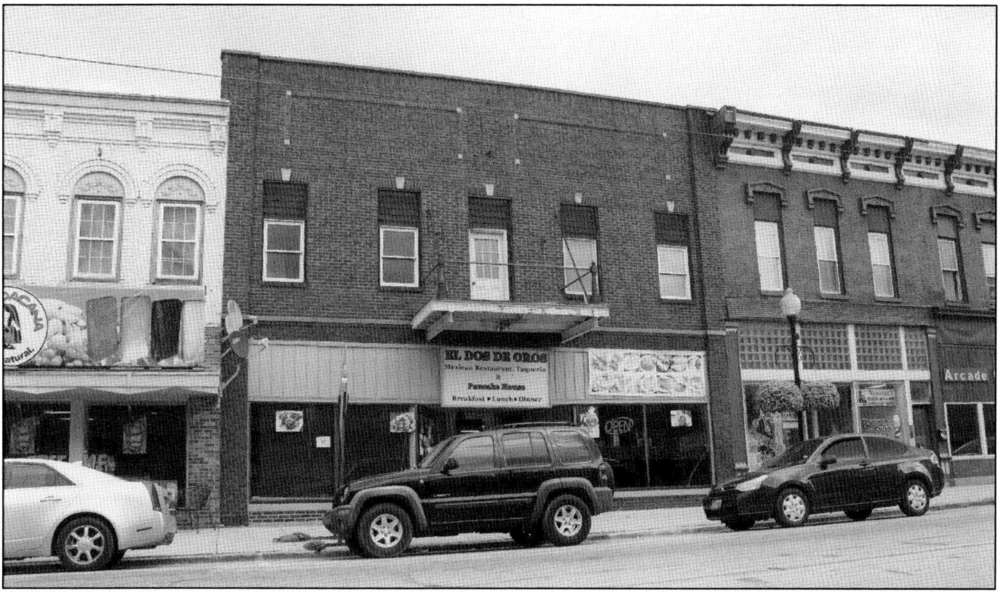


El Dos de Oros is the pancake restaurant at 115 South Cavin Street. Around 1900, this was the Hotel Mier. The balcony came in handy for watching parades. Seagley Hardware and Energy and Security Systems were previously here.

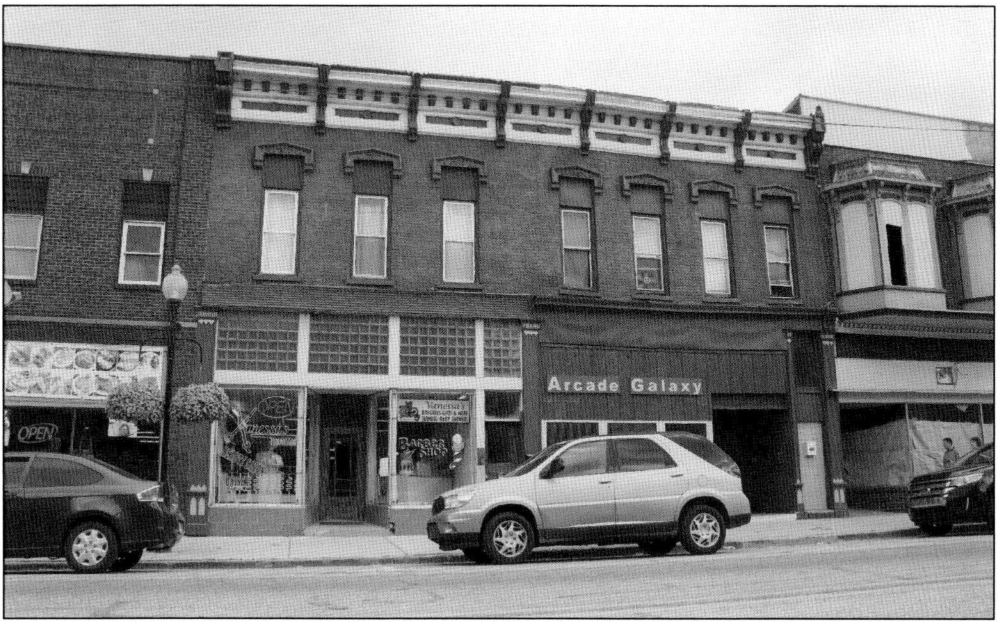


Vanessa Scissors and Barber Shop looks open. The Arcade Galaxy seems to be closed. A pair of bay windows projects out on the second floor of a vacant building on the right. Although the numbers are not shown, these are 117, 119, and 121 South Cavin Street. Formerly, at 117 South Cavin Street were the Adams Poolroom, Rice Poolroom, and Paddy's Tavern; at 119 were William A. Brown Furniture and Coffins, Kunkalman Plumbing, Delucenay Shoe Repair Shop, Stanley Card and Poolroom, and Midway Lounge; and at 121 were the Woodruff Drug Store, the office or the *Ligonier Leader* (a newspaper), Photographer's Studio (owned by a Mr. Sturtzbaugh), and the office of the *Advance Leader.*

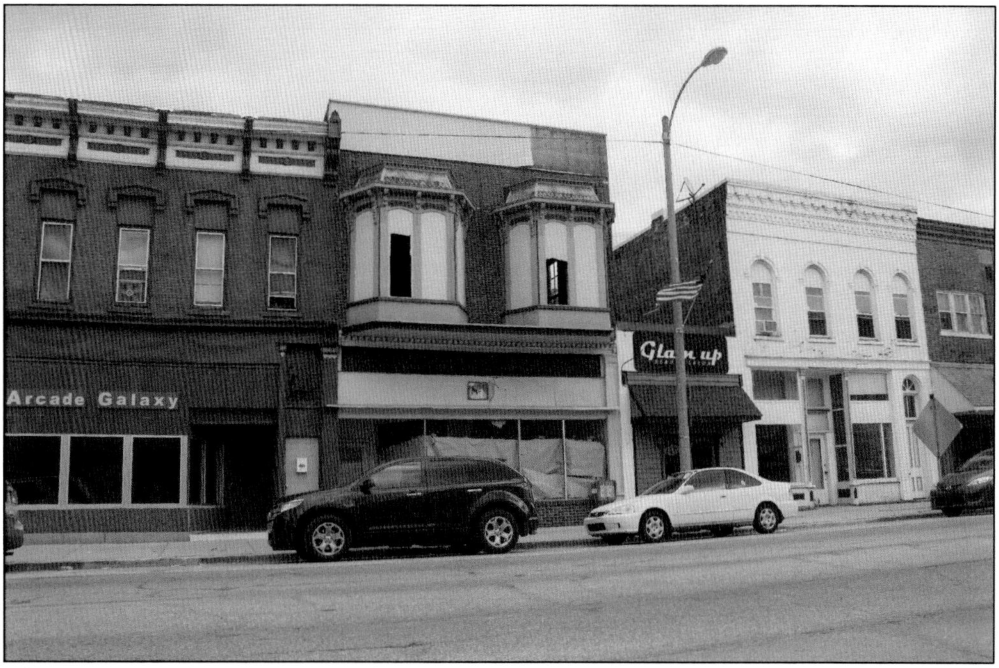


Glam Up beauty shop is at 201 South Cavin Street. Previous businesses here were Rigulo Barber Shop, Herman Sack and Garth Chrisman Haberdashery, the Wigton Law Office, and the Razor's Edge Barber and Beauty Shop. The vacant, white, two-story building is 203 South Cavin Street. This was previously the home of Green Meat Market, CA Meat Market, Stellar's Meat Market and Locker, and the Green Brothers and Oldfather Bank and Farmland.

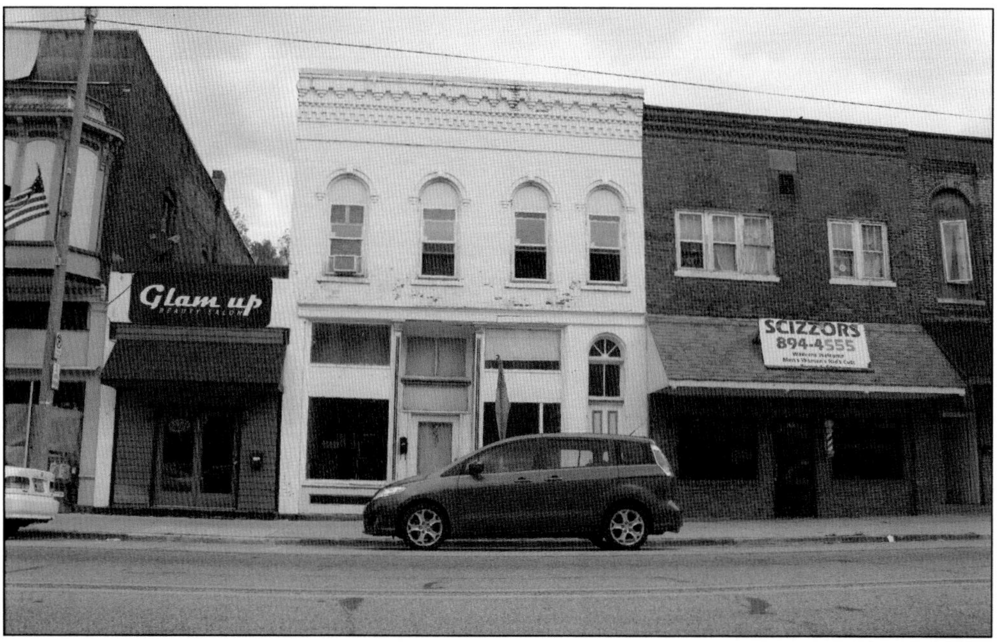


Pictured are Glam Up, the vacant building, and Scizzors Barber Shop, at 205 South Cavin Street. In the past, 205 Cavin Street has been the Cigar and Tobacco Shop, Cout's Barber Shop, Biddle's Cafe, Henry's Jewelry Store, and Hartsong's Insurance.

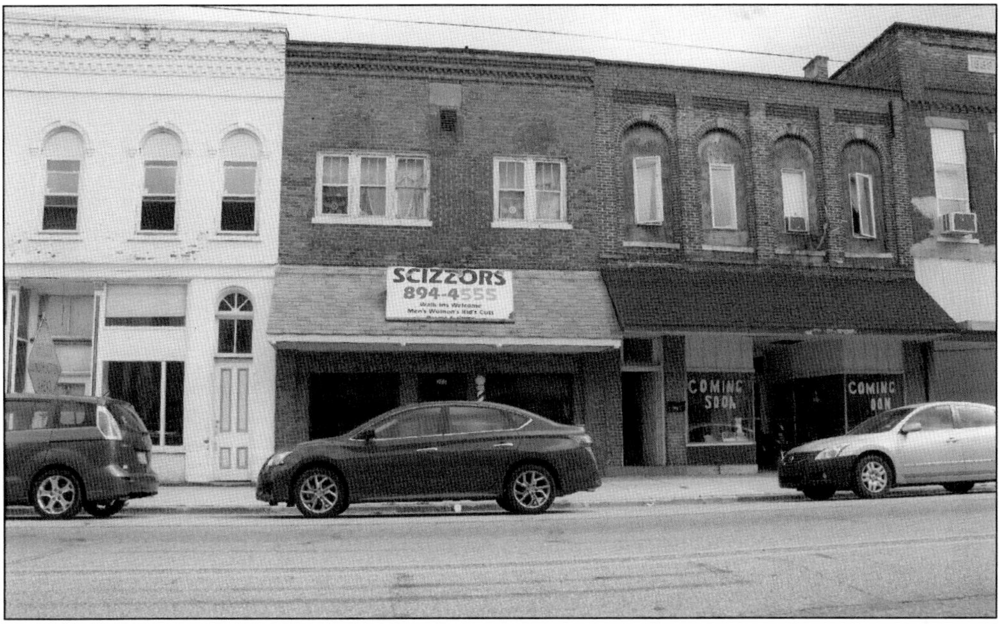


Here, a business is said to be "Coming Soon" to 207 South Cavin Street. This was previously the location of the American Café, Lowe Restaurant, Swan's Restaurant, Miller & Jones Shoe Store, and Signs & Things.

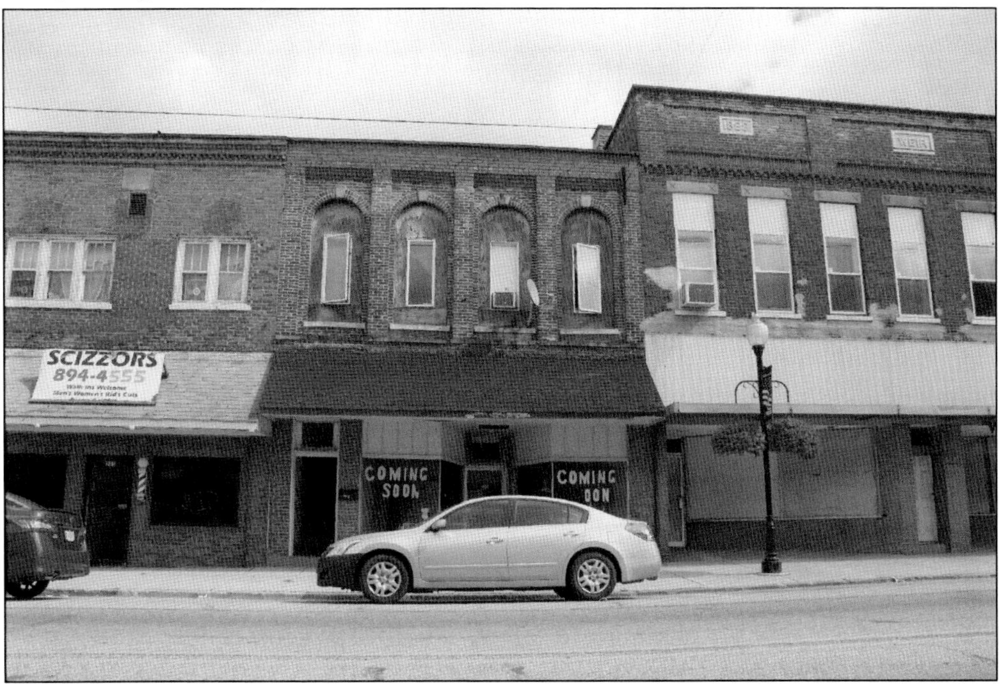


From left to right are Scizzors, "coming soon," and the vacant Weir Building (see the engraved stone near the top of the building), which occupies 209 and 211 South Cavin Street. Formerly at 209 were Art Newton Shoe Store, Jennie Hess Dress Shop, Dollar General, Bob Noe Jewelry, Sheppard's Restaurant, and Keidaish Pinball and Video Machines. At 211 were Weir & Cowley Hardware, Dale Hayes Home Store Grocery, Ton's Jewel Shoppe, and Krueger's Jewelry Shop.

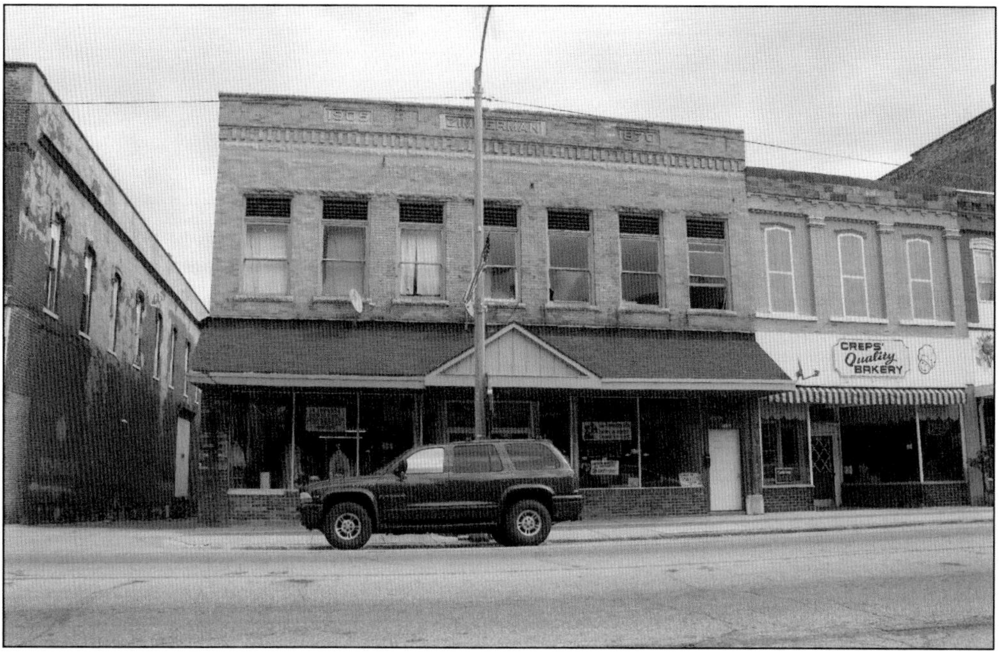


The engraved sign near the top indicates this is the Zimmerman Building. The signs in the window are for La Tampiquena. Zimmerman's Dry Goods Store, Gutelius Dime and Dollar Store, and Ben Franklin Store were once at 213 South Cavin Street. At 215 were Mel Hutchinson Jewelry Store, Mrs. Mel Hutchinson Ice Cream and Sodas, Holderness Jewelry Store, A&P Grocery, Western Auto, P.N. Hirsch Co., and Dollar General.

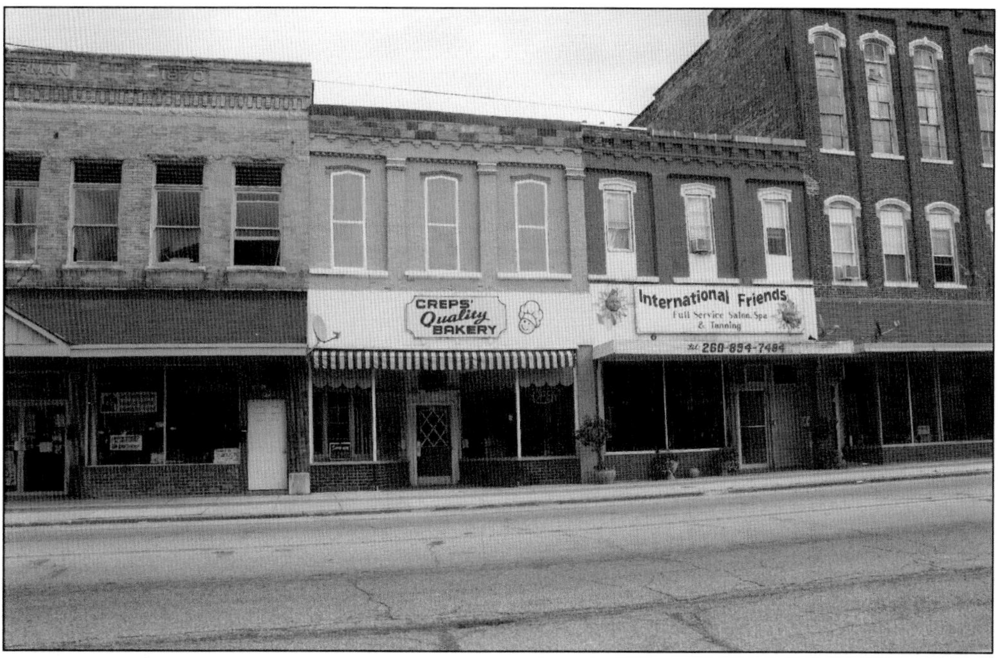


The corner of the Zimmerman Building is shown with Creps' Quality Bakery at 217 South Cavin Street and International Friends at 219. Bortner Saloon, Oyler Poolroom and Bowling Alley, Kirkwood Newspaper and Magazines, and Town Crier used to be at 219 South Cavin Street.

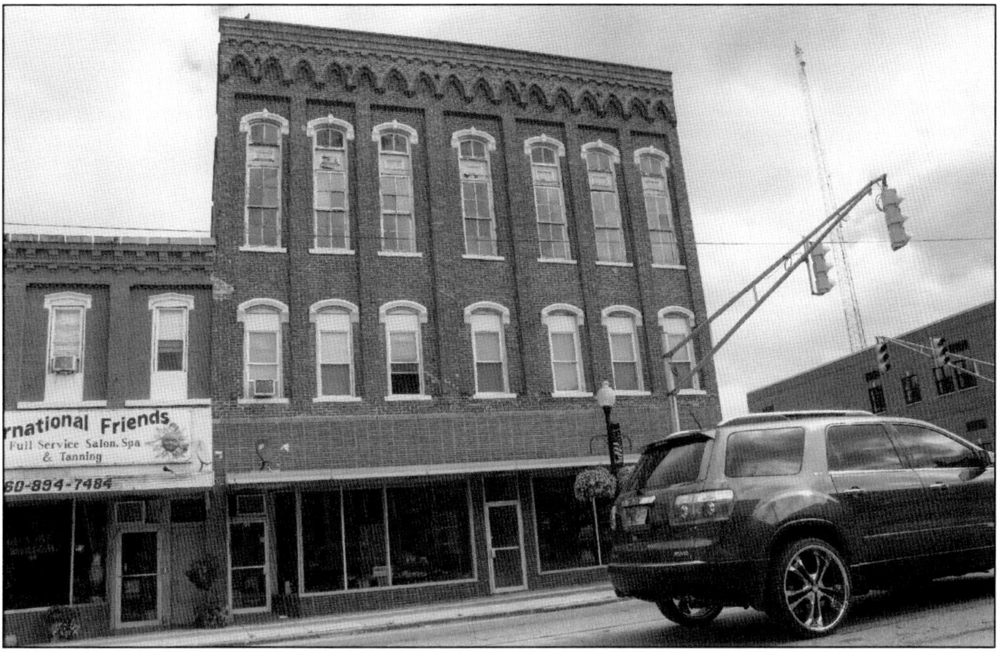


A three-story red-brown brick building, which is currently vacant, has three doors for good business entrances. The street numbers are 221, 223, and 235 South Cavin Street. This building formerly held the King and Weaver Hardware, William Cummings Tin Shop, A.W. Lyon, Weaver's Hardware, Cooper's Hardware, Stroman's Electronics, Western Auto, Seeley Brown Variety Store, Alice Schlemmer Yard Goods, and Jerry's Hardware.

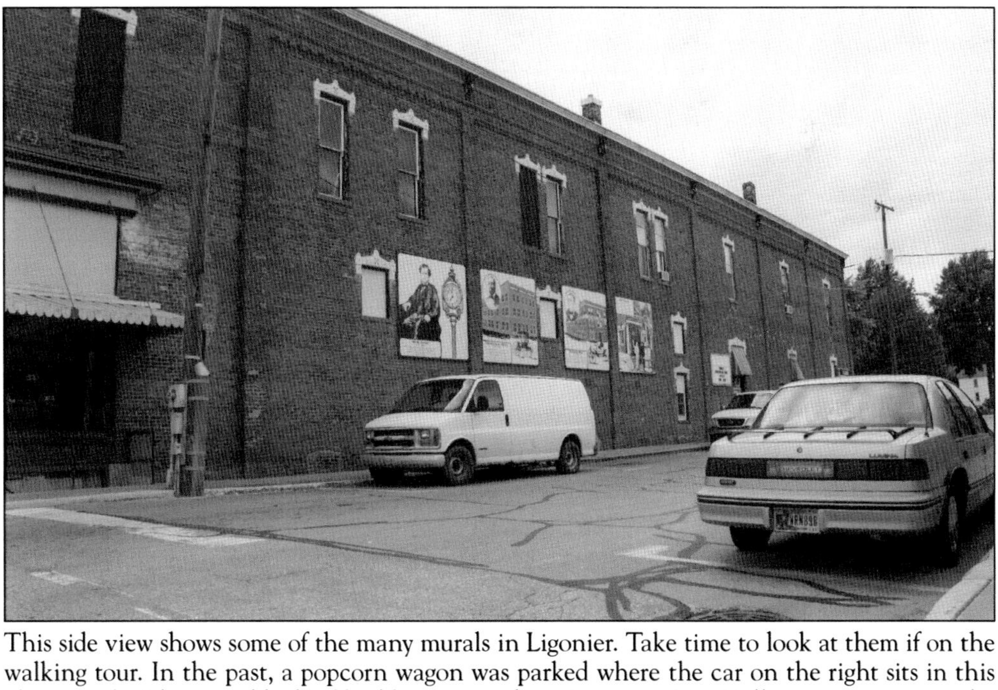

This side view shows some of the many murals in Ligonier. Take time to look at them if on the walking tour. In the past, a popcorn wagon was parked where the car on the right sits in this photograph. The next block of buildings was where Ligonier City Hall now sits, seen in the following image.

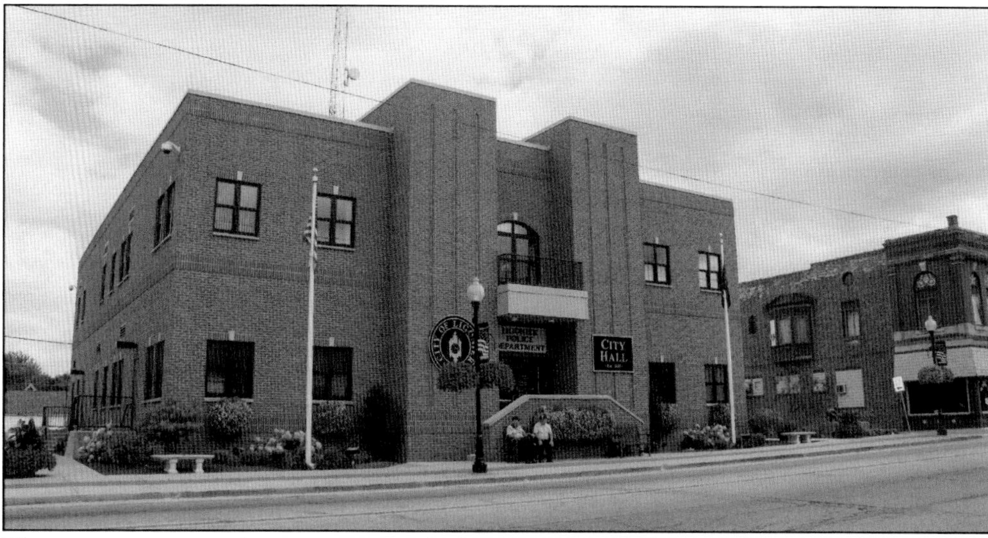


This impressive new, clean structure is the Ligonier City Hall, at 103 West Third Street. The building replaced many fine shops. The most important to the author was the Crystal Theatre, a movie theater that was bulldozed after it closed around 1970. At 301 were Jacob Sheet's Clothing Store, Levy's Furniture, Golden's Furniture, Dr. William Shobe, Dr. Arnold Elson, Dr. James Schutt, Opal Getts Beauty Shop, and Security Loan Office. Number 305 housed Burt Sisterhen's, Jet White, Schlotterback's Groceries, and Mrs. Lamb's Beauty Shop. Number 307 held Middleton Book, News, and Magazine Store; John Hoffman Book Store; Loy's Stationery, Gifts, and Book Store; Dirr's Book Store and Soda Fountain; Garl's Drug Store; Trowbridge Accounting Office; Gwenn's Dress Shop; Golden's Secondhand Furniture; and Tim's Sports and Wheels. Number 309 held Todd's Restaurant, Bellman's, Heckner's Law Firm, and Michi-Craft. Number 311 housed Simon Schloss Clothing, Sheets & Wertheimer, and the Crystal Theatre.

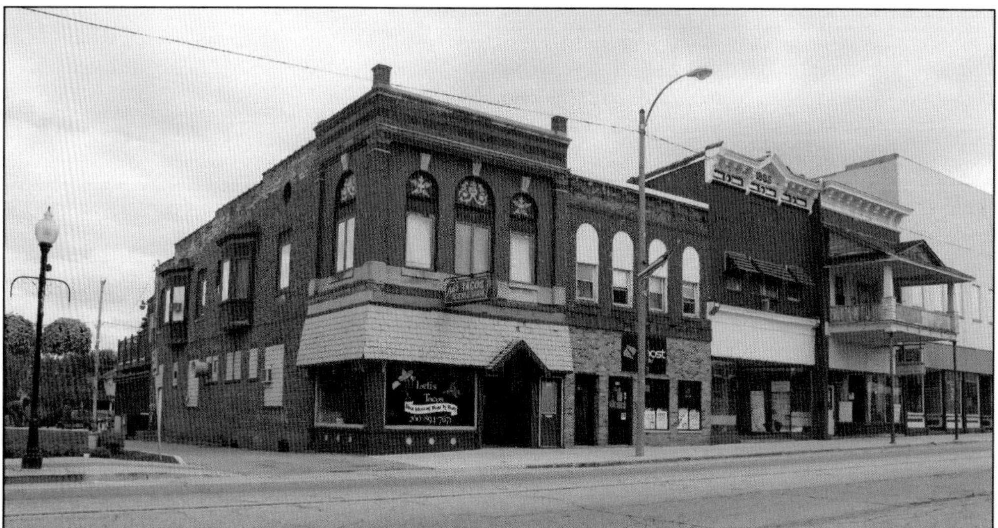

Leti's Tacos and Boost Mobile are next door at 313 and 315 South Cavin Street. The Dunning Grocery, the post office, W.R. Thomas 5 & 10, M&M 5 & 10, Leedy's Variety, Bucket & Brush, Pizza Shack, and Hopper Sister's Beauty Shop occupied 313 South Cavin Street in the past—the beauty shop on the second floor.

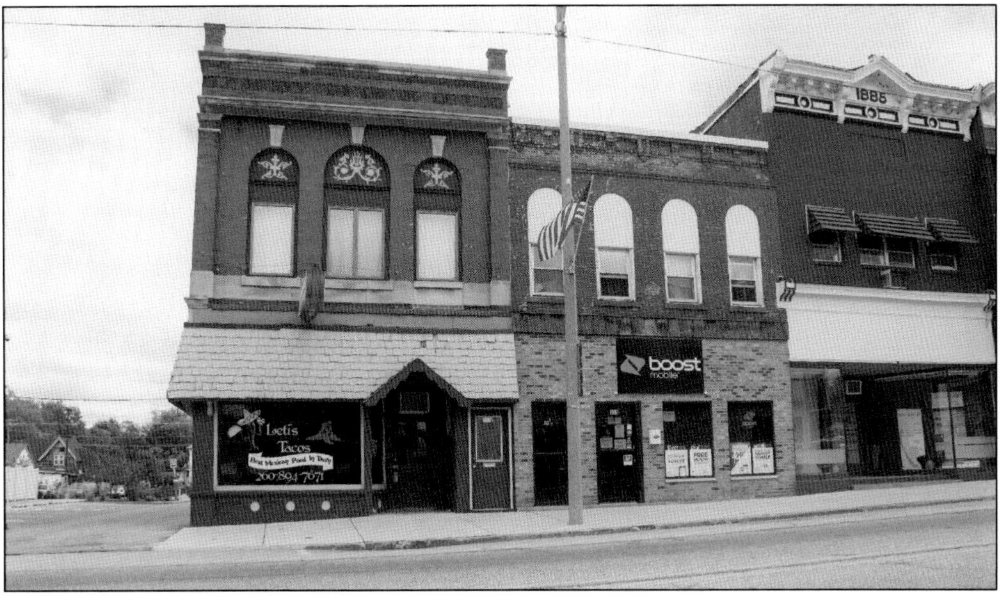


At 315 South Cavin Street were George Swan Restaurant, Lincoln Restaurant, Roy Gordon and Rollin Baker Barbershop, Ward Rimmell Gift Shop, and Bob Scott Insurance. One can see Leti's Tacos, Boost Mobile, and Wigent and Newman Law Office at 321 South Cavin Street. See the red brick, the 1885 sign at the top, and the Oeko-Tex on the sign in the window. At 317 South Cavin Street were William Casey Shoe Shop, Washing Machines, Denning and Cockley Insurance, Russell Smith's Toggery and Cleaning, and Toggery Cleaning.

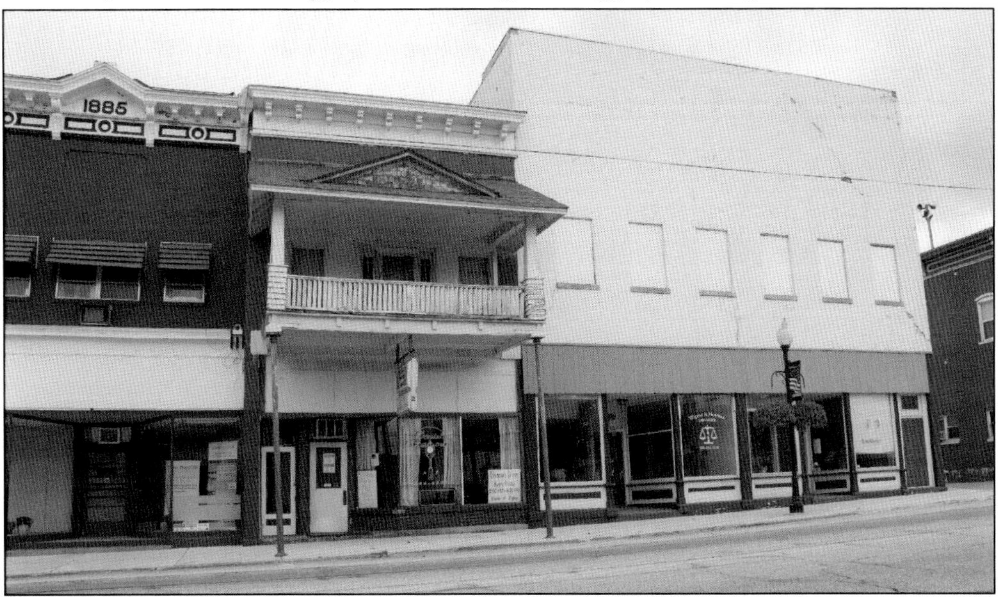


The tan or yellow building is Daniel's Ligonier Restaurant. On Fridays, Daniel serves Ethiopian food. His street number is 319. The next building to the right is Wigent and Newman Law Office at 321. Knapp Grocery, Wolfe Grocery, Fisher Poolroom, Bentz Poolroom, and Sheppard's Restaurant once inhabited 319. At 321 South Cavin Street were Eldred Drug Store, Griffith Drug Store, Dr. James Schutt, a Dr. Arnold, Dr. W.L. Harlan, Dr. Paul Webster, Dr. Robert Stone, Gene's Barber Shop, Wigent Law Office, and the post office.

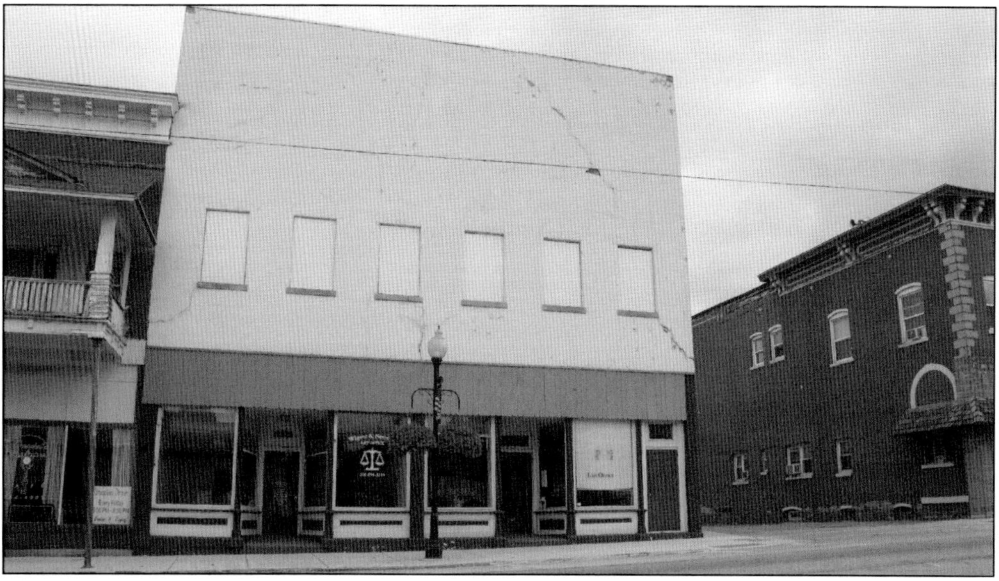

The vacant part of the building next to Wigent and Newman is number 323. Selig Meat Market, John Green Meat Market, Hassinger's Meat Market, Ligonier Electric Shop (located in the rear of the store), Smith Barber Shop, and Reflections Beauty Parlor were based at 323 South Cavin Street.

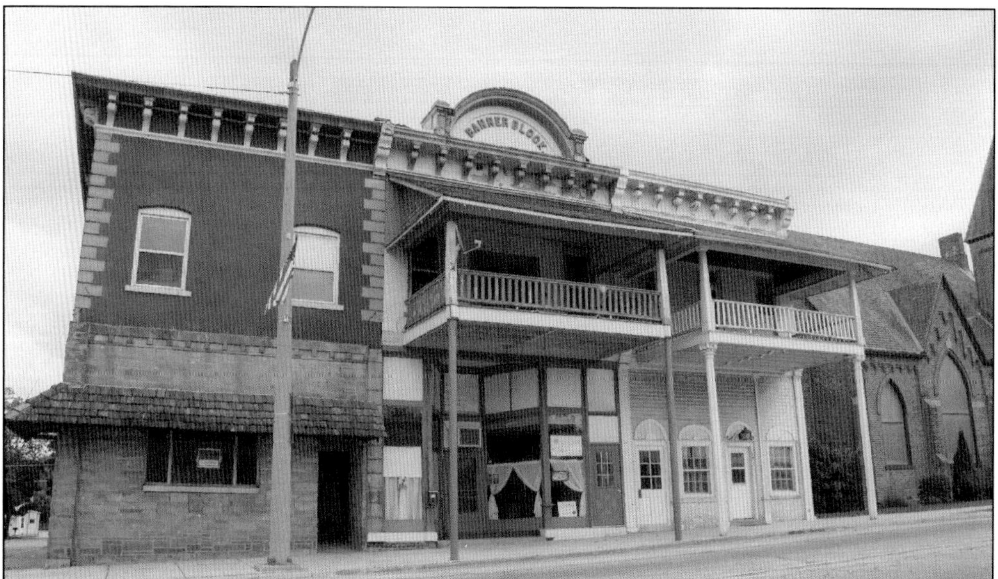

The next block of buildings is called the Banner Block (see the sign at the top of the building). The first shop is brown and is number 401. The second shop is green and is number 403. It contains Cindy's Hair Designs. The last shop in the block is white and is number 405. For 401, no listing for any businesses could be found. At 403 were Kunkalman's Millinery Shop, Nona Stuff Hat Shop, Rulison Law Office (in the rear of the building), Jan's Fashion Coiffures (in the rear of the building), Dr. Stoelting Dentist Office, and Fiandt & Rollins Insurance. At 405 were Banner Newspaper, Banner Printers, the first post office (located here in 1886), Inks Telephone Company (the predecessor of the Ligonier Telephone Company), and Dr. Robert Stone's office.

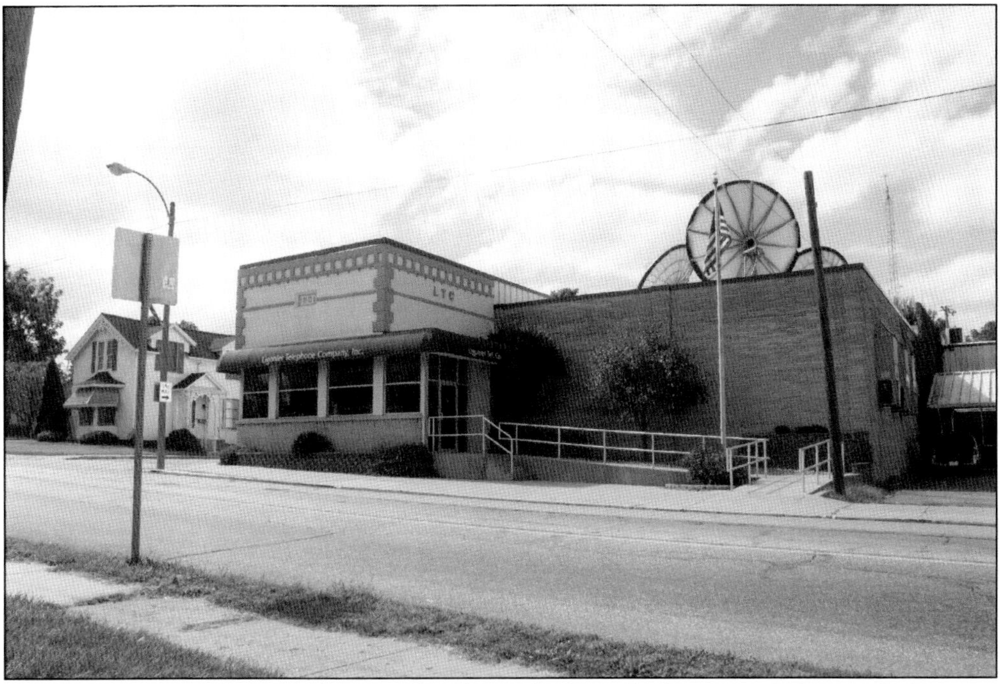

At 414 South Cavin Street is the Ligtel building, which was built in 1901. It houses the Ligonier Telephone Company, which will help with telephone, television, and Internet needs. The telephone was in Ligonier before 1900. Ligonier Telephone Company even made its own phones.

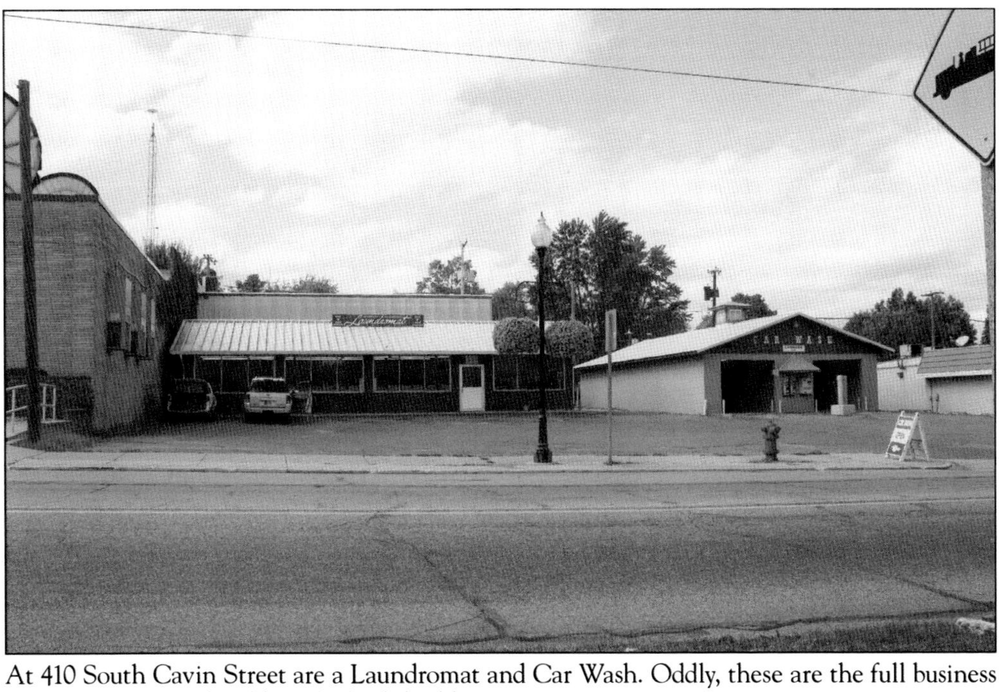

At 410 South Cavin Street are a Laundromat and Car Wash. Oddly, these are the full business names and the single address for both buildings.

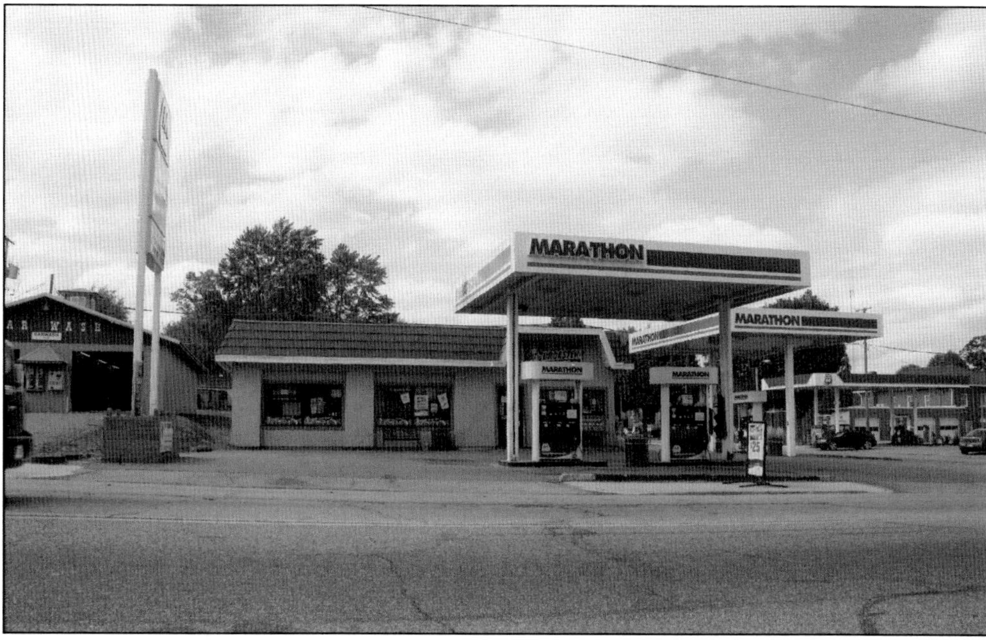

This site is home to the Ligonier Petro Marathon at 400 South Cavin Street. The history of this location includes Jacob Raubert Watchmaker, Pete Smith's Barber and Dr. O.H. Luse Dentist.

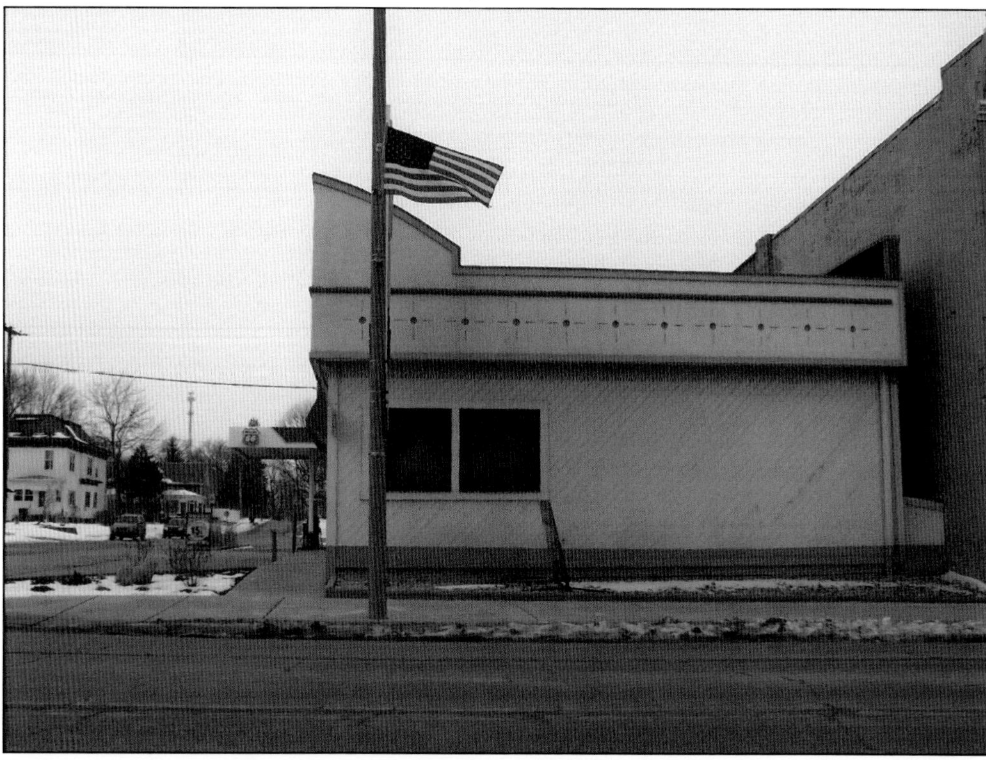
In the space where the Pac-a-Sak or Phillips 66 sits (102 West Fourth Street or 318 South Cavin Street) was Kerr Undertaking and Furniture. R.D. Kerr ran the business from 1858 to 1904, and Louis Kerr (his son) finished the history.

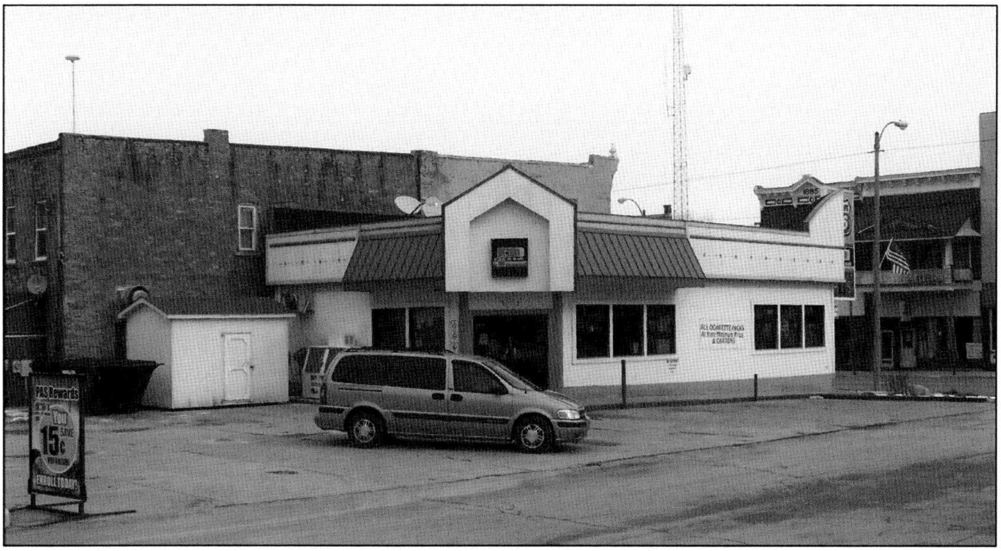

Orewiler Chevy Garage may also have been west of the Kerr Undertaking and Furniture. This space was 320 and 318 South Cavin Street. At 320, the businesses were Hugh Lundy Barber, Laura Mae Tea Room, and Orchid Beauty Shop; at 318 was Graves and Ona Dill Hat Shop. The numbering system may have changed after buildings were demolished.

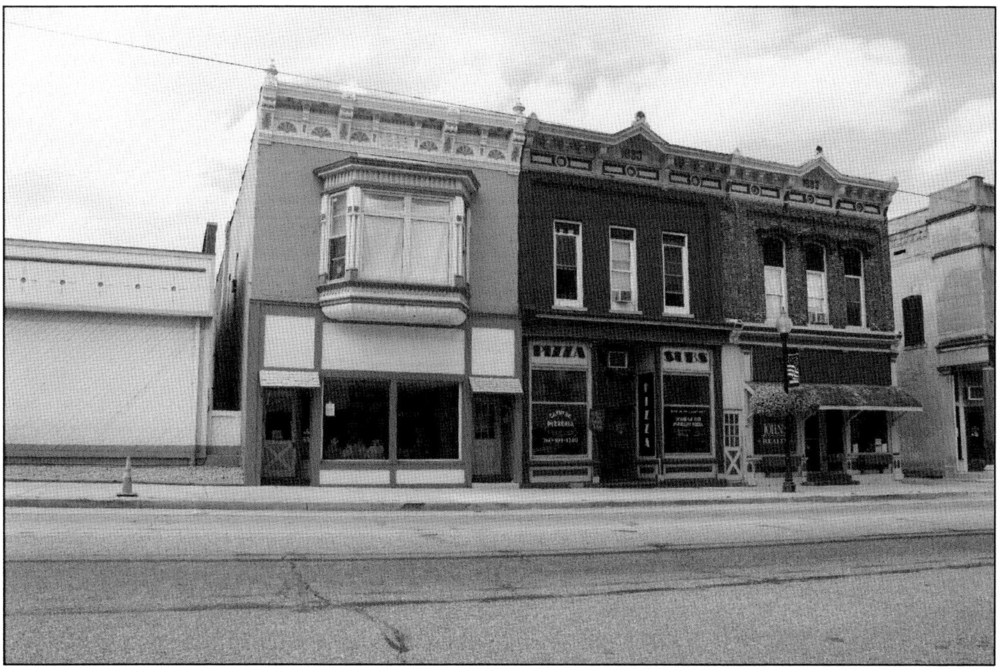

Note that three buildings are shown. They were built in 1889, 1883, and 1883. The first on the left, at 316 South Cavin Street, is presently vacant. Earlier businesses here were Mary Gordon Dress Shop, Bob Sedgwick's Laundromat, and Sears Catalog Store. The building in the center, at number 314, is now Cavin Street Pizzeria. Previously the address was Sack's Grocery, King Attorneys, and H&R Block. The structure at right houses John's Realty at number 312. Previously, this corner shop held Sisterhen's Shoe Store, McAdams Jewelry, Irene Mitchell's Beauty Shop, and J&M TV. In the back was Ed Keasey's blacksmith shop.

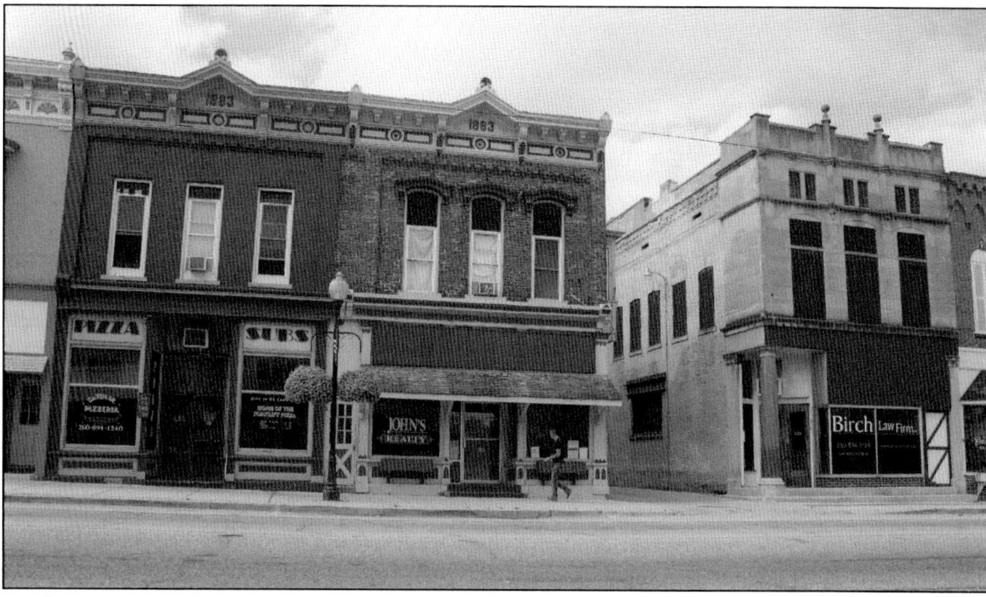


Birch Law Firm is at 310 South Cavin Street. This once was the home of the Banking House of Solomon Mier. Later, Frank's Sporting Goods got the attention of lots of men and boys. Tim's Sport-N-Wheels and Flooring Unlimited followed. Above this store were Ena Oliver's Beauty Shop, Opal Getts Beauty Shop, and offices for Dr. James Schutt, Dr. A.M. Timmis, Dr. Richard Stoelting, and Dr. Frank Black.

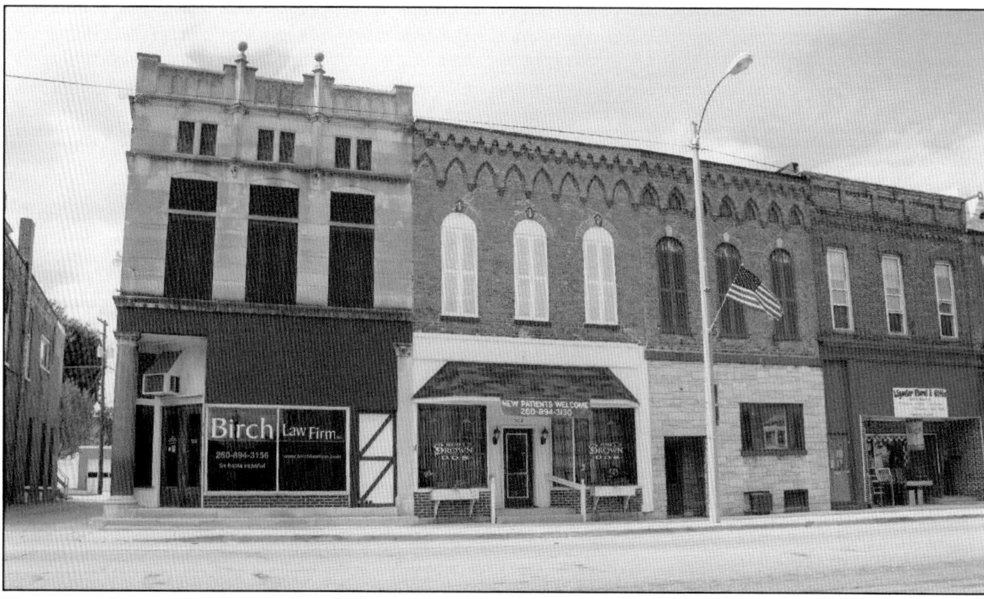


Four storefronts are shown: Birch Law Firm at 310 South Cavin Street, Brown Dental with Dr. Richard D. Brown and Dr. Peter J. Brown at 308, a vacant storefront at 306, and Ligonier Floral and Gift at 304 South Cavin Street. Number 308 used to offer Essi Candy Kitchen, the Philadelphia, Sheppard's Restaurant, and Ligonier Accounting. At number 306, the fine businesses of Sheets & Wertheimer Feeds, Wertheimer & Sons Feed, and Ligonier Eagles once flourished. At number 304, one could buy scrips from Sam Williams Drug Store, Knights Drug Store, Meyers Drug Store and Soda Fountain, Blues Drug Store, and Shoemaker's Drug Store.

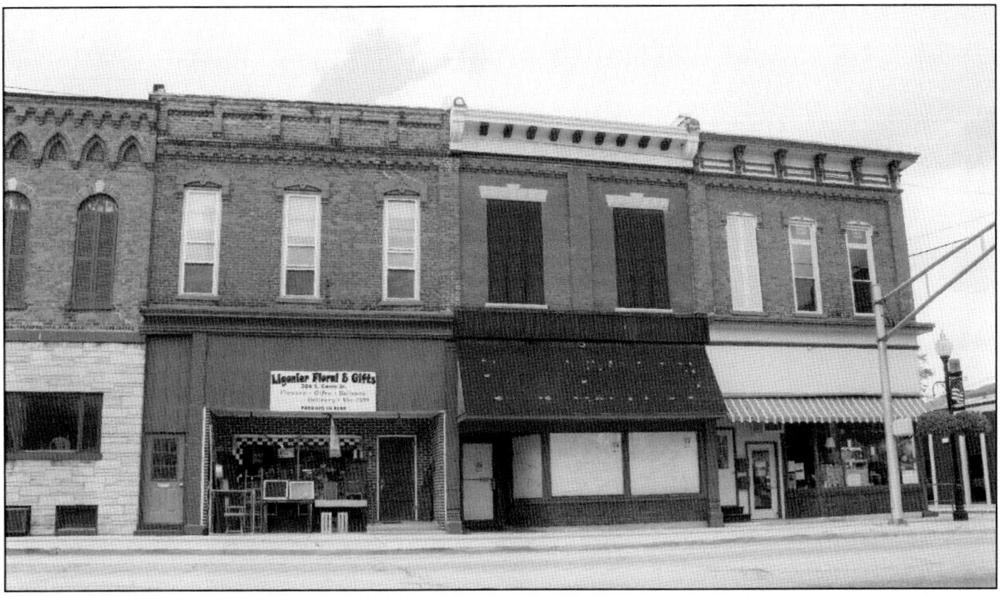


Two new storefronts are shown. Number 302 is vacant. Number 300 looks occupied, but the sign that tells the name of the store is missing. Lou Kerr Undertaking once occupied these addresses. Then Guy Calbeck Hardware, Frank Christlieb, and E&T Auto Pro Parts occupied this choice location. It is believed that 302 and 300 connected in the past. 300 was home to E.B. Gerber Hardware, Stellar's Meat and Butcher Shop, Raubert's Jewelry, Dr. F.N. Stratton, South's Grocery, and Ligonier Hardware, with Pete's Barber Shop in the basement. The author was told by Mayor Patty Fisel that there were five businesses on this site at the same time. Many small businesses were in the basement. Their names may be lost to history.

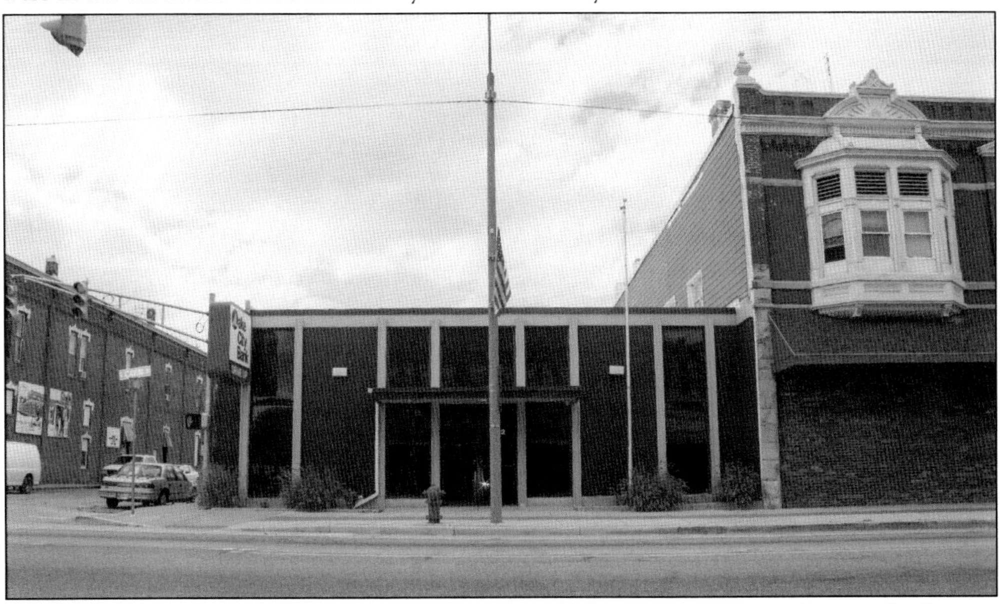

This modern-looking building is Lake City Bank at 222 South Cavin Street. Previously, this site housed Citizen's Bank and American State Bank. To the west of this building were Lepird Livery Barn, Foster Sales Barn, S&H Farm Implements, veterinarian Dr. G.O. Smith, Kiser Insurance, and Bill Kitson Barber Shop. The building to the right with the bay window is 220 South Cavin.

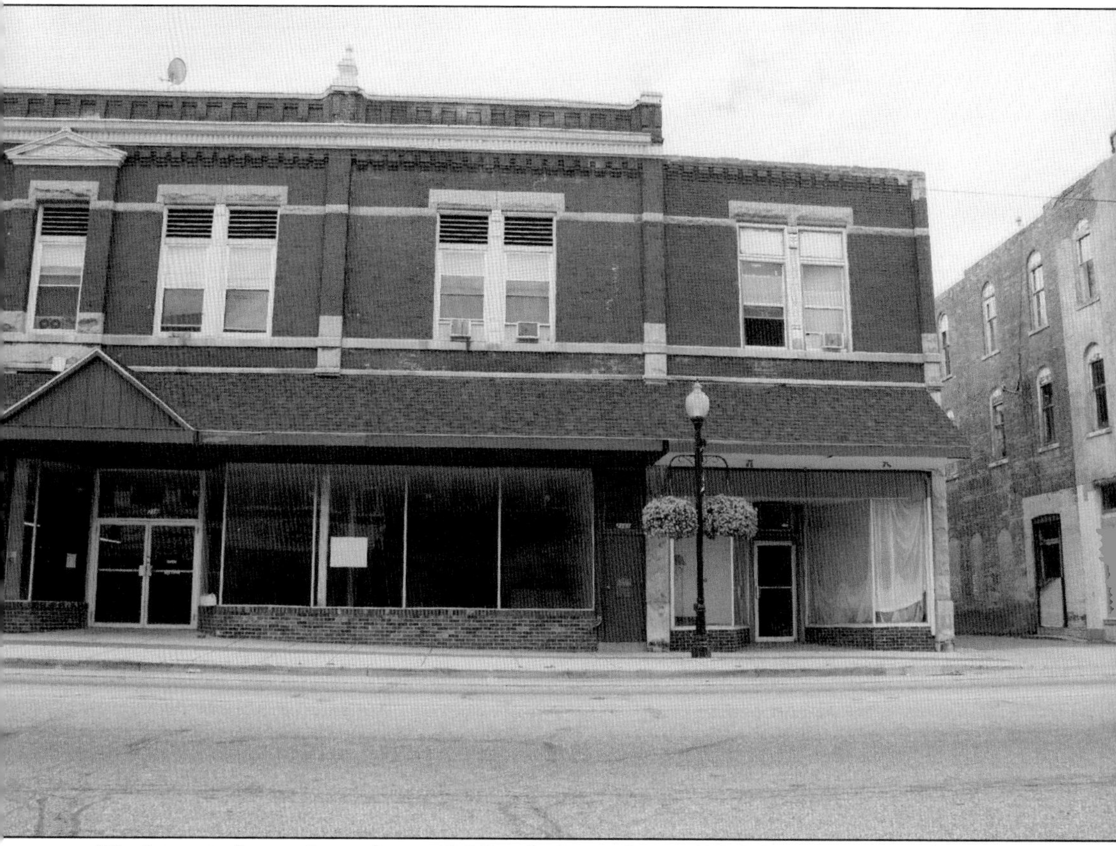

The historical records say that at 220 South Cavin Street, B&S Carpets was on the second floor and on the first floor were Goldsmith and Jacobs Dry Goods, Goldsmith & Jacobs Ladies Ready to Wear, Jacob & Hess Clothing Store, and Atz Furniture Store. At 218 South Cavin Street were Addis Beauty Shop (likely a second-floor business), Orchid Beauty Shop, Tillman Pool Room, Koons Pool Room, Koon's Bar & Restaurant, and the Hoosier Club. At 216 South Cavin Street were Henry Israel Saloon, Shirt Factory, Lepird Shoe Store, Galloway Shoe Store, Miller & Jones Shoe Store, and Paul Delucanay Shoe Repair. There is another vacant building at the north end at 214 South Cavin Street. This was formerly the home of J.P. Carney Men's Clothing Store, Sack's Bakery, Oscar Barch, American Insurance Agency, and Ligonier Chiropractic Center.

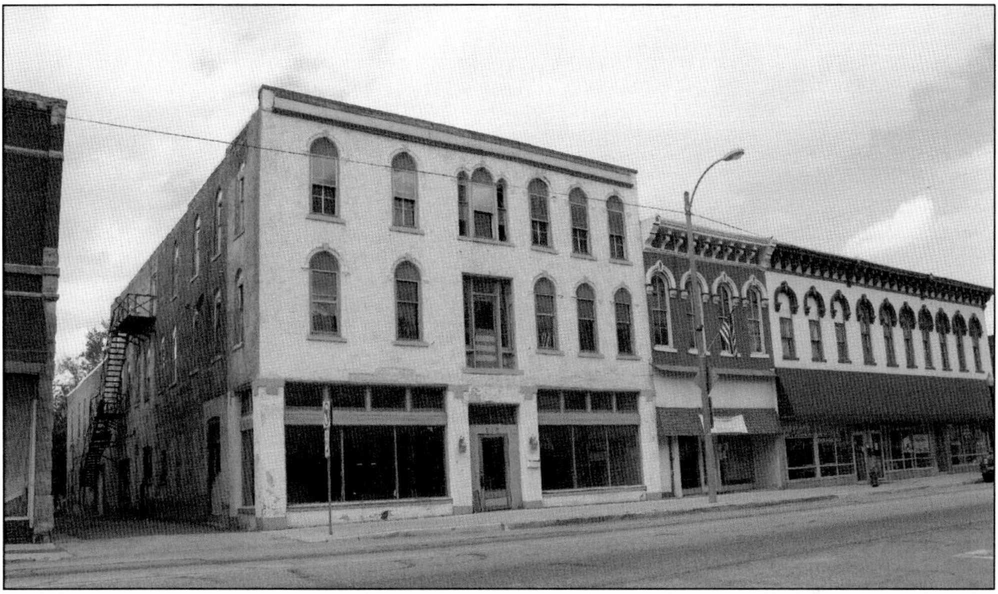

This impressive-looking three-story building is now vacant, but it used to be hopping. It housed the Goldsmith Hotel, which later became the Ligonier Hotel. There is a very visible "212" sign but the older maps mark this as 210 and 208. Also on the second floor at this site were Dr. Frank Black, Isaac Rose, and Dr. A.M. Timmis. In the back was the Blue Room Cocktail Lounge. Later, this was Ankersons.

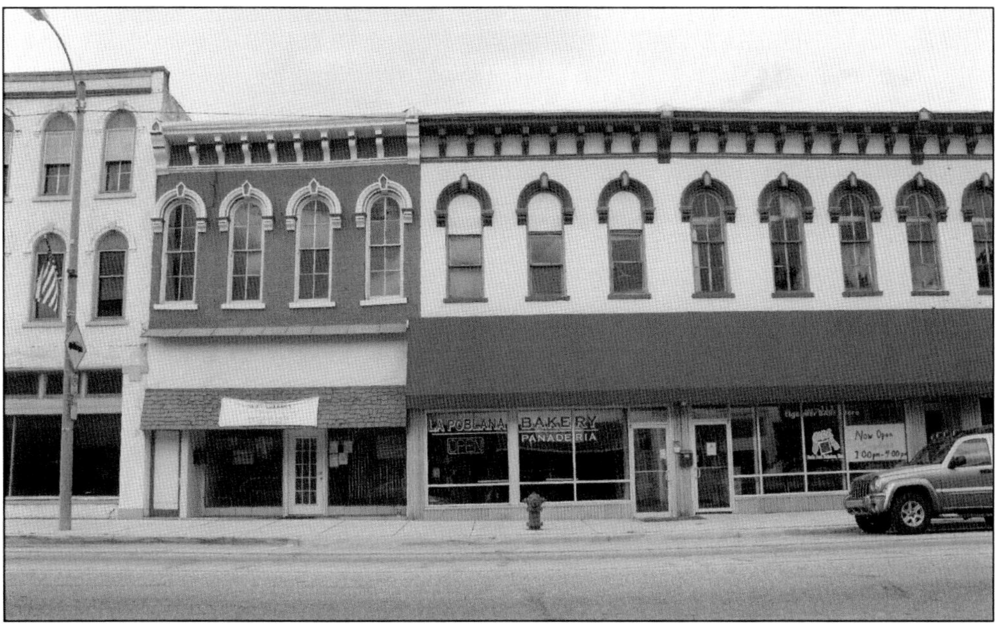


The next business, at 208 South Cavin Street, is Nuevamerika. The author believes that this site was part of the businesses listed above when the hotel was 210 and 208 South Cavin Street. Also shown in this photograph are 206 South Cavin Street, La Poblena Bakery Panederia; a vacant number 204; and number 202, Ligonier Babe Store. The Whitelite Theater, Wertheimer & Sons, Newton Shoe Store, Miller's Shoe Store, Miller & Jones Shoe Store, the Shoe Shack, and Craft Shop previously occupied 206 South Cavin Street.

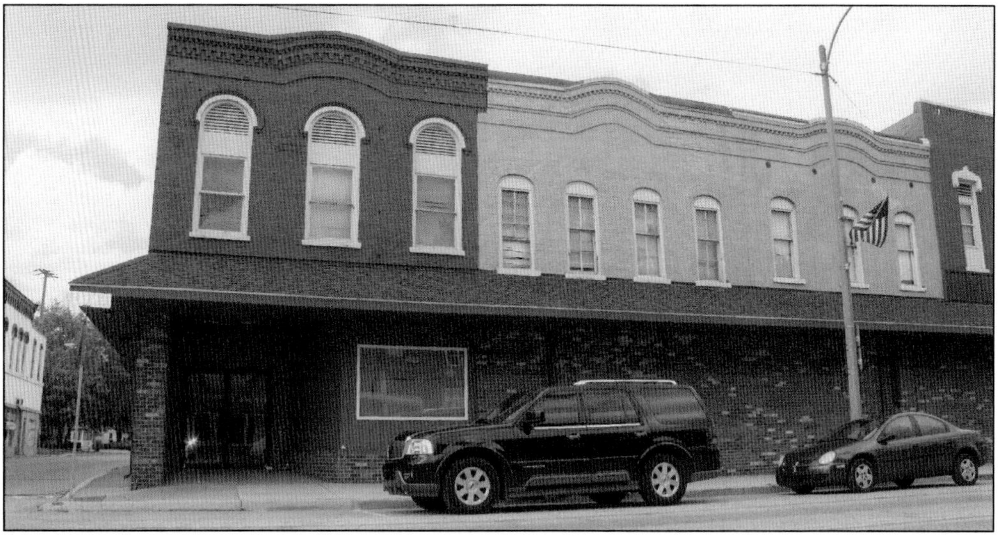

At 204 South Cavin Street were Green Meat Store, C&A Green Meat Market, Henry Green & Sons, Farmers & Merchants Trust Company of Ligonier, Green Bros. & Oldfather, and S.J. Williams Drug Store. Ligonier had major fires in 1860, 1870, and 1873. Many structures were built in 1883 and 1888, likely as the result of those fires. The vacant site above is at number 202, although no sign is posted. Zimmerman's Bakery & Grocery with Dressmaker used to be on the second floor. Others included John Kegg Bakery, 5 and 10, Economy Grocery, Kerr Undertaking, Jet White Groceteria, Herman Sack Clothing Store, and Pettit & Galloway Clothing.

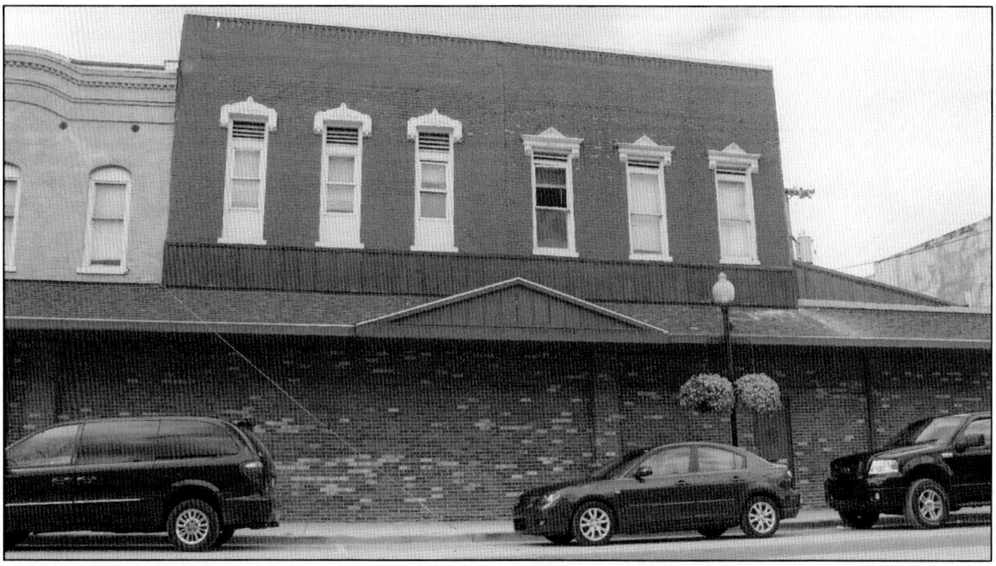

Previous businesses at this vacant site were Reed's Drug Store, *Banner Newspaper*, Stellar's Meat and Butcher Shop, Banner Drugs, Banner Laundry, Radio Shack, and Ligonier Electronics. Number 116 housed Brown Furniture and Undertaking, then later the loan office and city clerk's office, DePew's Plumbing, and Fritz TV. Numbers 114 and 112 were the sites of the famous Stansbury Dry Goods and Stansbury Grocery. Number 110 was Reed Grocery and Drugs, Jess Dewey's Laundry and Cleaners, Caldwell Bicycle Shop, Jorg's Hatchery, Mazlin Hatchery, and Neuhoser Hatchery. Number 108 housed an open-air theater (in other words, an empty lot), followed by the Indiana & Michigan office, Kimmell Realty Office, Sheppard's Light Lunch Counter, and Village Market.

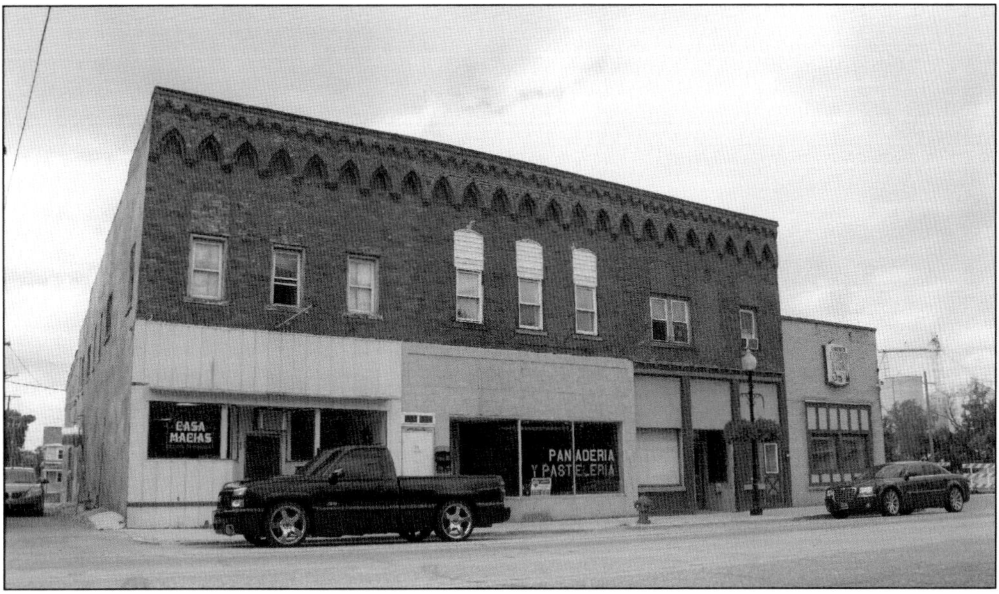


Casa Macias is at 106 South Cavin Street. Previously, the building hosted a hardware business, Kauffman Garage, and Ligonier Liquor Store. The author's grandfather, William Furkis, kept the light on in the Ligonier Liquor Store. A vacant building is at 104 South Cavin Street, which previously was Joe Scovial Furniture, Elijah Motors, Cloverleaf Creamer, S&H Implements, and Noble Auto Parts. The last vacant building is 102. This site used to be the Fruit Dryers storage (in 1866), followed by Billman's Pump Shop, Sprague's Card Room, Union Hall, and Kay Shearer Ceramics.

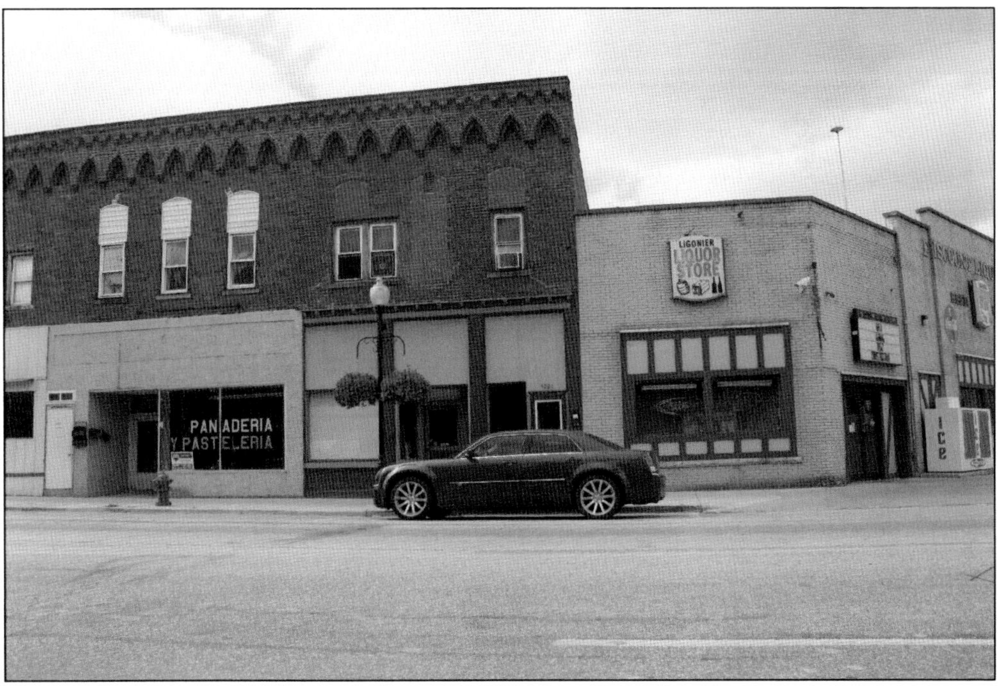


The Ligonier Liquor Store is seen from the side at South Cavin Street, although no address is posted.

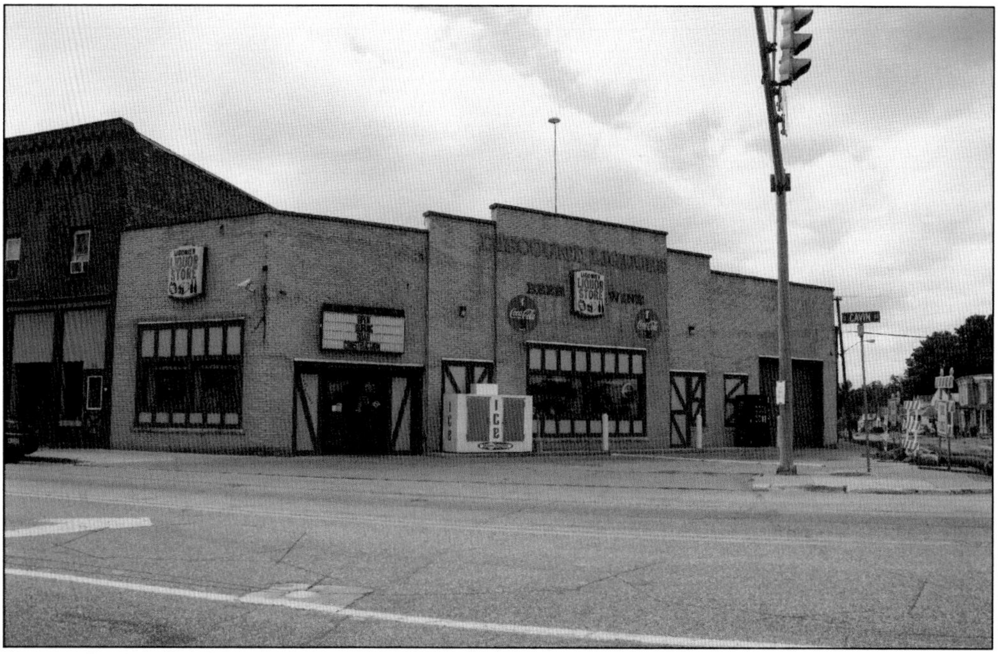


Here is the front of the Ligonier Liquor Store at 100 South Cavin Street. This was a watchmaker shop in 1866, followed by Bryan's Ford Garage, Whitaker's Chevy Garage, Edd Tyler Oil and Kerosene, and Noble County Beverage Company.

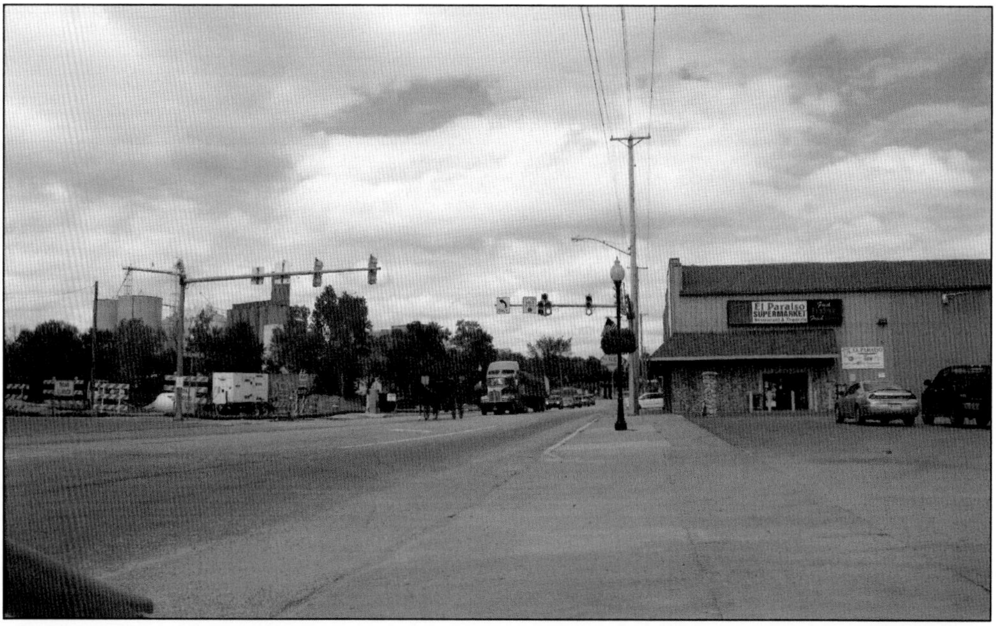


The Star of the West Milling Company can be seen in the distance. At the stoplight is an Amish horse and buggy, which is a common site in Ligonier. This corner on the west side of the stoplight used to be the site of the Ligonier Carriage Company. Later, it was the Ligonier Refrigerator Company. Then it was the US Rubber Company, and at last, Essex Wire. This is why there were two or three lunch counters within a block. Photographs of these businesses are shown elsewhere in this book.

# *Three*

# The Government Helps Organize

Whenever a large group of people gathers, there is the need for organization and for someone to provide services. The people pick someone to represent them, attend meetings, make decisions, and spend money in their behalf.

Some of the highlights in this chapter are the waterworks, bridges, police, library, post office, schools, band, and the parks. The author knows some of these might not be considered a part of the government, but because this books needs organization they are placed in this chapter.

The need for clean water (as opposed to Elkhart River water) was seen early on. The job should be controlled by the city, not by an individual. In other words, water is too important to be controlled by one private company. This role of the government was established in 1888 thanks to Solomon Mier (a Jewish citizen and leader of Ligonier). Around this same time, the need for sewage treatment was viewed as another governmental job, but this book does not delve into that. Few pictures of making a sewer or working in sewage exist.

Without roads and bridges, commerce would grind to a halt. The government was put in charge of making and maintaining roads and bridges. Cavin Street has a major bridge over the Elkhart River. The viaduct under the railroad tracks might be viewed as an underground bridge.

Ligonier once had a jail and an Indiana State Police post. A police department is found in the city hall to this day. There is also a fire department. Both are vitally needed to protect citizens, property, and businesses.

The public library performs a service for all citizens, and the post office performs a vital function. For the purposes of this book, they are discussed in this chapter.

Schools are a big part of the government. Schools and libraries are supported by taxes paid to the government.

The last roles of government in this chapter will be related to bands and parks. Many bands are featured, but only one park.

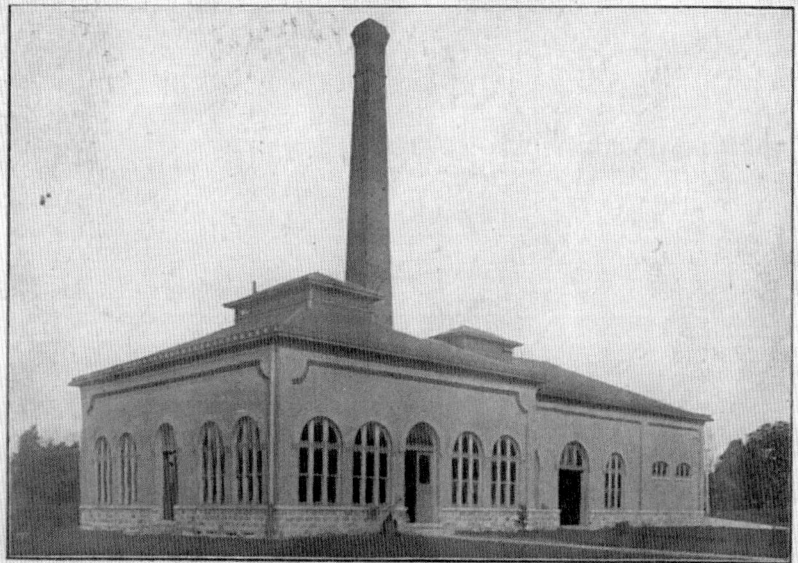

Water Works, Ligonier, Ind.

This c. 1890 photograph may be the earliest of the Ligonier Water Works building. In 1889, Solomon Mier proposed the idea that the waterworks should be publicly owned.

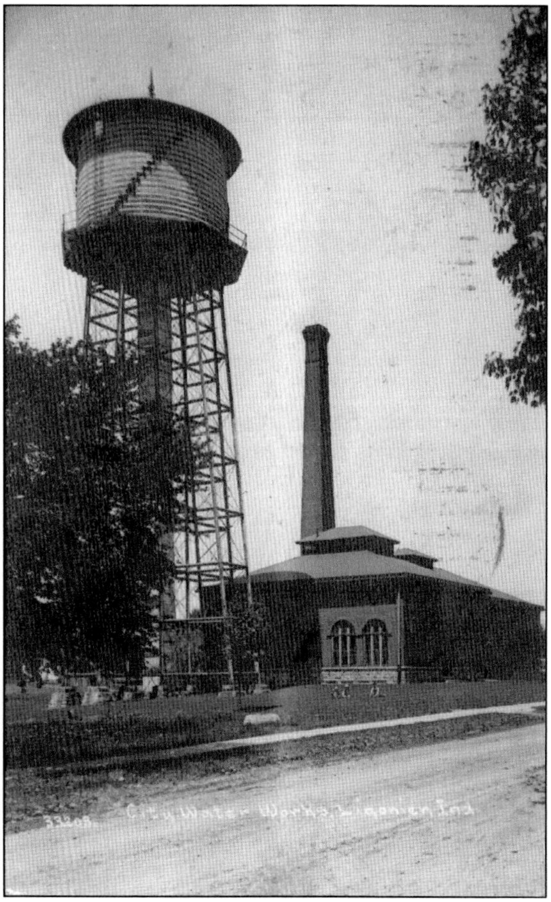


The water tower stores the water. When people do not need large amounts of water (such as at night when they are sleeping), the water is pumped up into the tower. When businesses are humming and people are showering or watering the horses and cattle, the tank is drained. The pressure in the line to the homes is greater if this method is used. The pressure would vary greatly if the tank were not there.

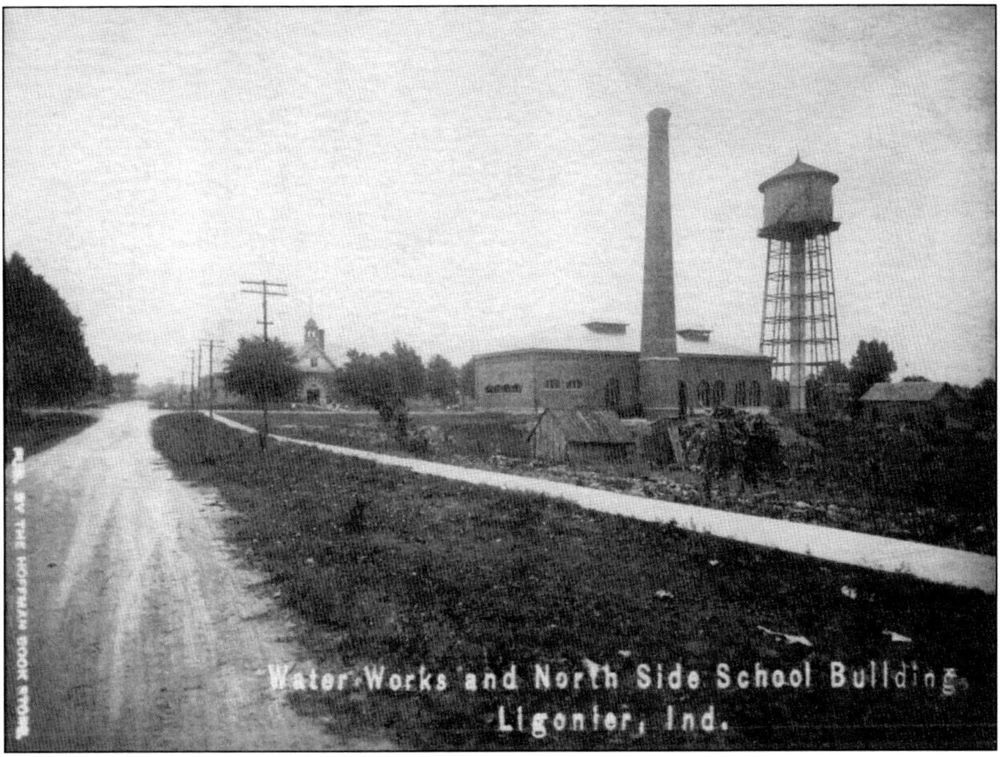


This early photograph shows the Northside School (built in 1889) and the waterworks. The waterworks is on Water Street. It is unknown which was named first, the street or the building.

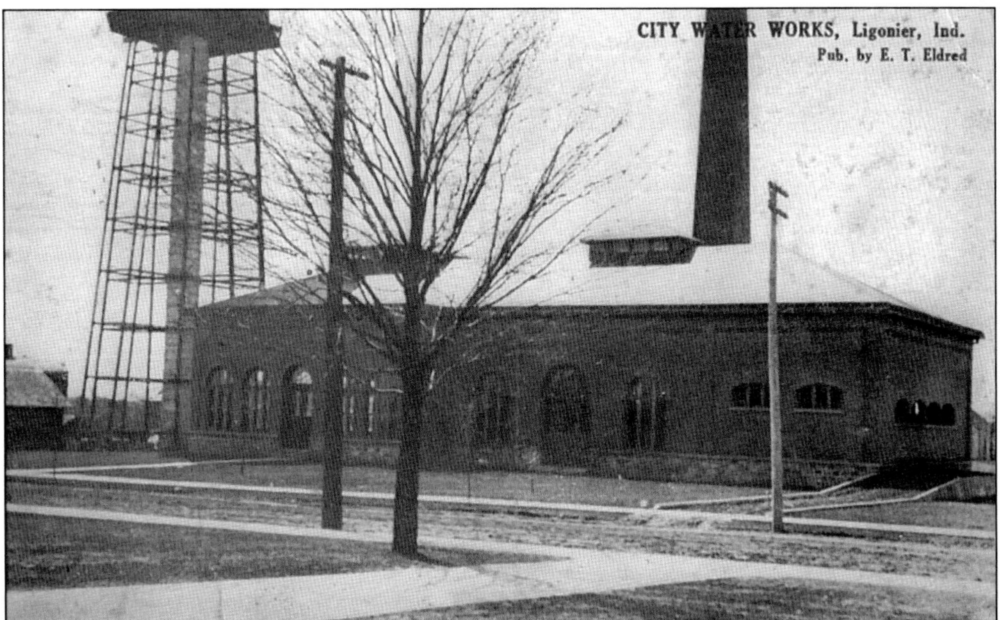


The waterworks pumped 2 million gallons of water each day in 1985 for industrial use and home use. Car washes and Laundromats in Ligonier also use water. This building shows where the process was started by the Ligonier city government before 1900.

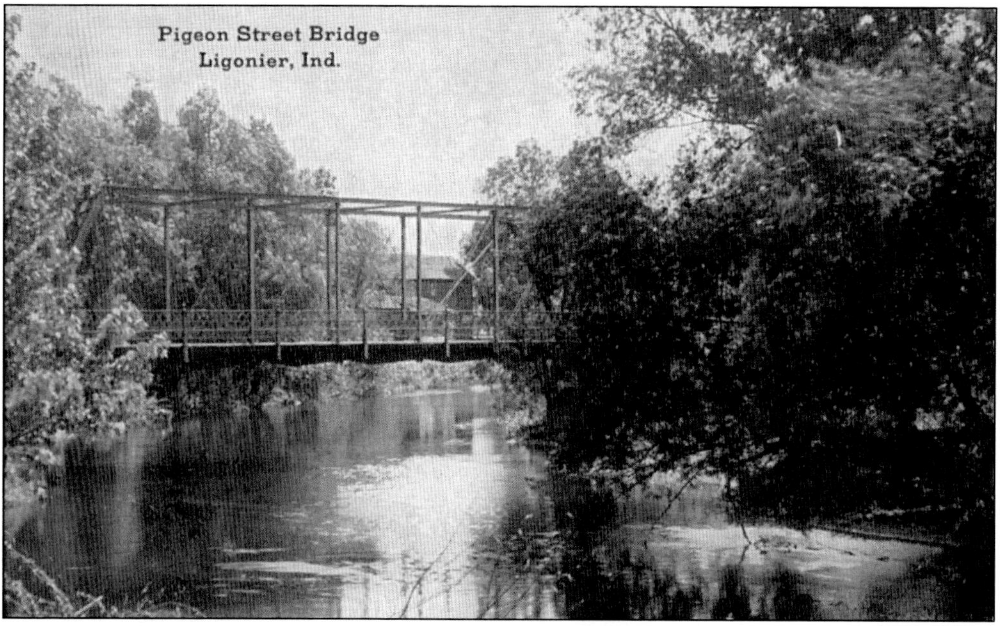


This bridge is like the one that went over the Elkhart River on Cavin Street, but it is not the Cavin Street Bridge. It is the Pigeon Street Bridge. The bridge over Cavin Street would have been larger and wider, because Cavin Street has heavier traffic.

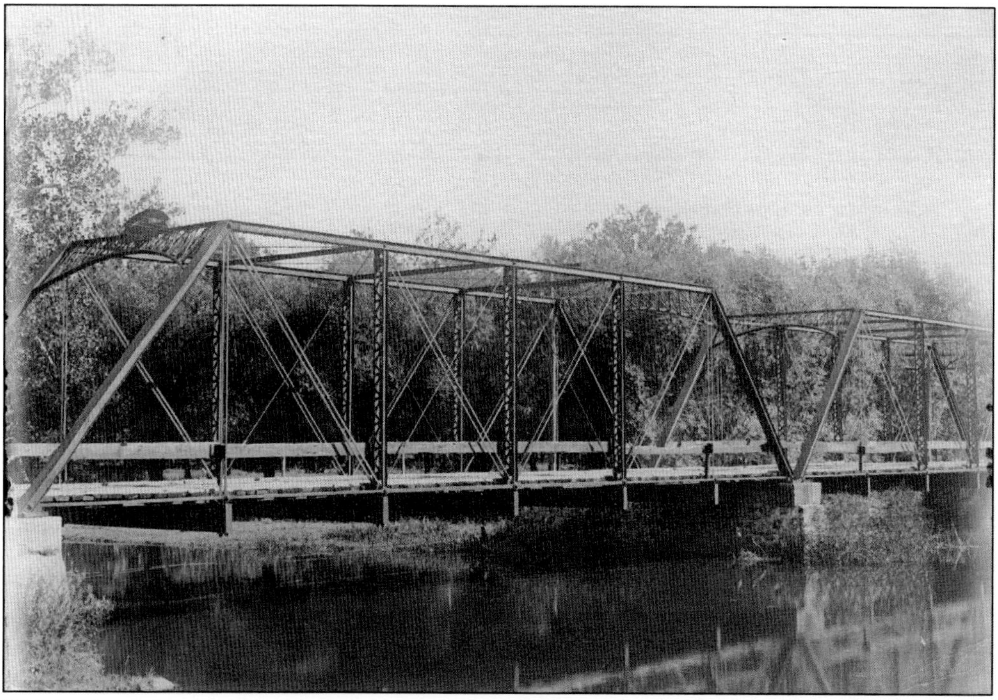

This bridge is larger than the Pigeon Street Bridge. It is for a larger river that needs a support in the middle of the span. The author is unsure if this is like the Cavin Street Bridge or the bridge at Rochester, one mile east of Ligonier. It is shown here merely as an example of a larger steel bridge.

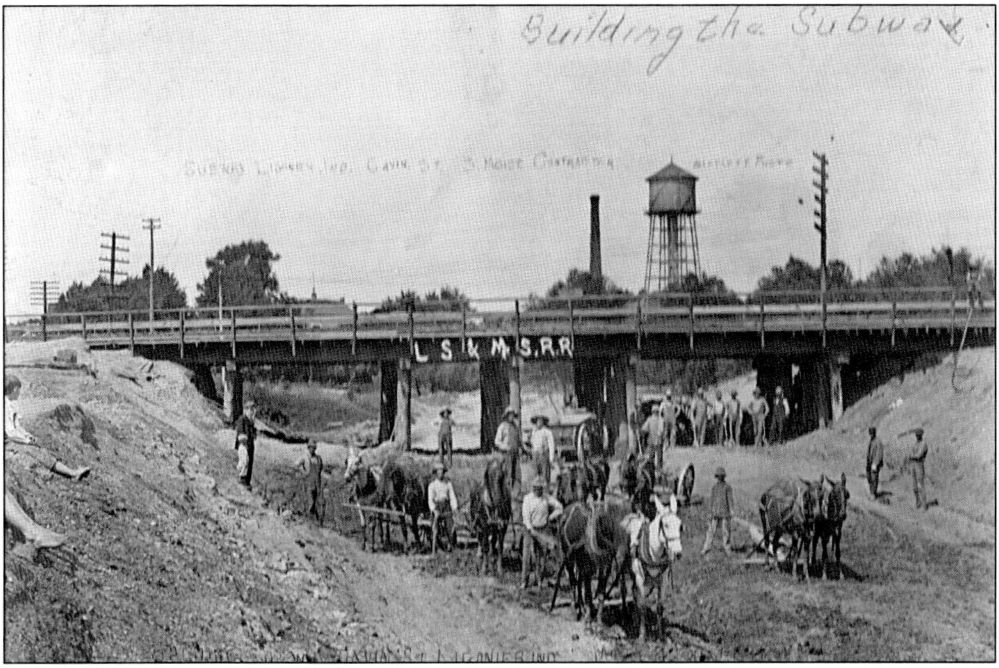


This was preparatory road work to get the ground leveled so that traffic on Cavin Street could go under the railroad viaduct. It is not bridge construction but it is similar in that lots of dirt must be moved and one does not want to just use a shovel to do it. The Cavin Street Bridge replacement caused a lot of headache to the traffic through Ligonier.

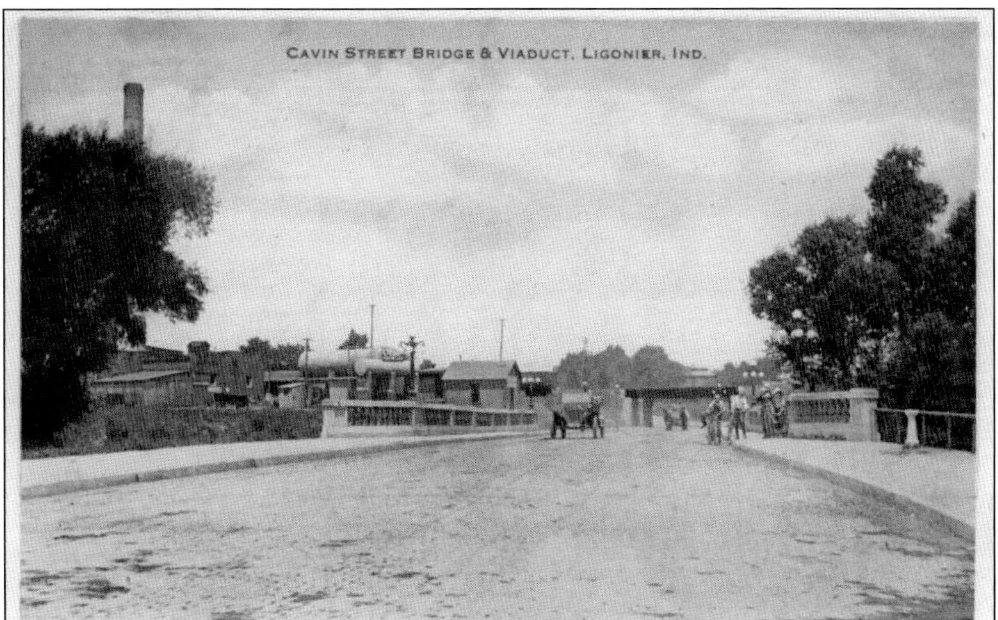


This photograph shows the traffic after the bridge has been replaced. Note how light the traffic appears. In the background on the left is the Ligonier Milling site. Just seeing that site should remind citizens why they need the Cavin Street Bridge and why they want a heavy-capacity bridge hauling semis full of wheat to the mill.

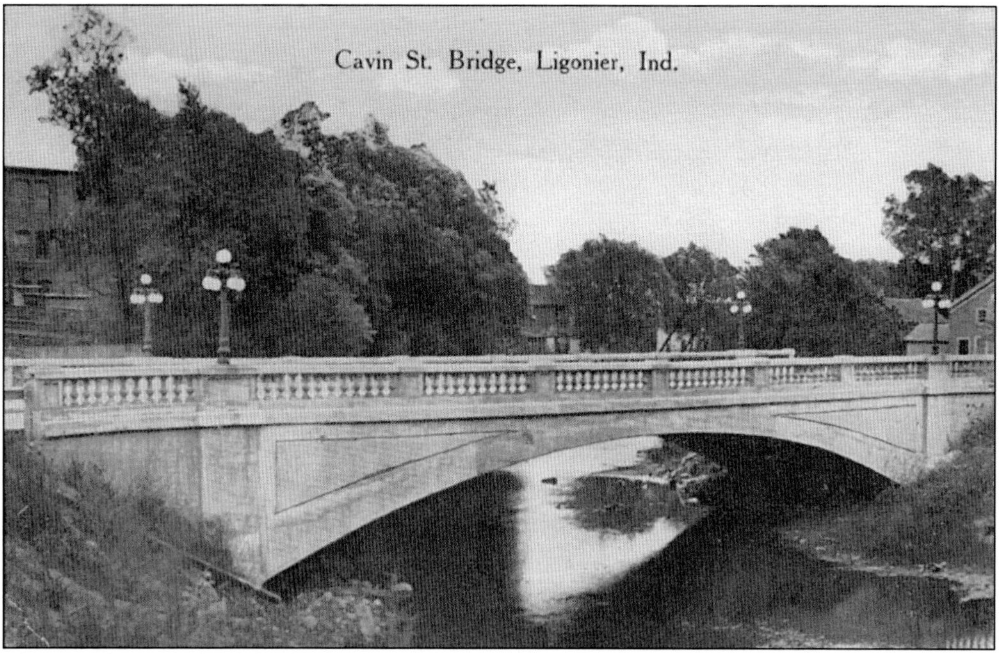


This is a photograph of the finished Cavin Street Bridge. Note the cluster lamps and the view of the Mier Carriage Company (or Wirk Garment) in the background.

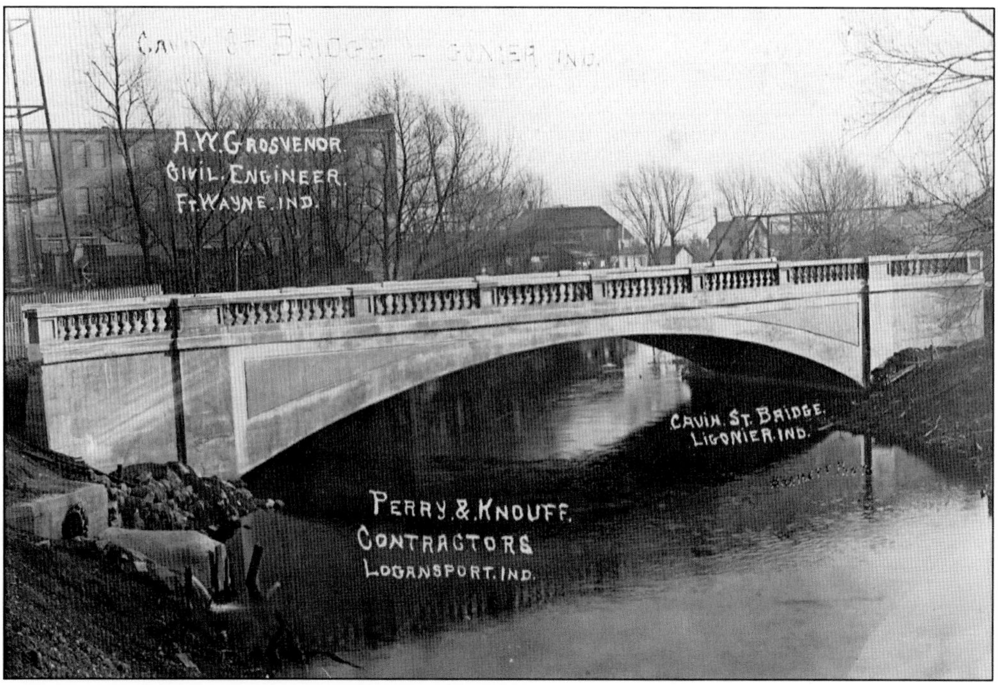


This photograph shows the Pigeon Street Bridge just above the Cavin Street Bridge on the right side. Mier Carriage Company (or Wirk Garment) is in the background on the left. Note that the lamps are not on this bridge, so this is an earlier view of the new bridge.

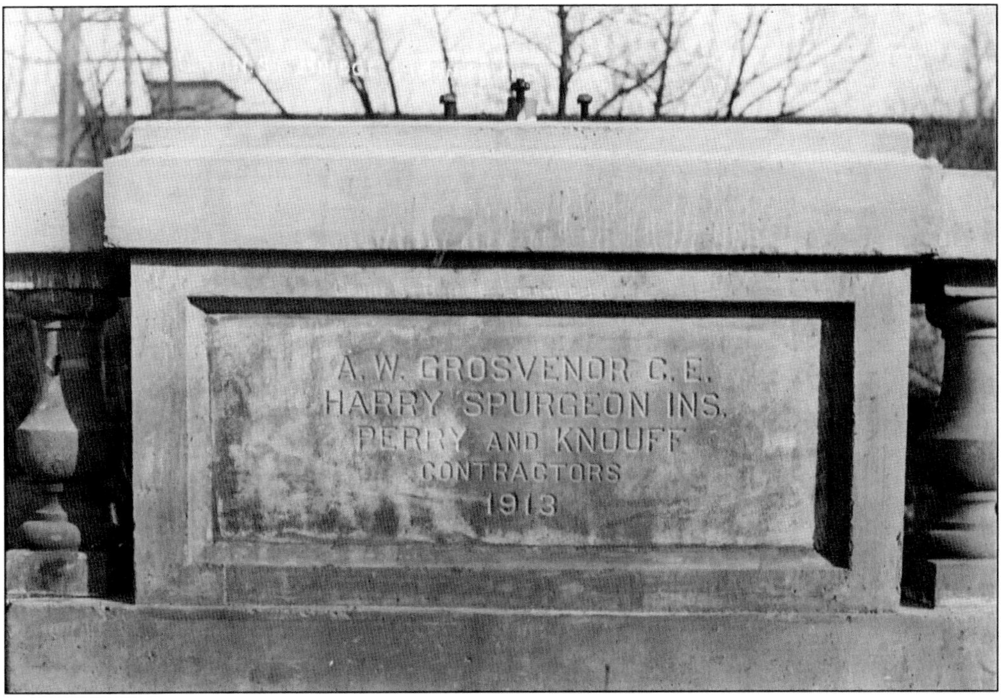


This photograph shows a plaque on the bridge that states who the contractors were in 1913. The plaque lists A.W. Governor, C.E. (civil engineer?); Harry Spurgeon, Ins. (inspector?); and Perry and Knouff, contractors. Employees of that company actually did the physical work.

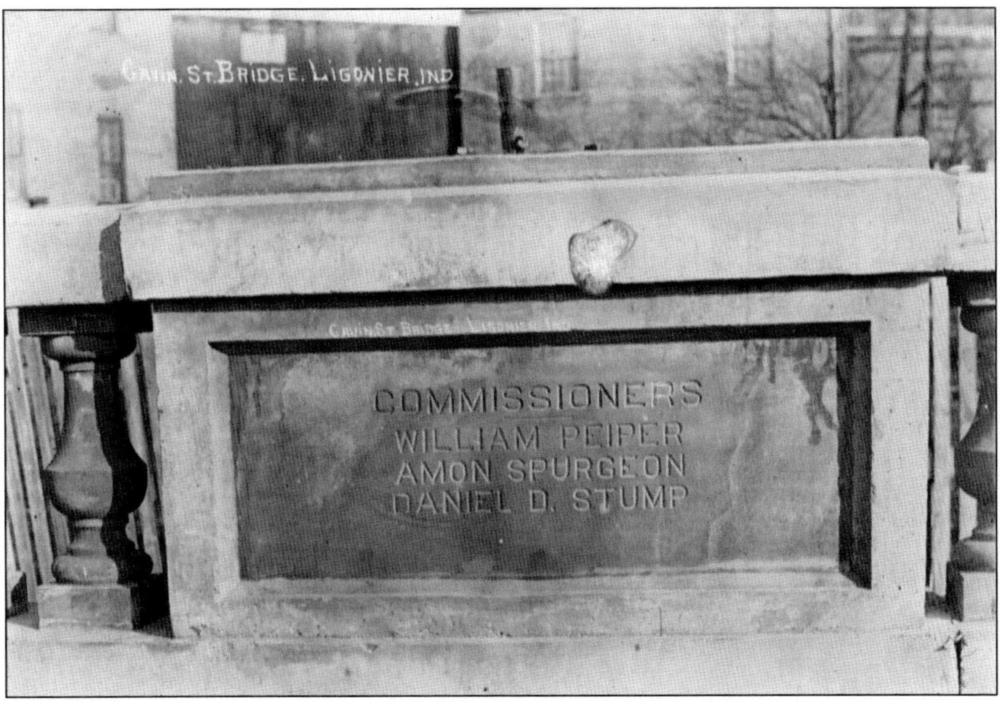


This plaque tells who the commissioners were when the bridge was built: William Peiper, Amon Spurgeon, and Daniel D. Stump.

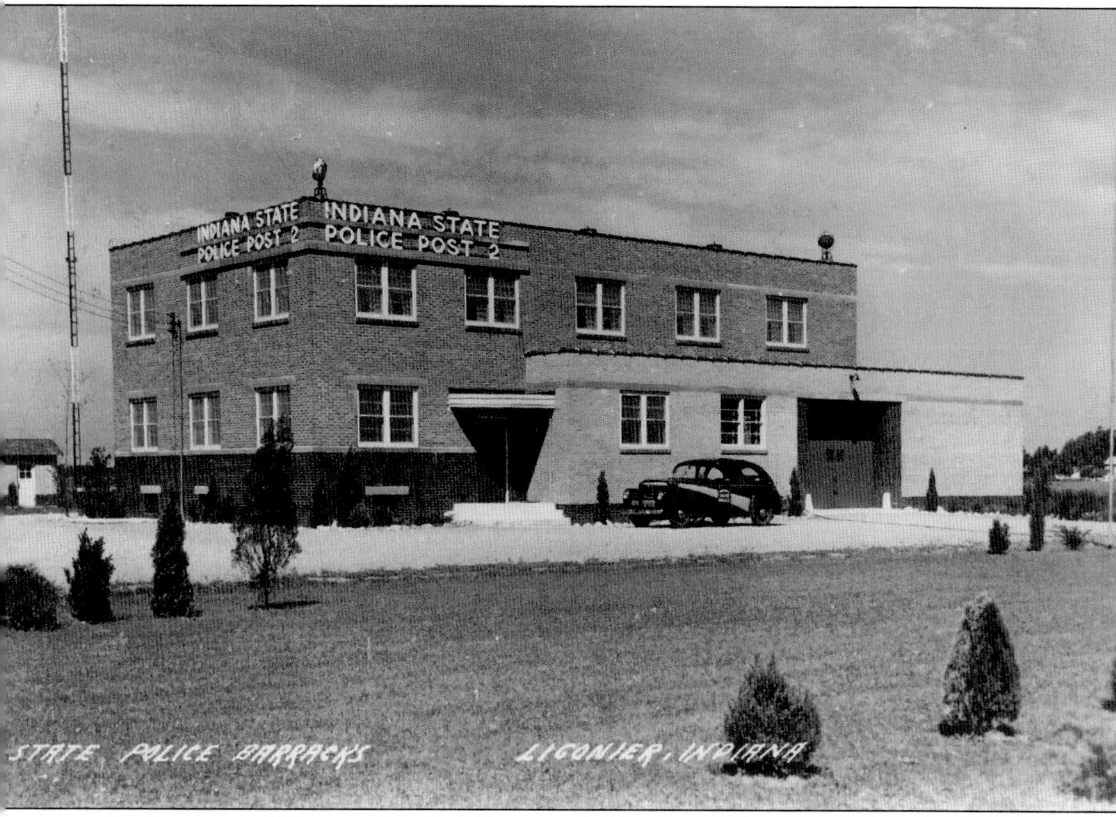


Another postcard shows a slightly different and older view of the Indiana State Police barracks. The age is revealed by looking at the patrol car. The structure was built in 1943. There were 30 people working at the post at that time. The post had a photo lab, a garage beneath the building, and a mechanic. It also had an indoor gun range and an attached garage.

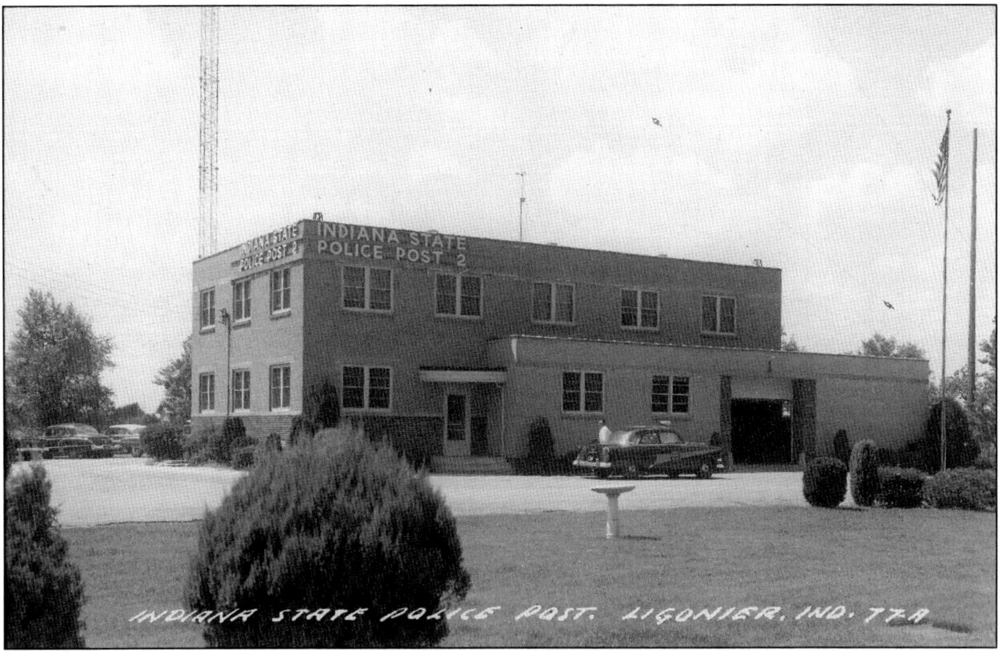


The photograph shows the Indiana State Police post near US 6 and on US 33 and State Road 5 in Ligonier. The post was built in 1943. It was abandoned and demolished sometime after 1971, possibly in 1978. In 1970, there were 64 people working at the post, compared to only 30 in 1943. There was 4,000 square feet of floor area.

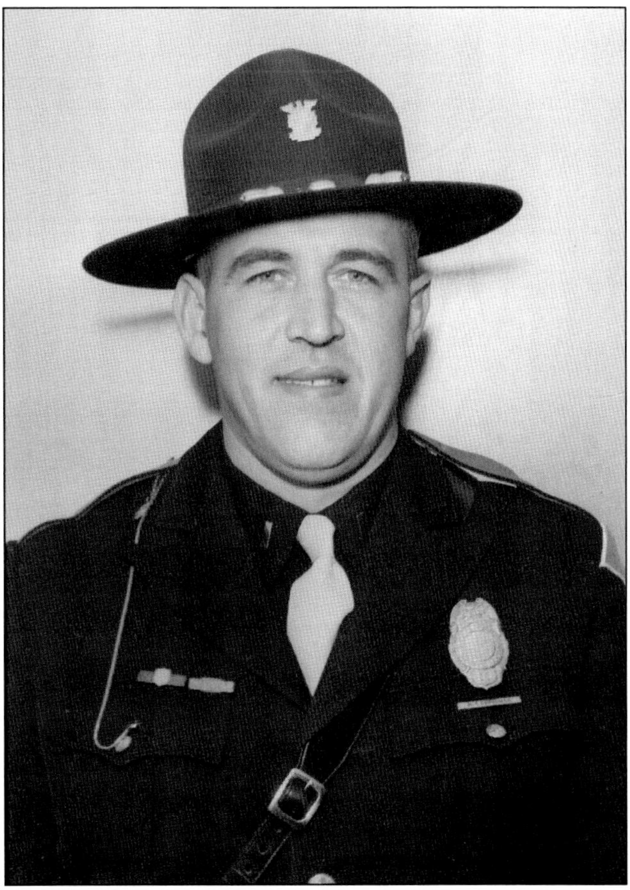

This officer worked out of the Indiana State Police Post No. 2. His name is Howard "Hookie" Crisman. The photograph was taken in 1956. The author estimates that approximately 50 people worked out of the post then. Paul Beverforden was one of the officers who worked at this post.

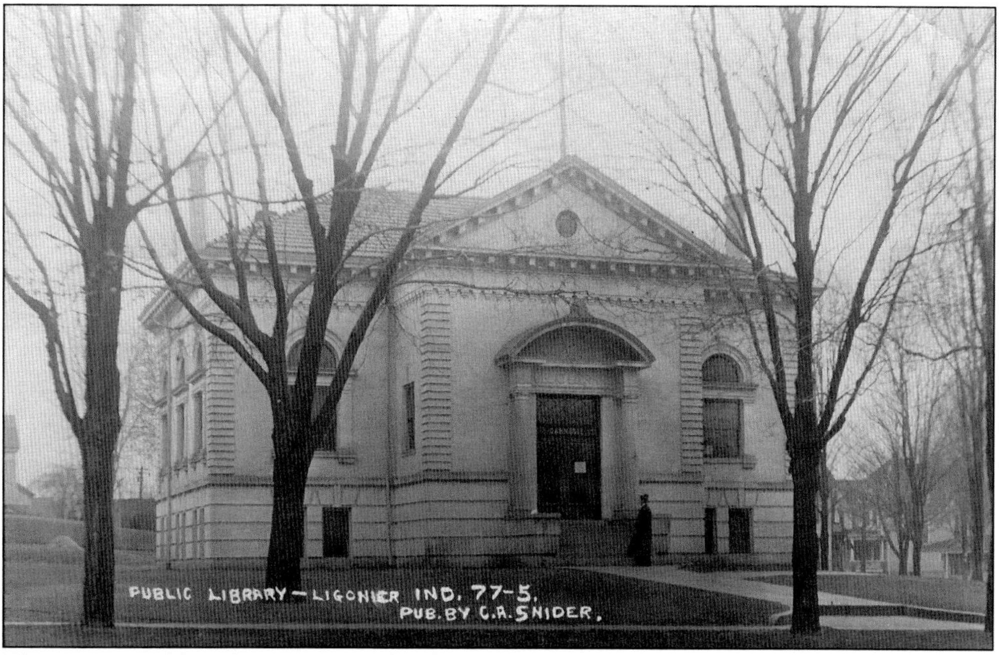


The Ligonier Public Library was completed in 1908. Ligonier was able to build it, in part, due to a generous gift from Andrew Carnegie. Built on the public square on the site of a former schoolhouse, the library sits between Third and Fourth Streets along South Main Street.

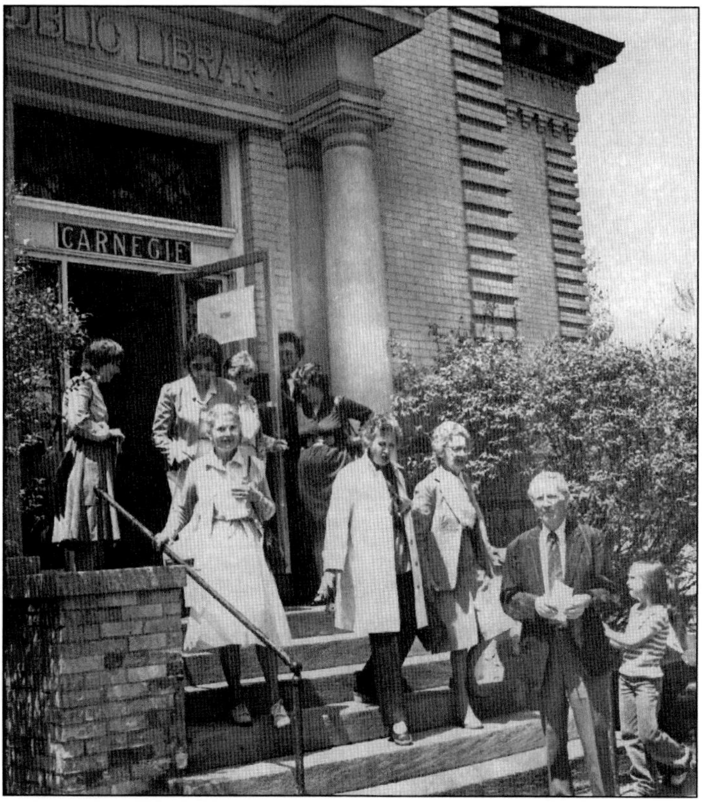


No library can survive unless people use it. People use the Ligonier Public Library every day it is open. The services provided in 2016 would never have even been imagined in 1908, when the library started. Of course, computers and DVD players did not exist in 1908.

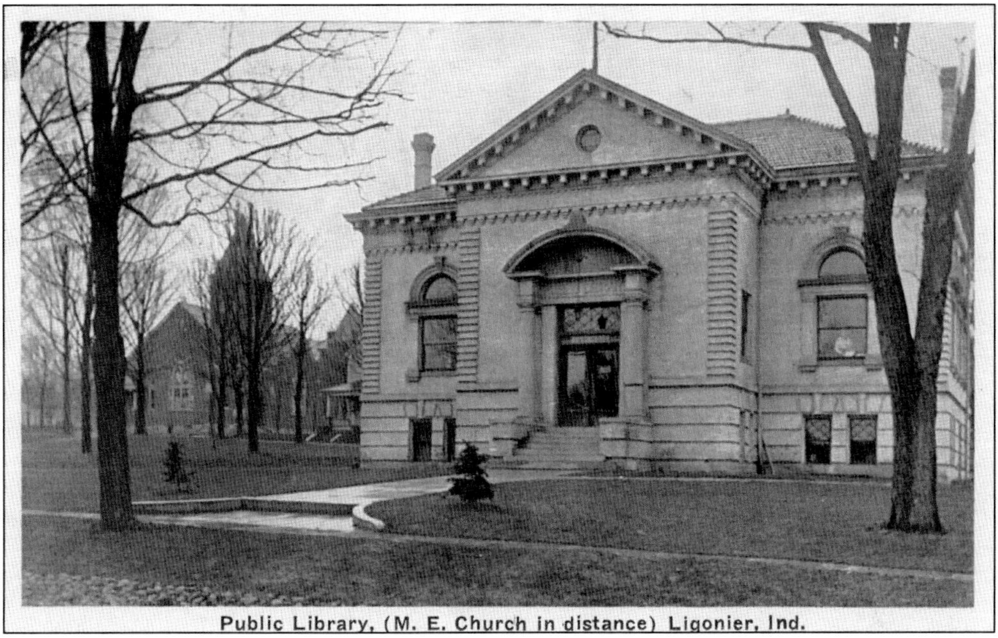


This c. 1910 postcard image of the Ligonier Public Library, at 303 South Main Street, shows a church in the background. This is the Methodist Episcopal church at 207 West Fourth Street, at the corner of Martin Street; it burned down in 1933. A new Methodist church was built at the same site, but it was sold to Trinity Lutheran Church in 1973.

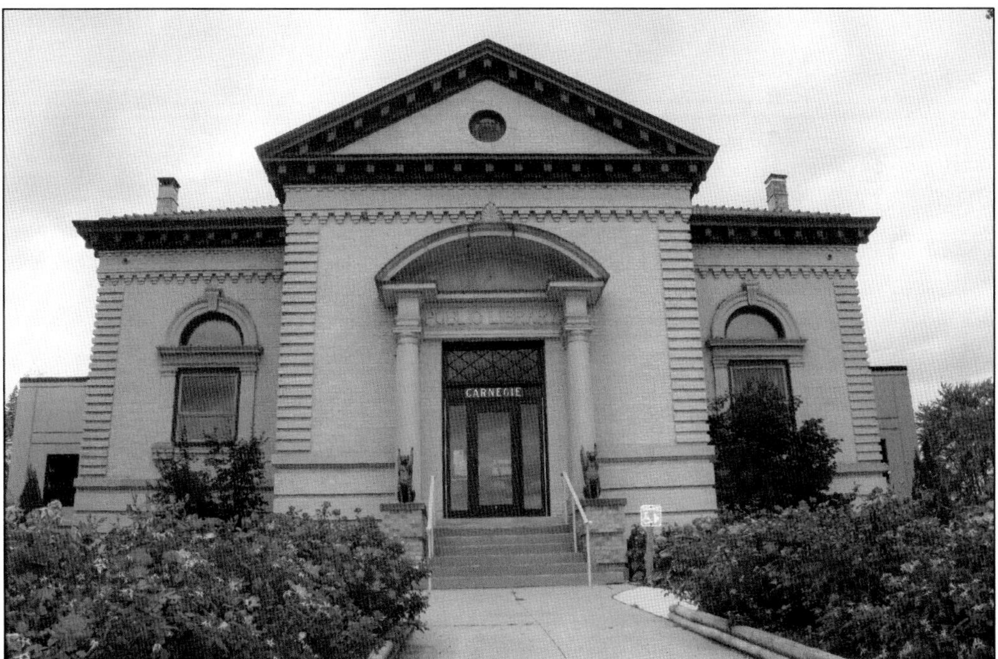


This beautiful library has had two remodeling jobs. The latest remodeling was completed in 2015. The library is bigger than ever, and the staff is always extremely courteous and helpful. Besides the wonderful people, the author enjoys the microfilm reader so old newspapers can be researched.

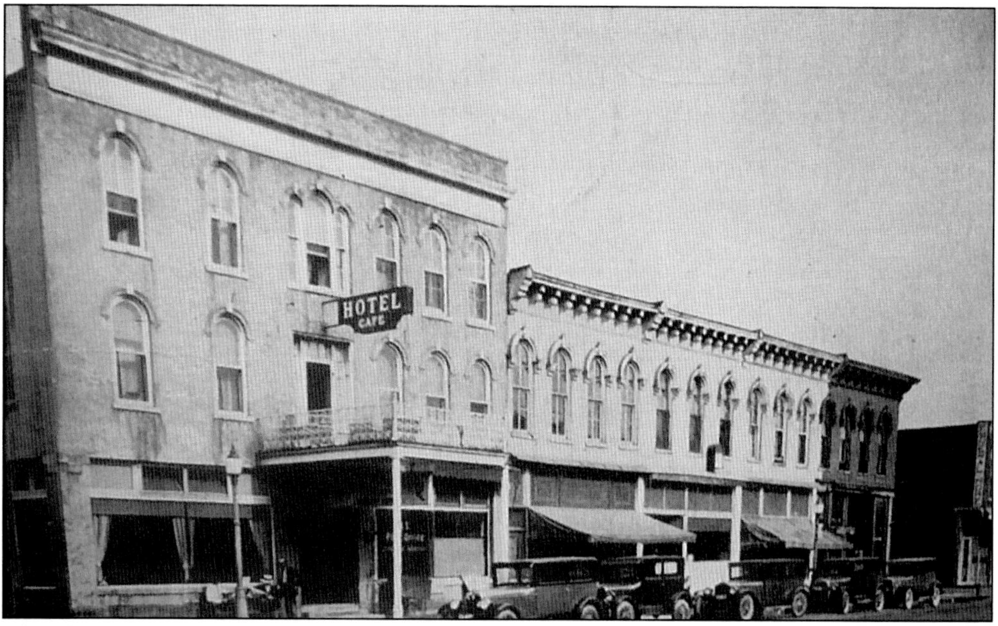


This photograph shows the post office when it was in a store on Cavin Street. The store was in the Gentry Hotel at that time. This hotel has had at least three names. The former hotel building is at 212 South Cavin Street today. The post office is directly on the right of the hotel entrance.

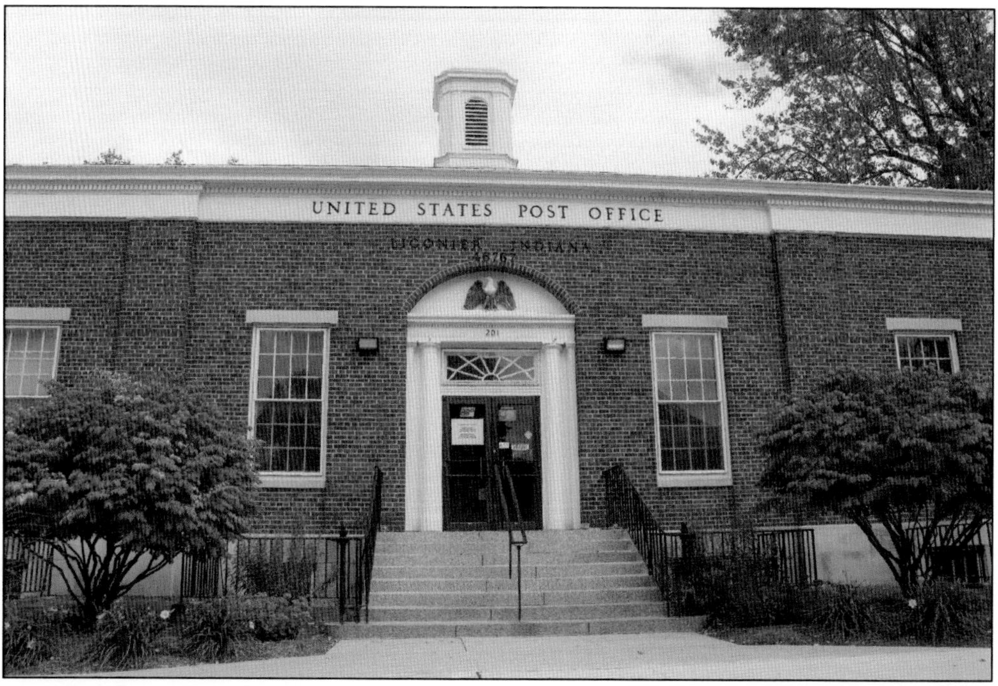


This 2015 photograph of the Ligonier Post Office shows the beauty and good care the building has had since 1935, when it was built. Inside the post office is a mural painted as part of the Federal Art Project during the Depression. The facility is now rated a first-class post office. Home delivery started in 1912, followed by parcel post service in 1913.

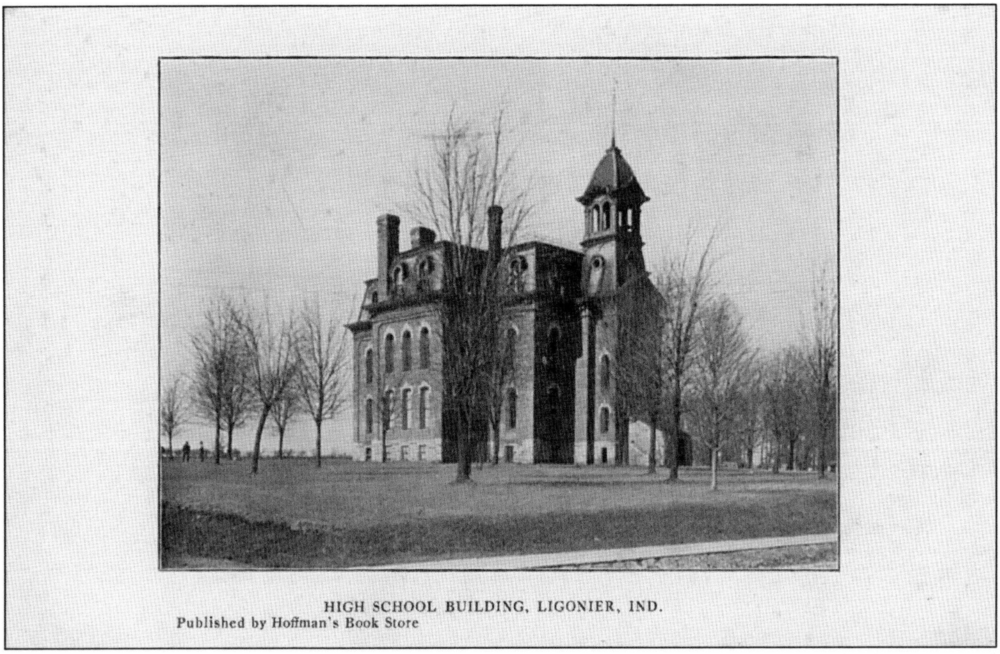


This photograph shows Ligonier's school in 1877 or soon after. This school was built on Grand Street a bit north of where the Ligonier Elementary School sits now. The address of Ligonier Elementary, although the two boys playing on the left side of the photograph would not call it that, is 610 Grand Street.

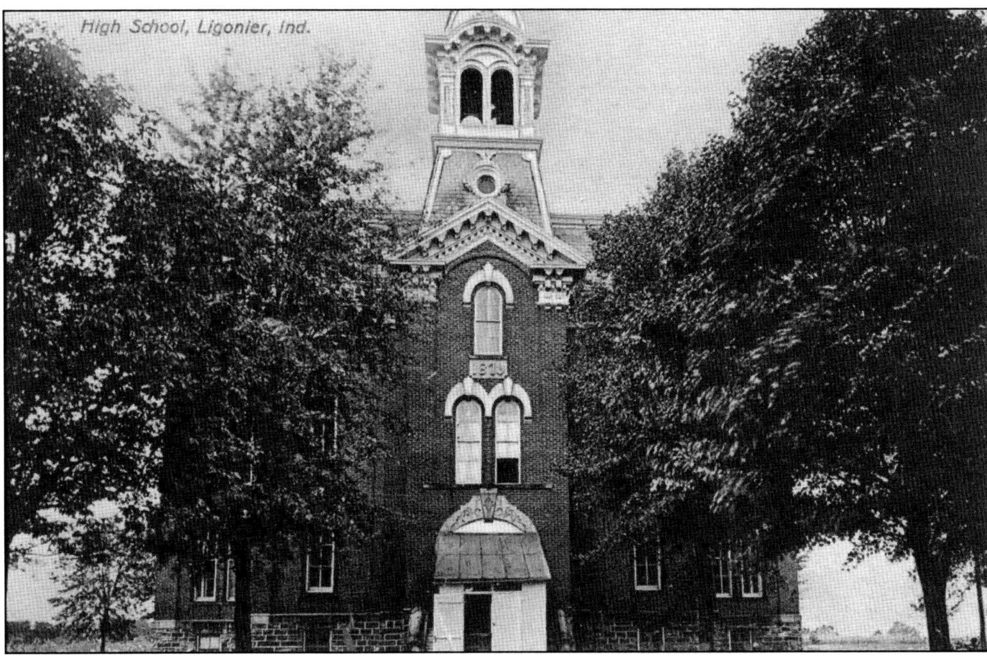


This photograph shows a closer view of the same school, built in 1876. The trees seem to have grown since the earlier photograph seen at the top of the page was taken. This image must date from between 1877 and 1910, because the school had an addition built onto it in 1911.

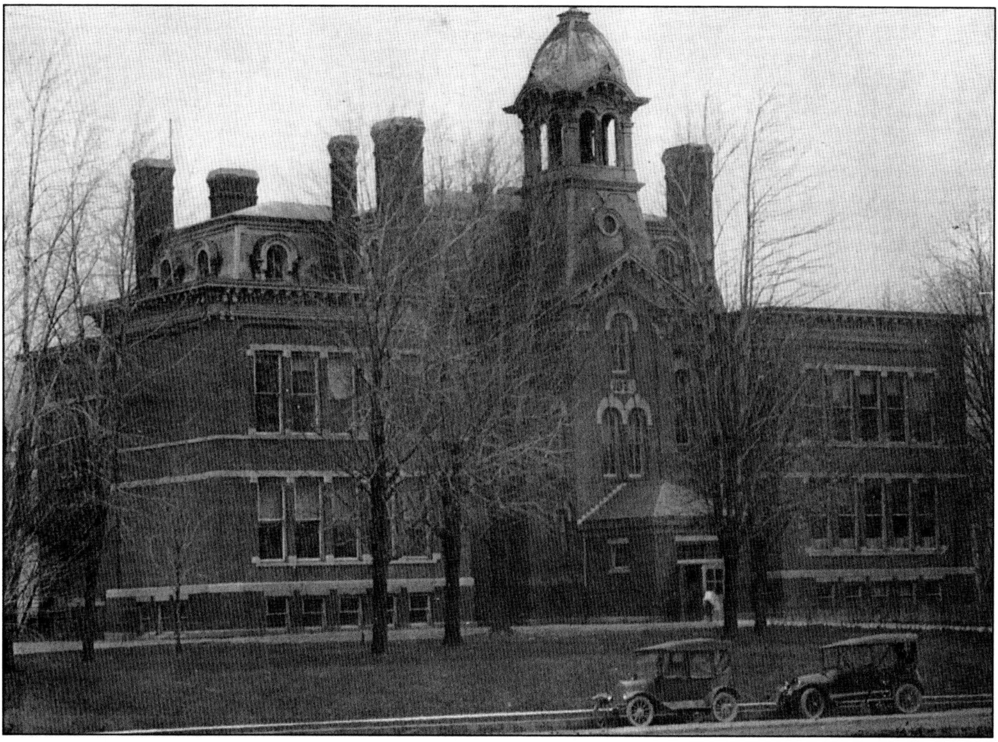

This photograph shows the 1876 school with its two additions. One was built on the north side of the school, and the other was built on the south side. Note the cars sitting in front of the school. The larger school was needed because the population of Ligonier was growing.

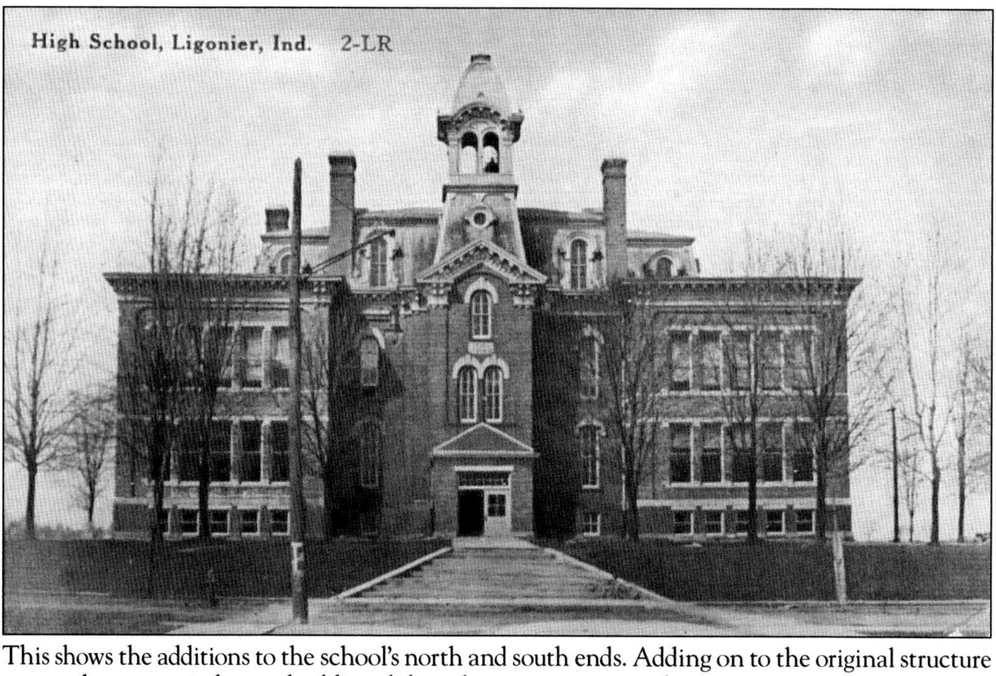


This shows the additions to the school's north and south ends. Adding on to the original structure meant that an entirely new building did not have to constructed.

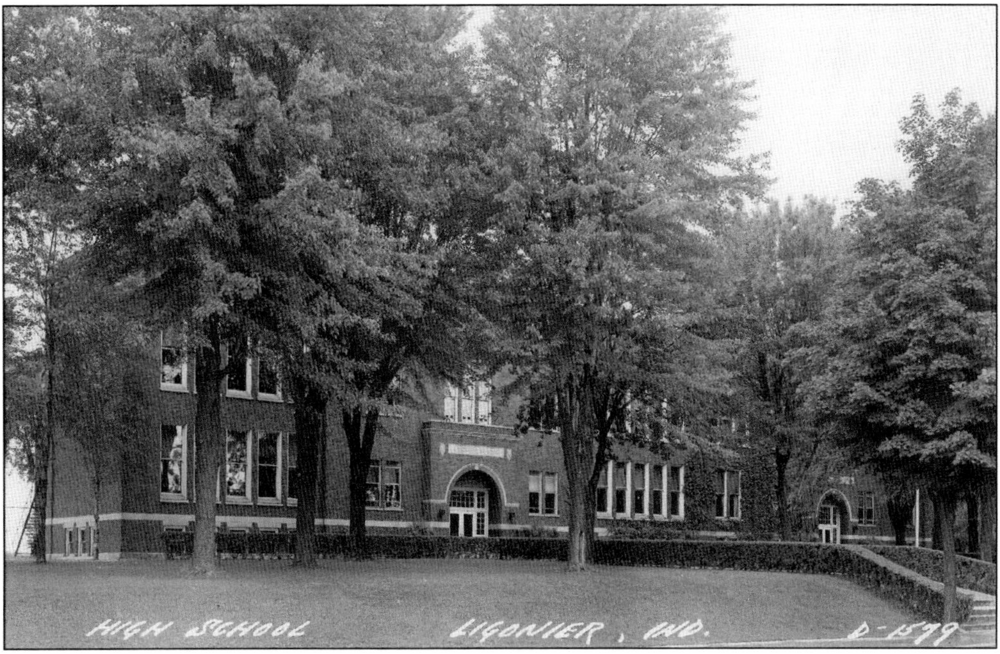


This shows a more modern photograph of the school, but there is a puzzle. Note the fire escape on the left side. The author remembers a tube in the 1950s that came out of the school on this side. It is suspected that the tube preceded the fire escape steps.

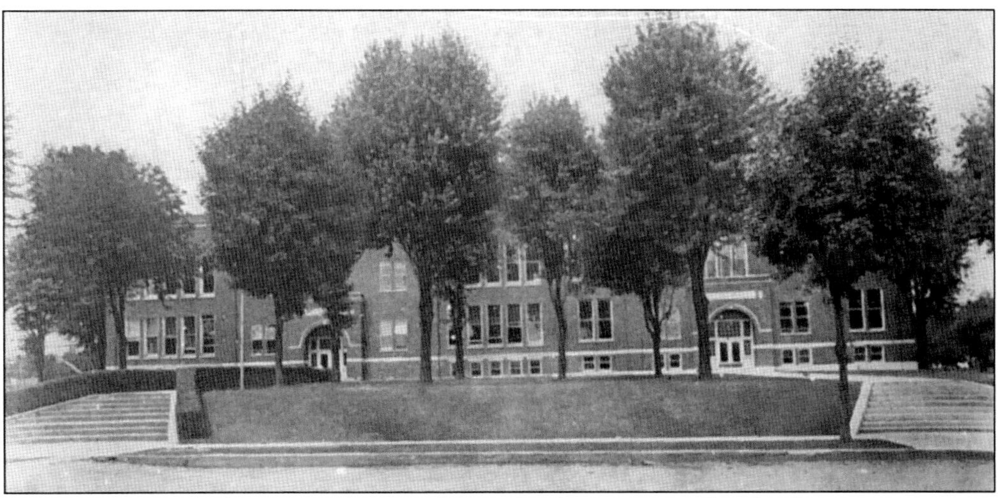

This shows the broad north-south view of the school. Ligonier High School was an impressive school with quite a character. Its students must have been very proud of their facilities and also of the care their teachers gave them. The education was top-notch. Remember too that the Jewish leaders helped organize the schools. They wanted a good education for their children and for all children in Ligonier.

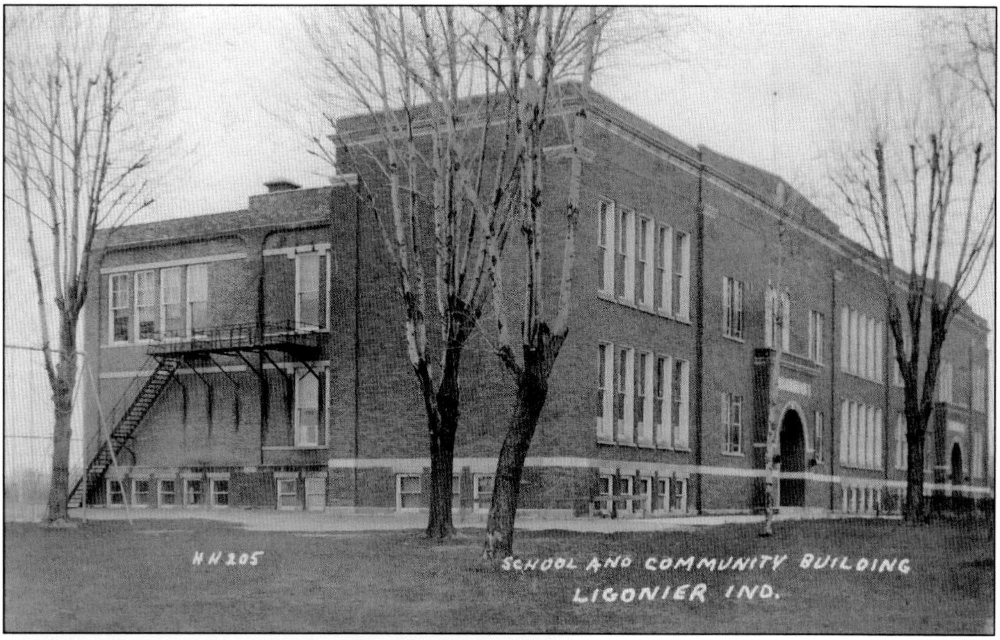


This high school served Ligonier from 1876 through 1976.

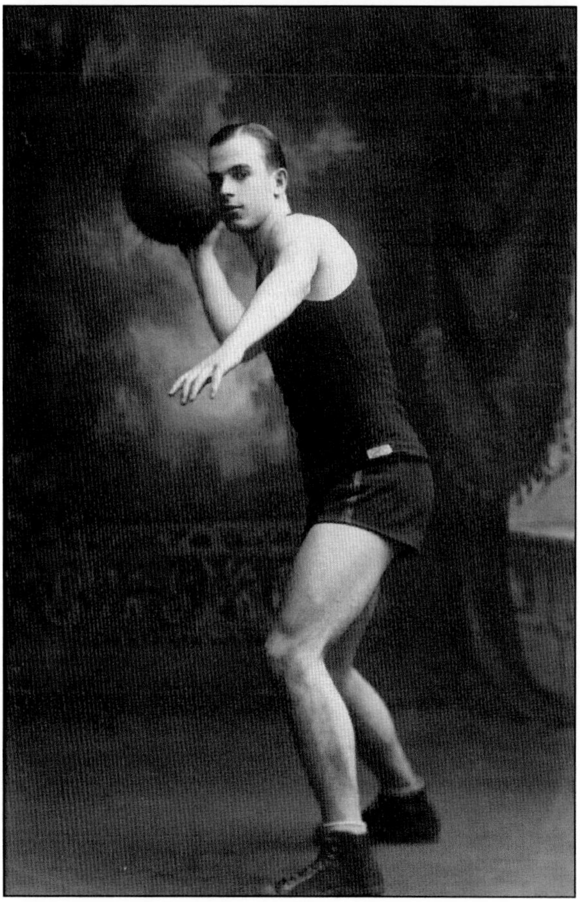

This proud basketball player remains anonymous because no one wrote his name or the year or the place on the back of the photograph. It is believed that the photograph is from around 1930.

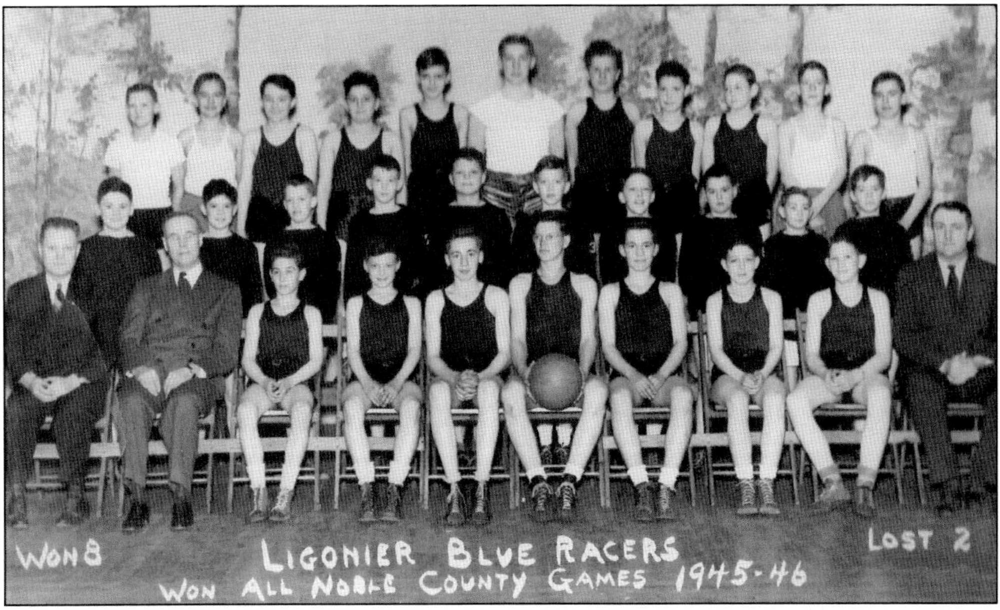


The Ligonier Blue Racers are pictured during the 1945–1946 school year. The photograph wisely lists the names and date. This is a good reference to estimate the date of other photographs. O.R. Bangs, sitting in the front row, second from the left, is seen in other pictures, as he was the superintendent of Ligonier Schools from 1933 to 1946.

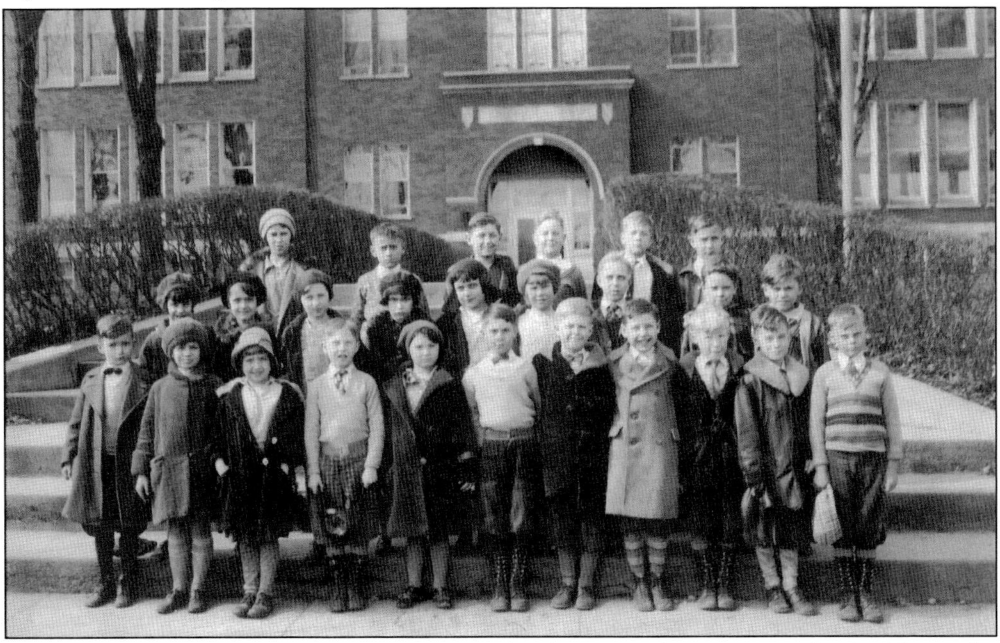

Ligonier students are in front of the Ligonier School on Grand Street around 1920. Notice the shoes with laces and hooks that almost go to their knees. The boys seem to prefer this style. The boys' pants come slightly below the knee. The girls all wear a similar style of cap. Even the teacher is wearing a cap of this style. Such features are useful to date the photographs if one is fortunate enough to find guides that interpret the era when certain styles were popular, along with a photograph of what they are describing.

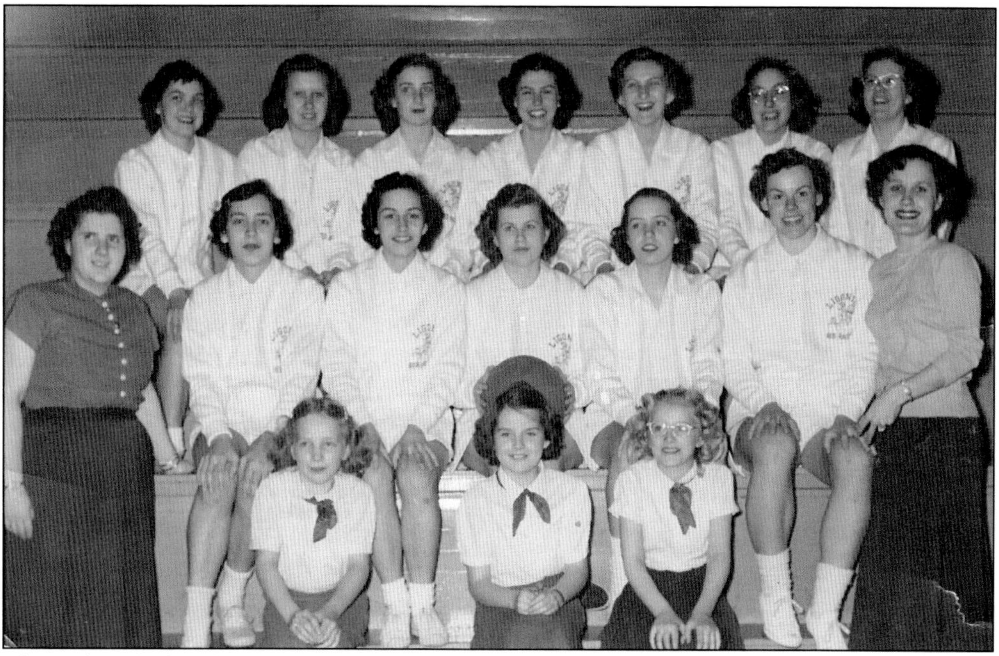

Those identified in this c. 1955 Ligonier High School girls' basketball team are, from left to right, (second row) Joyce L. Kaplan (first), Gretchen A. Stoltz (fifth), and Marilyn Shock (sixth); (third row) Sherry Nighsonger, Betty West, Judy Loeser, Shirley A Henry, Mary M Shell, Marjorie Adams, and Jane Sprague.

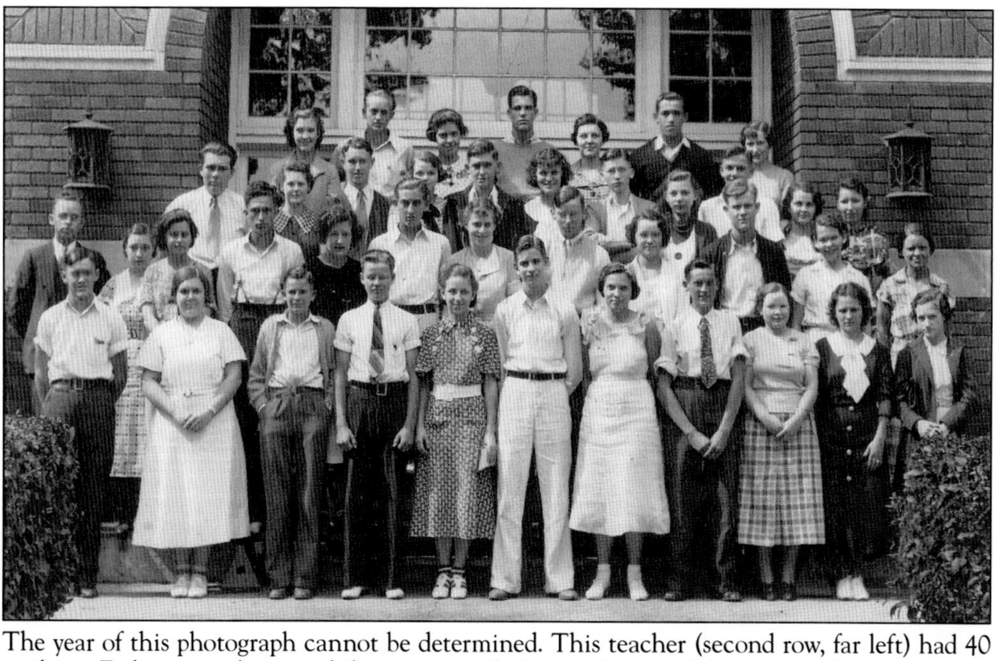

The year of this photograph cannot be determined. This teacher (second row, far left) had 40 students. Eighteen are boys, and the rest are girls. It is unknown if this is a total senior class or mixed grades. Yearbooks are unavailable because the school stopped making them for a decade or two.

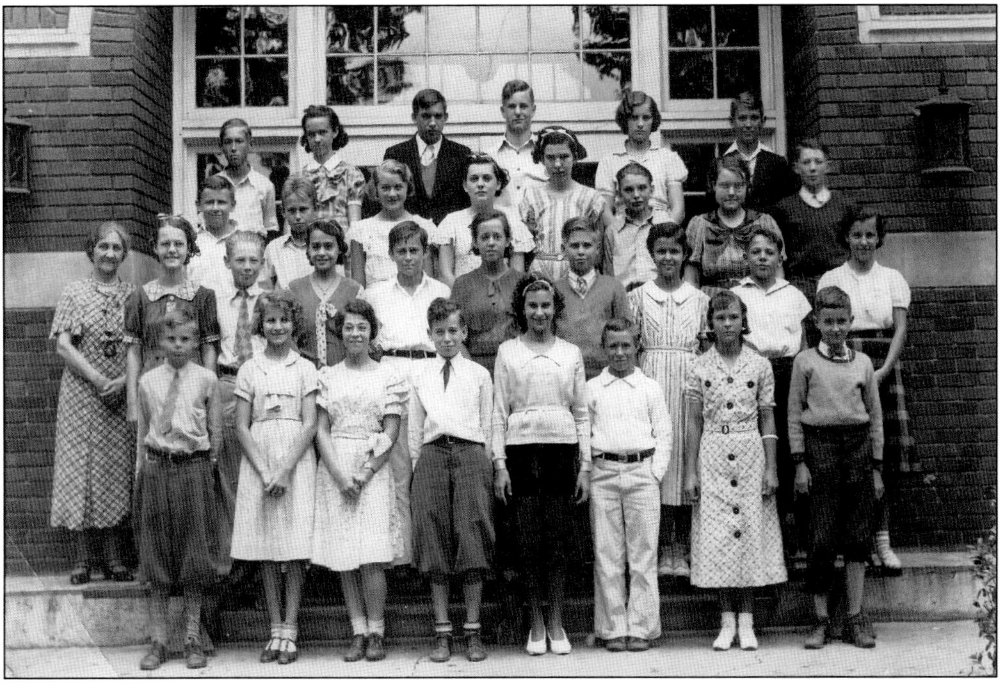

The date of this photograph cannot be determined. This teacher poses with 31 students. Sixteen are boys, and 15 are girls.

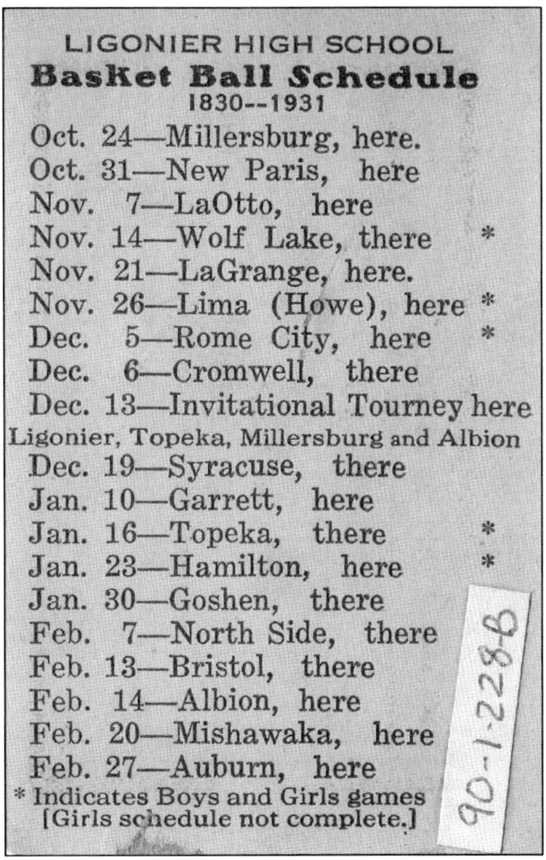

LIGONIER HIGH SCHOOL

**Basket Ball Schedule**

1830--1931

Oct. 24—Millersburg, here.
Oct. 31—New Paris, here
Nov. 7—LaOtto, here
Nov. 14—Wolf Lake, there *
Nov. 21—LaGrange, here.
Nov. 26—Lima (Howe), here *
Dec. 5—Rome City, here *
Dec. 6—Cromwell, there
Dec. 13—Invitational Tourney here
Ligonier, Topeka, Millersburg and Albion
Dec. 19—Syracuse, there
Jan. 10—Garrett, here
Jan. 16—Topeka, there *
Jan. 23—Hamilton, here *
Jan. 30—Goshen, there
Feb. 7—North Side, there
Feb. 13—Bristol, there
Feb. 14—Albion, here
Feb. 20—Mishawaka, here
Feb. 27—Auburn, here

* Indicates Boys and Girls games
[Girls schedule not complete.]

This basketball schedule may have confused some when it was first published. The schedule starts in 1830 and ends in 1931. Obviously, it should state 1930–1931. Nineteen games are listed for the boys' team, and asterisks indicate dates when the girls' team has a game.

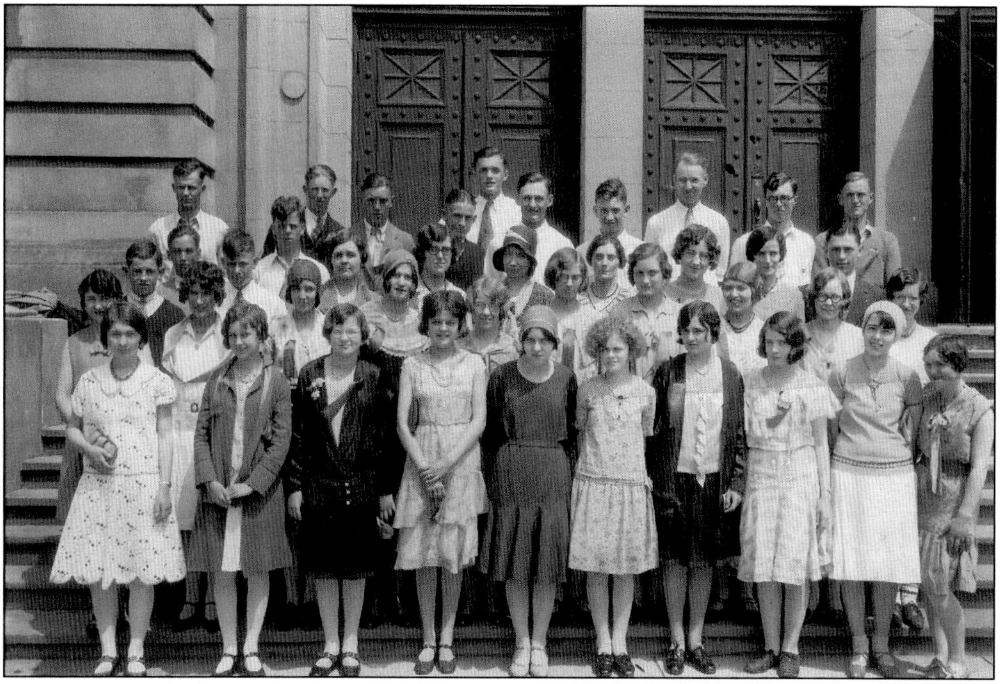

A class is on a field trip. Notice the nice dresses on the ladies and the ties on some of the men. Also notice the door. The author thinks these doors are either at Purdue or in Chicago at the Field Museum. No date is given, and none of the students are identified.

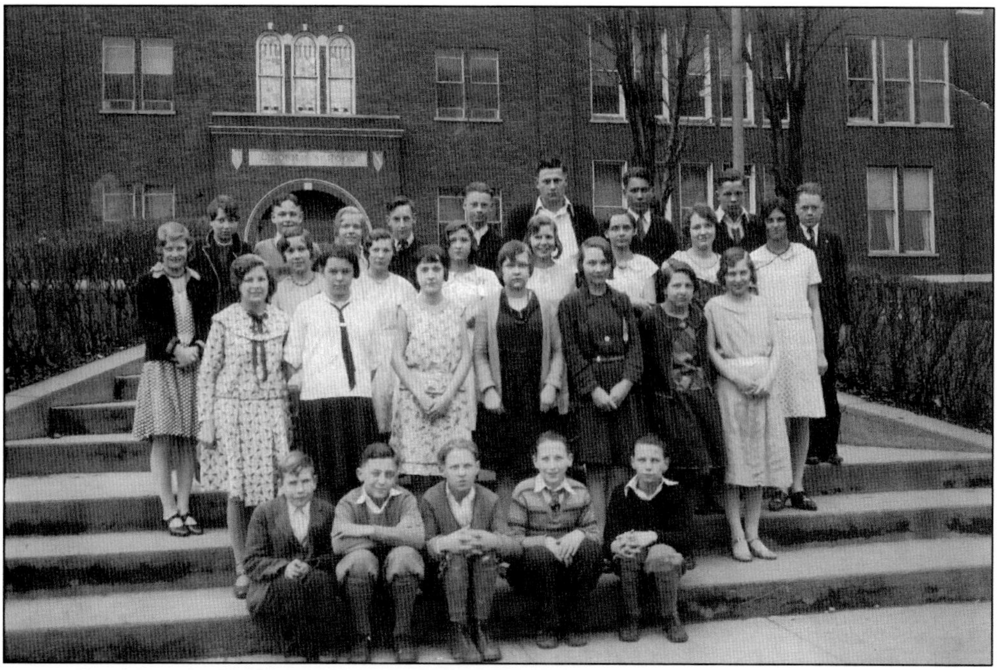

No yearbooks are available to look up a match to this picture, because the school stopped making them for about two decades. This leaves a large information gap. Yearbooks are an excellent source for matching photographs to students and student groups.

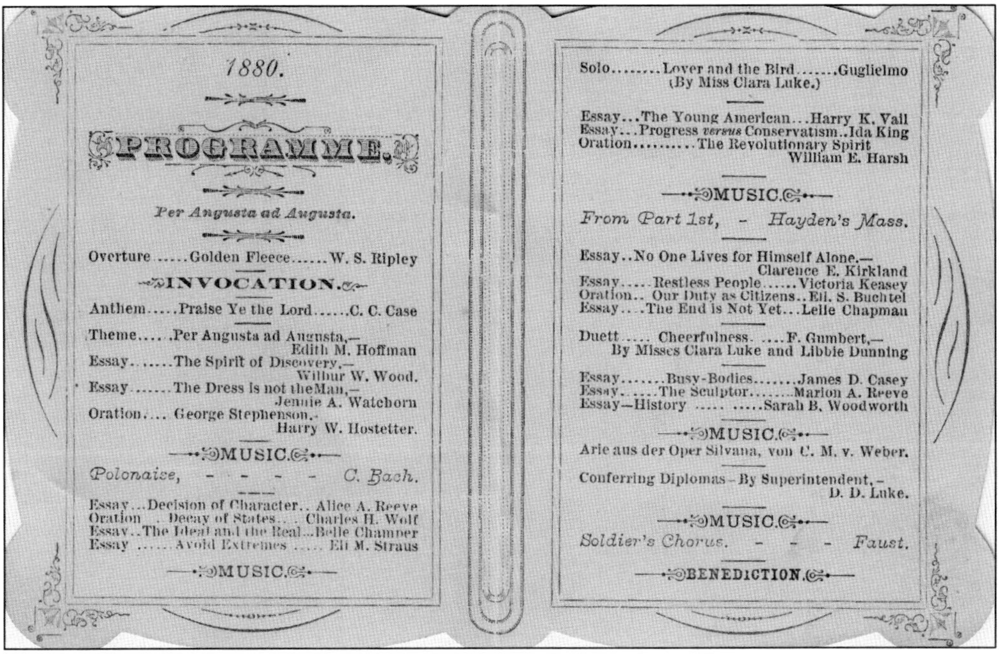

1880.

PROGRAMME.

*Per Angusta ad Augusta.*

Overture......Golden Fleece......W. S. Ripley

INVOCATION.

Anthem.....Praise Ye the Lord......C. C. Case

Theme.....Per Angusta ad Augusta,—
Edith M. Hoffman
Essay.......The Spirit of Discovery,—
Wilbur W. Wood.
Essay.......The Dress is not the Man,—
Jennie A. Watchorn
Oration.... George Stephenson,-
Harry W. Hostetter.

MUSIC.

*Polonaise,* - - - - *C. Bach.*

Essay...Decision of Character.. Alice A. Reeve
Oration ..Decay of States... Charles H. Wolf
Essay..The Ideal and the Real...Belle Champer
Essay ......Avoid Extremes ...... Eli M. Straus

MUSIC.

Solo........Lover and the Bird.......Guglielmo
(By Miss Clara Luke.)

Essay...The Young American...Harry K. Vail
Essay...Progress *versus* Conservatism..Ida King
Oration.........The Revolutionary Spirit
William E. Harsh

MUSIC.

*From Part 1st,* - *Hayden's Mass.*

Essay..No One Lives for Himself Alone.—
Clarence E. Kirkland
Essay.....Restless People......Victoria Keasey
Oration.. Our Duty as Citizens..Eli. S. Buchtel
Essay....The End is Not Yet...Lelle Chapman

Duett..... Cheerfulness. ....F. Gumbert,—
By Misses Clara Luke and Libbie Dunning

Essay.......Busy-Bodies.......James D. Casey
Essay......The Sculptor........Marion A. Reeve
Essay—History ...... .....Sarah B. Woodworth

MUSIC.

Arie aus der Oper Silvana, von C. M. v. Weber.

Conferring Diplomas—By Superintendent,—
D. D. Luke.

MUSIC.

*Soldier's Chorus.* - - - *Faust.*

BENEDICTION.

This 1880 program shows a lot of music (10) and a lot of speeches (20). Also note the separate presentation of diplomas and commencement program.

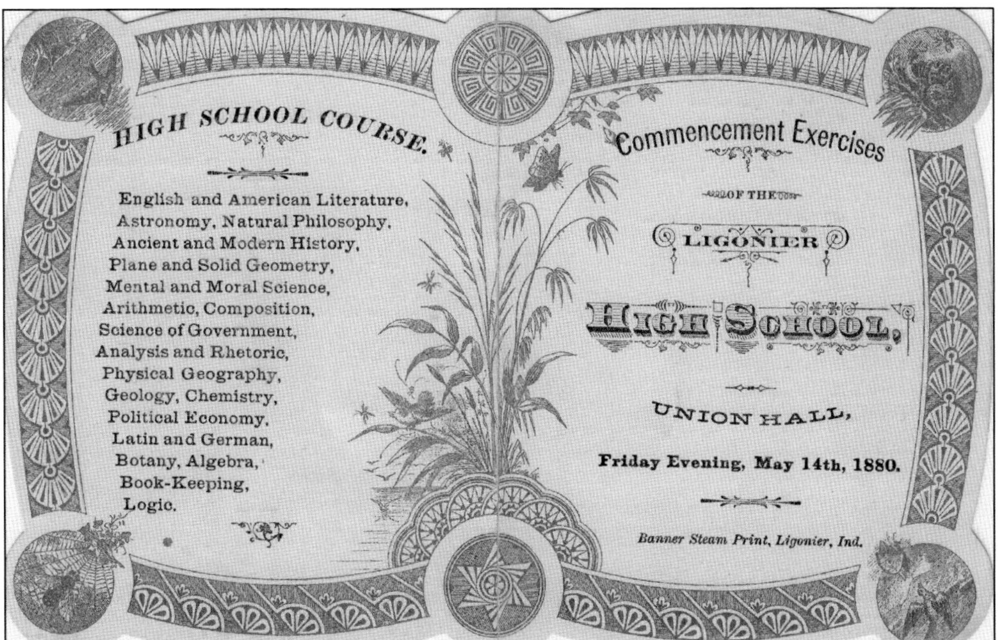

HIGH SCHOOL COURSE.

English and American Literature,
Astronomy, Natural Philosophy,
Ancient and Modern History,
Plane and Solid Geometry,
Mental and Moral Science,
Arithmetic, Composition,
Science of Government,
Analysis and Rhetoric,
Physical Geography,
Geology, Chemistry,
Political Economy,
Latin and German,
Botany, Algebra,
Book-Keeping,
Logic.

Commencement Exercises

OF THE

LIGONIER

HIGH SCHOOL,

UNION HALL,

Friday Evening, May 14th, 1880.

*Banner Steam Print, Ligonier, Ind.*

The 1880 commencement program has some very fancy printing. It lists almost 20 courses. Among other courses, a student could have taken Latin or German—or perhaps both.

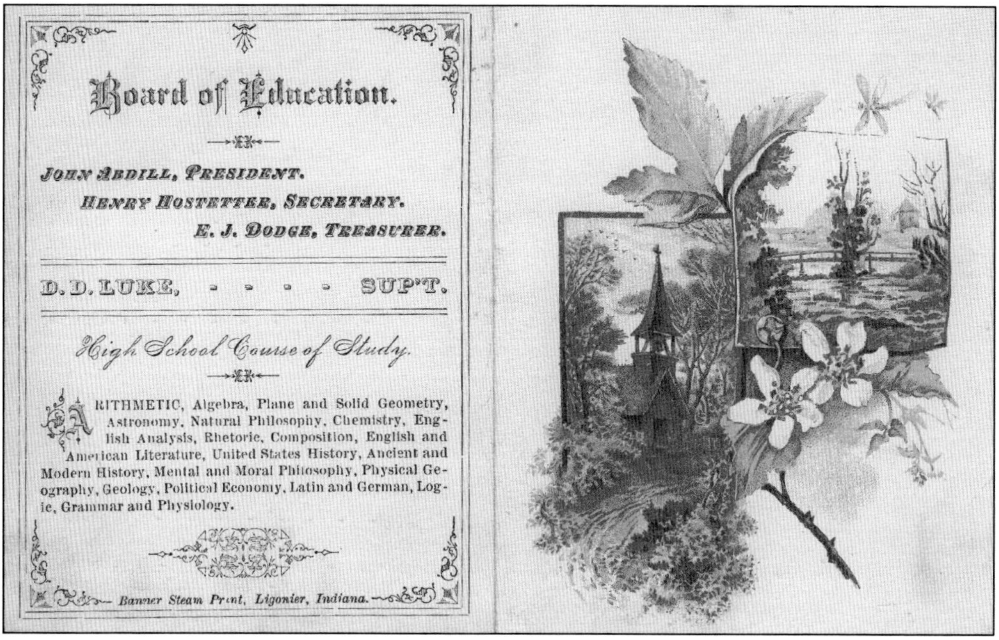

Board of Education.

JOHN ABDILL, PRESIDENT.
HENRY HOSTETTER, SECRETARY.
E. J. DODGE, TREASURER.

D. D. LUKE, - - - - SUP'T.

High School Course of Study.

ARITHMETIC, Algebra, Plane and Solid Geometry, Astronomy, Natural Philosophy, Chemistry, English Analysis, Rhetoric, Composition, English and American Literature, United States History, Ancient and Modern History, Mental and Moral Philosophy, Physical Geography, Geology, Political Economy, Latin and German, Logic, Grammar and Physiology.

Banner Steam Print, Ligonier, Indiana.

The printing technique is incredible. The work is very professional. The course of study does not look easy. This printing was done in 1880.

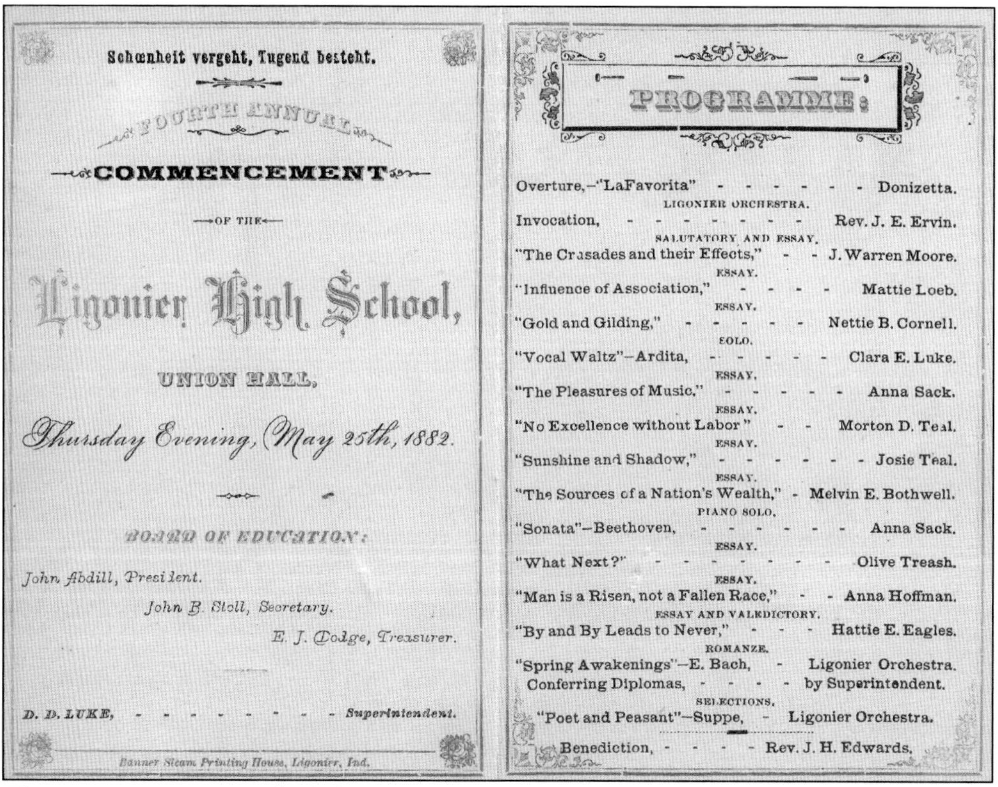

Schœnheit vergeht, Tugend besteht.

FOURTH ANNUAL

COMMENCEMENT

OF THE

Ligonier High School,

UNION HALL,

Thursday Evening, May 25th, 1882.

BOARD OF EDUCATION:

John Abdill, President.
John B. Stoll, Secretary.
E. J. Dodge, Treasurer.

D. D. LUKE, - - - - - - - - Superintendent.

Banner Steam Printing House, Ligonier, Ind.

PROGRAMME:

Overture,—"LaFavorita" - - - - - - Donizetta.
LIGONIER ORCHESTRA.
Invocation, - - - - - - - - Rev. J. E. Ervin.
SALUTATORY AND ESSAY.
"The Crusades and their Effects," - - J. Warren Moore.
ESSAY.
"Influence of Association," - - - - Mattie Loeb.
ESSAY.
"Gold and Gilding," - - - - - Nettie B. Cornell.
SOLO.
"Vocal Waltz"—Ardita, - - - - - Clara E. Luke.
ESSAY.
"The Pleasures of Music." - - - - - Anna Sack.
ESSAY.
"No Excellence without Labor" - - Morton D. Teal.
ESSAY.
"Sunshine and Shadow," - - - - - - Josie Teal.
ESSAY.
"The Sources of a Nation's Wealth," - Melvin E. Bothwell.
PIANO SOLO.
"Sonata"—Beethoven, - - - - - - Anna Sack.
ESSAY.
"What Next?" - - - - - - - - Olive Treash.
ESSAY.
"Man is a Risen, not a Fallen Race," - - Anna Hoffman.
ESSAY AND VALEDICTORY.
"By and By Leads to Never," - - - Hattie E. Eagles.
ROMANZE.
"Spring Awakenings"—E. Bach, - Ligonier Orchestra.
Conferring Diplomas, - - - - by Superintendent.
SELECTIONS.
"Poet and Peasant"—Suppe, - Ligonier Orchestra.
Benediction, - - - - Rev. J. H. Edwards.

This 1882 commencement looks heavy too. There are 10 essays or speeches and five presentations of music. There was even an orchestra for this event in 1882.

This student-produced newspaper/magazine is from the 1905–1906 school year. The publication is printed, which in itself is impressive. The author can remember using mimeographed handouts during the 1950s that were wet, cold, and had a distinct smell.

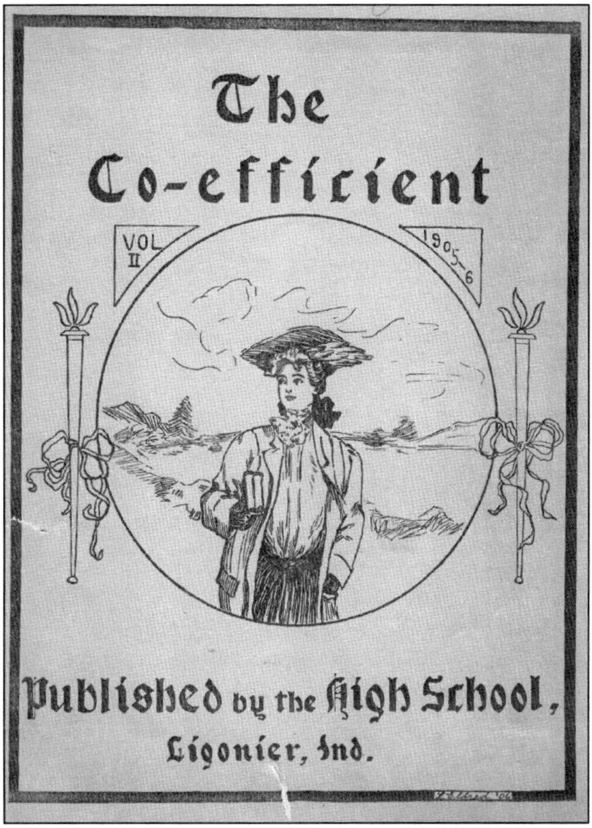


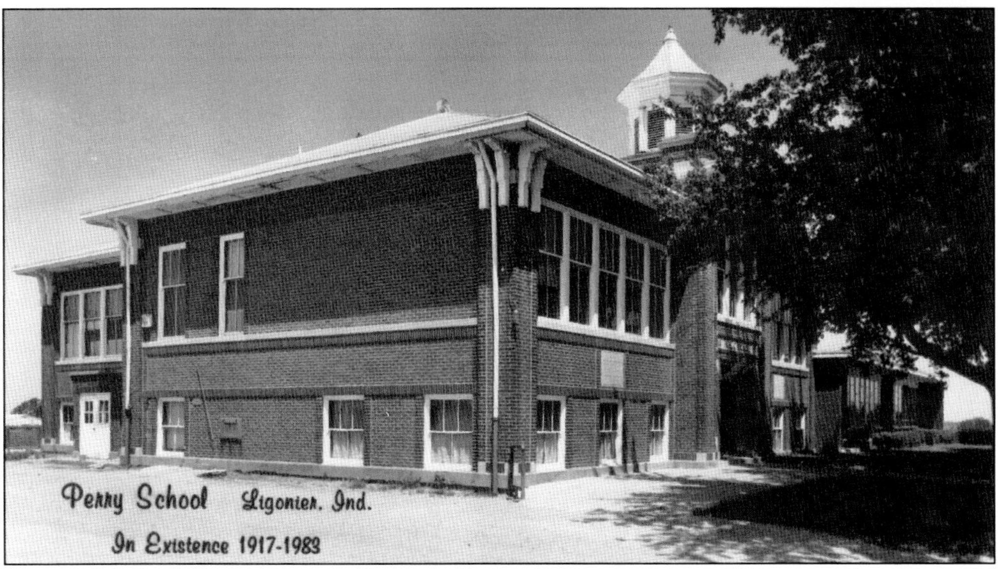


Perry School, pictured here, was north of Ligonier, about a mile out of the city. The school had nice facilities, and its teachers had a good reputation. Perry School was in existence from 1917 until 1983. An addition was built in 1955. A tornado struck the school in 1974. It damaged the gym and some classrooms. The people in the school were very fortunate that the tornado did not injure or kill them. Some cars outside were not as lucky.

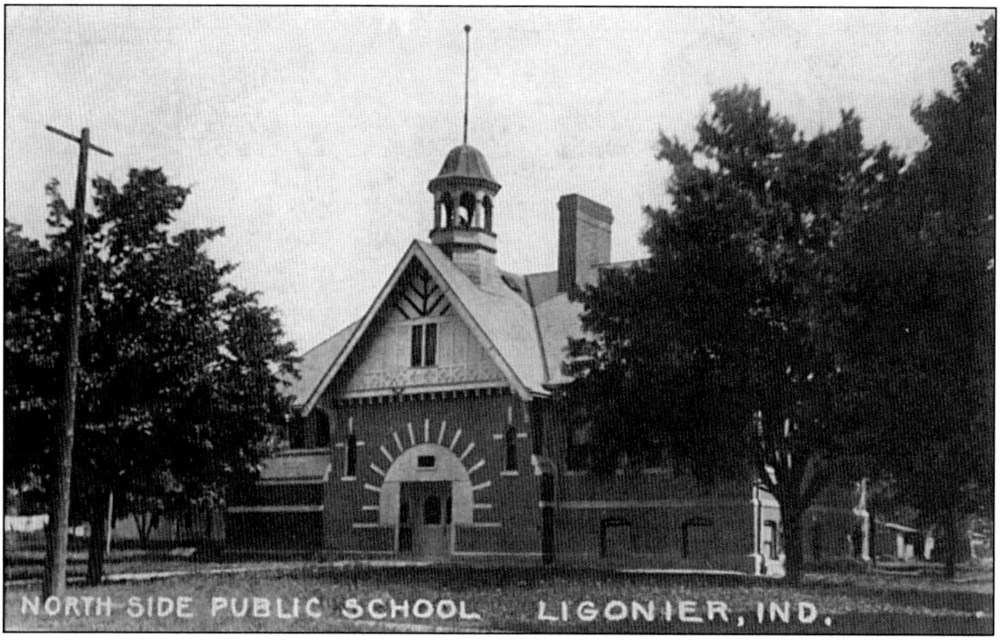


Northside School is pictured sometime between 1890 and 1910. The author attended kindergarten here in the early 1950s, and his aunt was a teacher at Northside. Northside was north of the railroad viaduct and about one block east of Cavin Street at Miller Street. It was by the waterworks on Water Street.

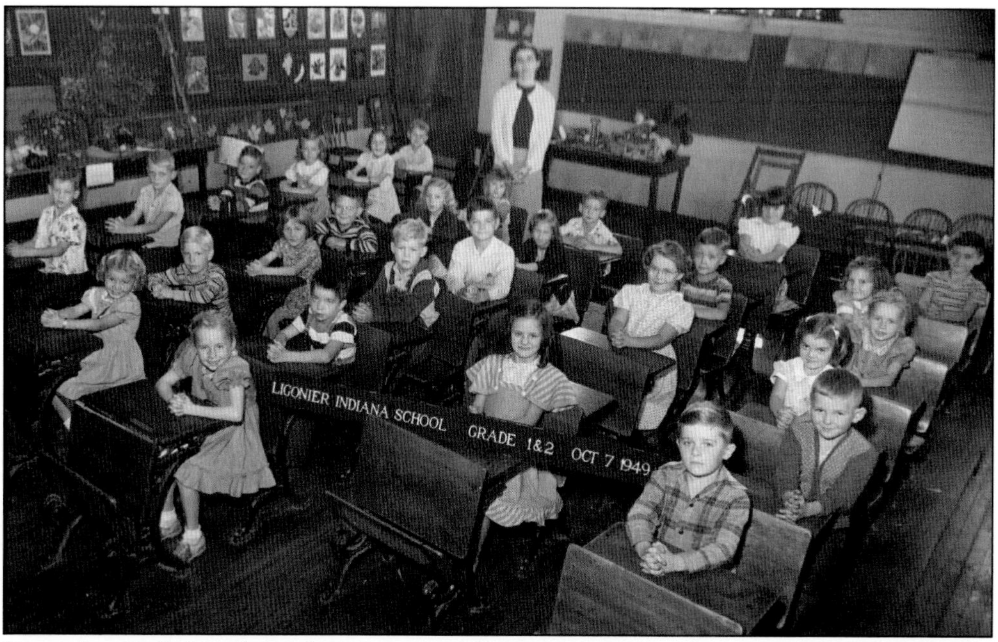


Here is Louise Furkis, the author's aunt, proudly posing with her class of grades one and two in 1949. Furkis dedicated her entire life to helping children get an education, which equaled a chance to have a happy life. Furkis paid for her nephew to attend kindergarten at Northside, even though he lived in a different town.

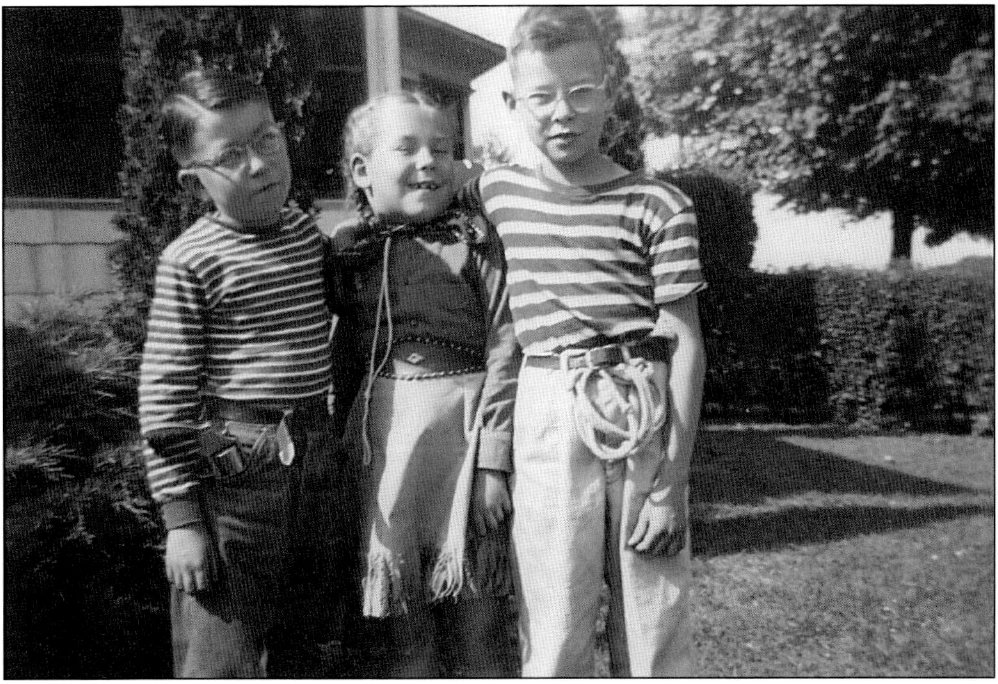

These children live near the Northside School. One can tell the approximate date of the photograph (early 1950s) by the guns and ropes and cowgirl clothes. These were the duds of Gene Autry and Roy Rogers fans.

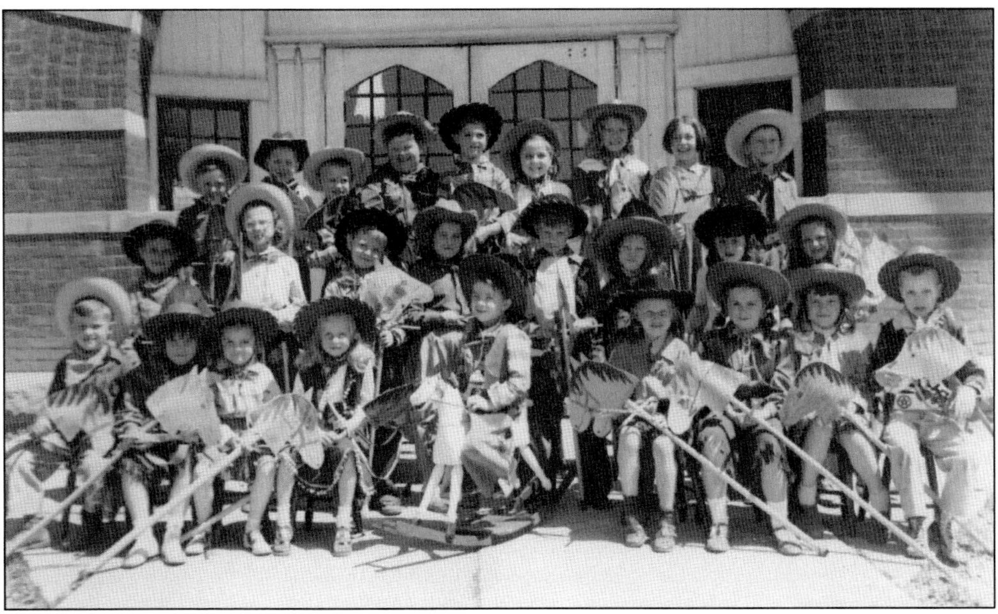

These first- and second-grade students are posing in front of the main doors at Northside School in the early 1950s. Each student has a horse to ride for this photograph.

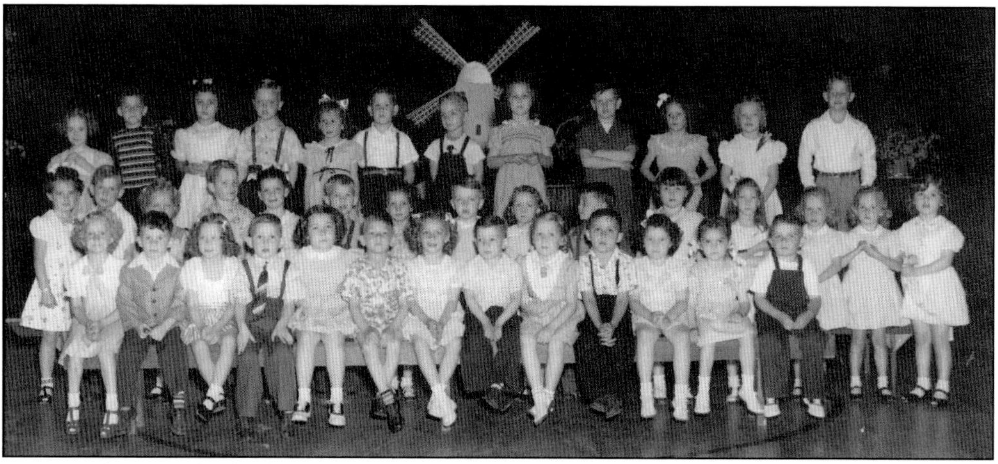

Twice each year, Elizabeth Mentzer would have programs for the parents and grandparents of the kindergartners at Northside School. The children who participated in such events learned about performance jitters, but the memory of kindergarten brings many positive things to mind for most.

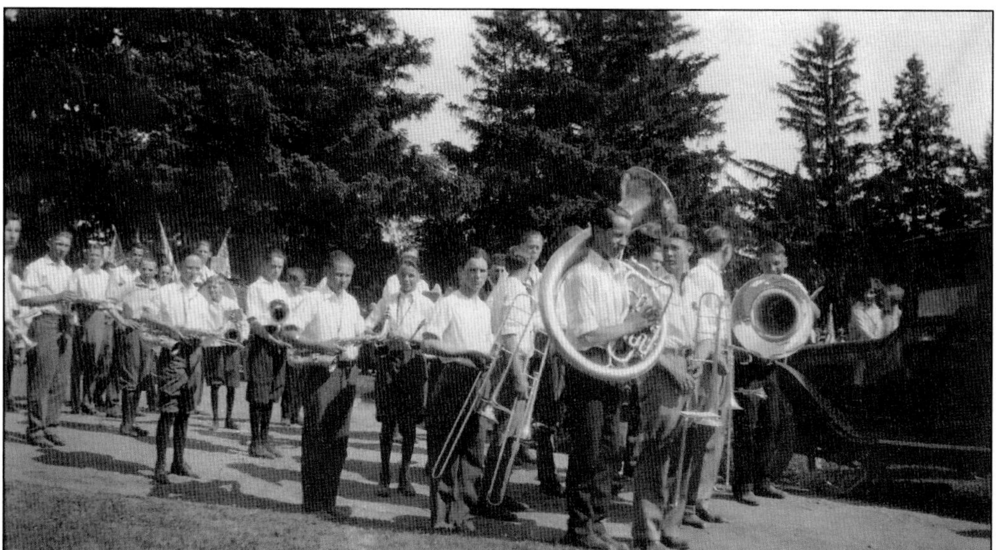

This band is marching at the Oak Park Cemetery for a Memorial Day or Decoration Day event. Decoration Day was started after the Civil War and later became Memorial Day. The old car on the right (even if it was a new car then) dates the photograph to around 1920. Note the shorts for the boys fall just below their knees.

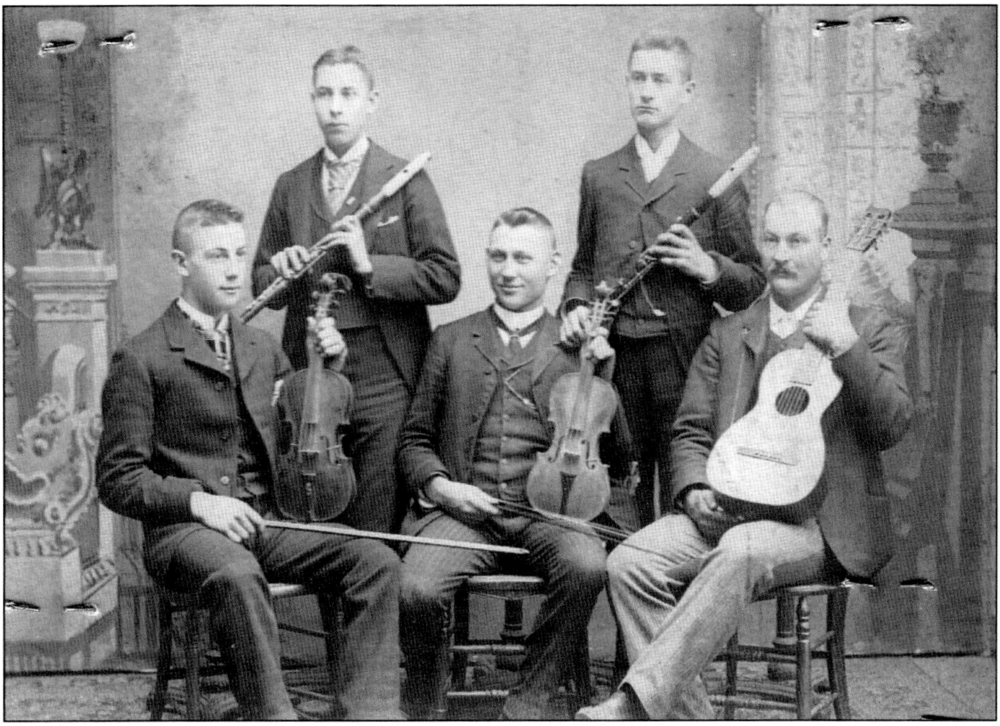

This band is from 1880. The names of the people are known because William Cochran wrote the information on the back. Pictured are, from left to right, (front row) Charley McLean, Charles Joray, and Frank Reese; (back row) Sam Gants and Zack Cook The image was made by Henry Cornell, a famous Ligonier photographer.

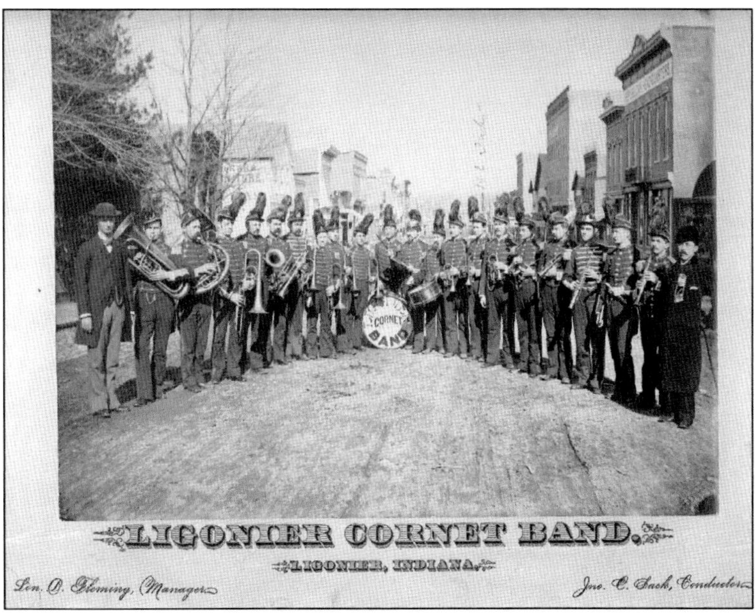


This is the famous Ligonier Cornet Band. It was formed by Crist Sack in 1875 and morphed into the Ligonier Military Band. It was extremely good and won a worldwide competition in 1887 in Chicago. That year, the band won over $4,000 worth of instruments and cash prizes. There are 22 men pictured.

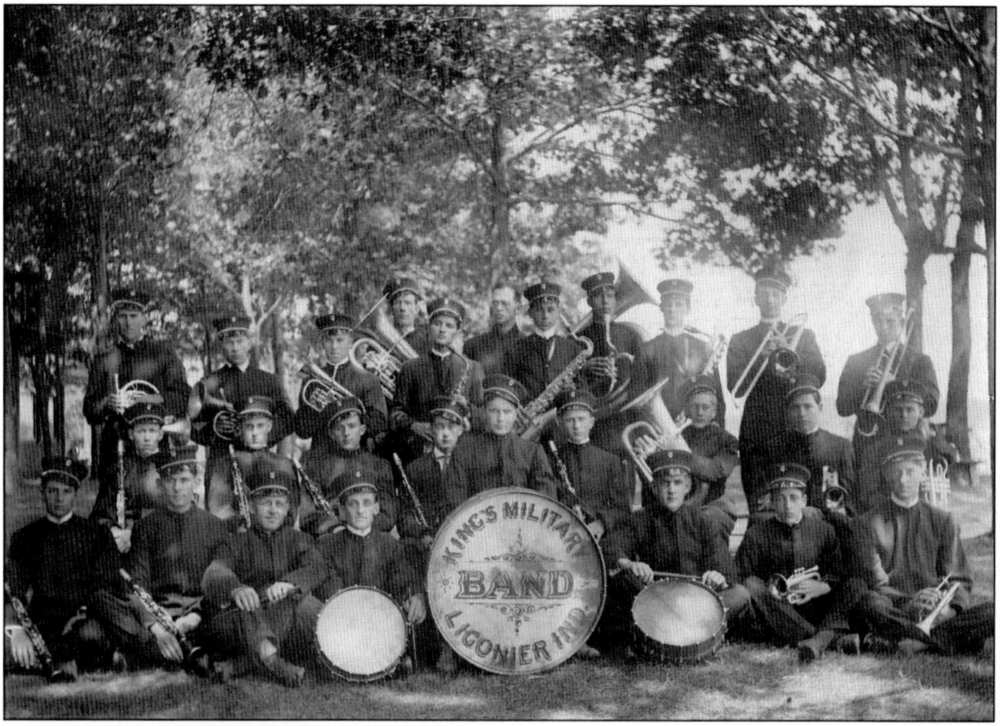


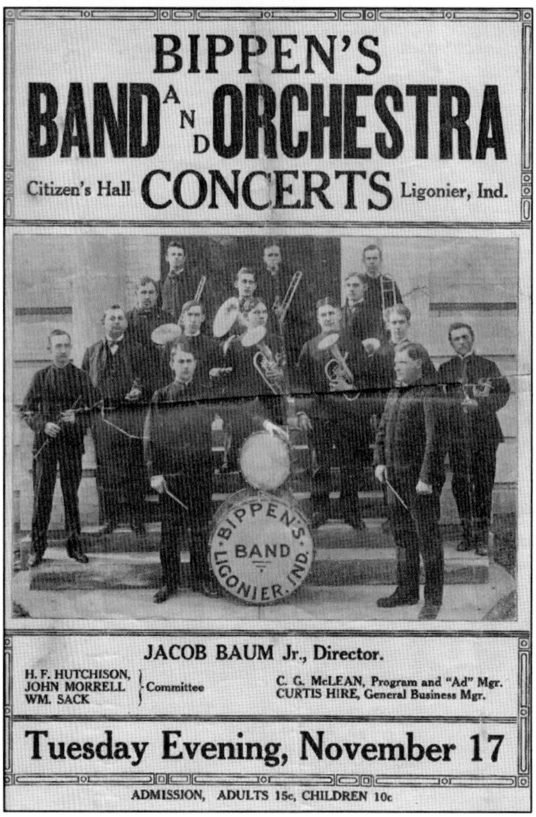


This band is the famous Ligonier Military Band. The name on the drum reads "King's Military Band Ligonier Ind." There was a hardware store in Ligonier called Kings Hardware. Perhaps Kings Hardware supported the band and thus was entitled to put its name on the drum. The practice was grueling, and the band members aged. They disbanded around 1915. This photograph is also featured on the cover of this book.

This advertisement is for a performance by the Bippens Band and Orchestra. Christ Sack was called "Bip," and his band members were dubbed Bippens. Research found an approximate date for the band of before 1911, when Jacob Brown died.

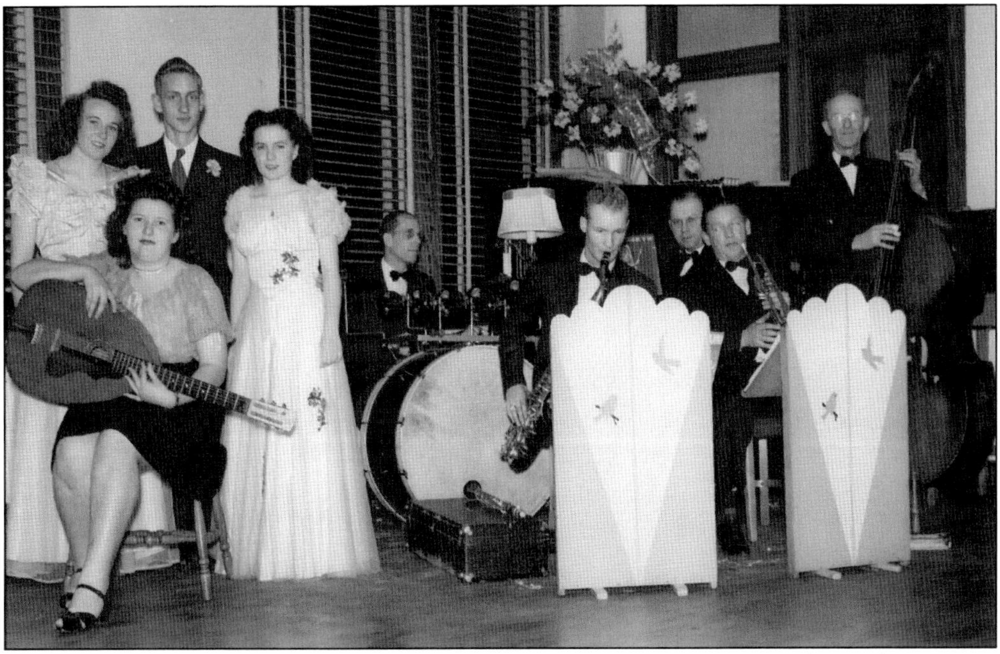

This is the William Cochran 1946 Blue Birds Band. They are playing at the Wirk Garment factory dance. The Blue Birds are the older men at the right of the photograph. Russell Smith is on drums, Cochran plays piano, Max Emery plays fiddle, Dutch Selentright plays sax, and John Leming plays trumpet.

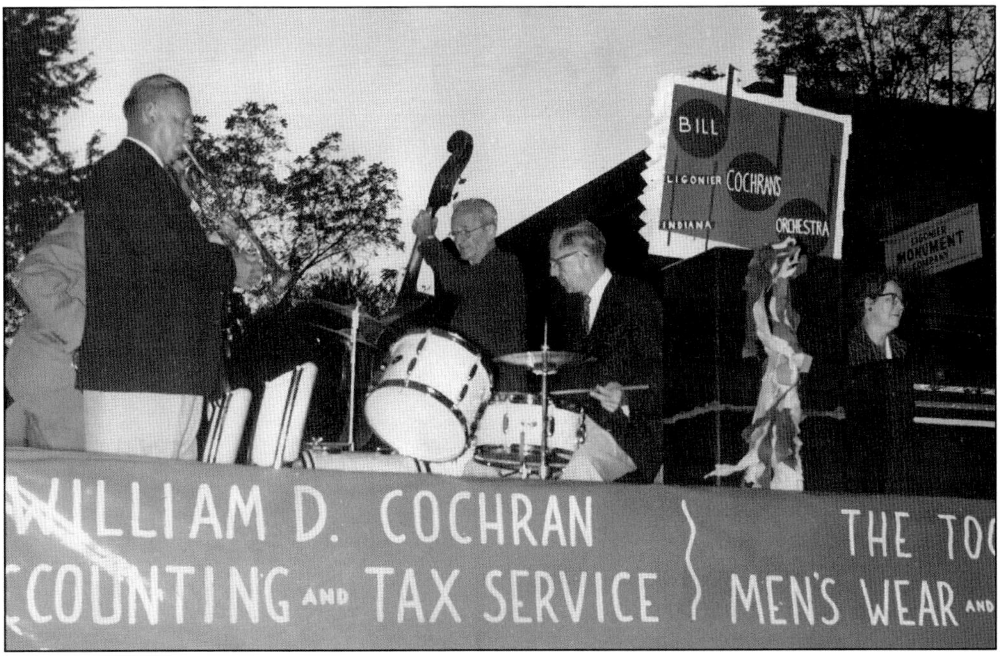


This is the William Cochran band again. This time, the men are riding a float in either the Strawberry Festival or the Marshmallow Parade. The Strawberry Festival morphed into the Marshmallow Festival. The musicians are Russell Smith on drums, Bernice and William Cochran on piano, Max Emery on fiddle, Dutch Selentright on sax, and John Leming on trumpet.

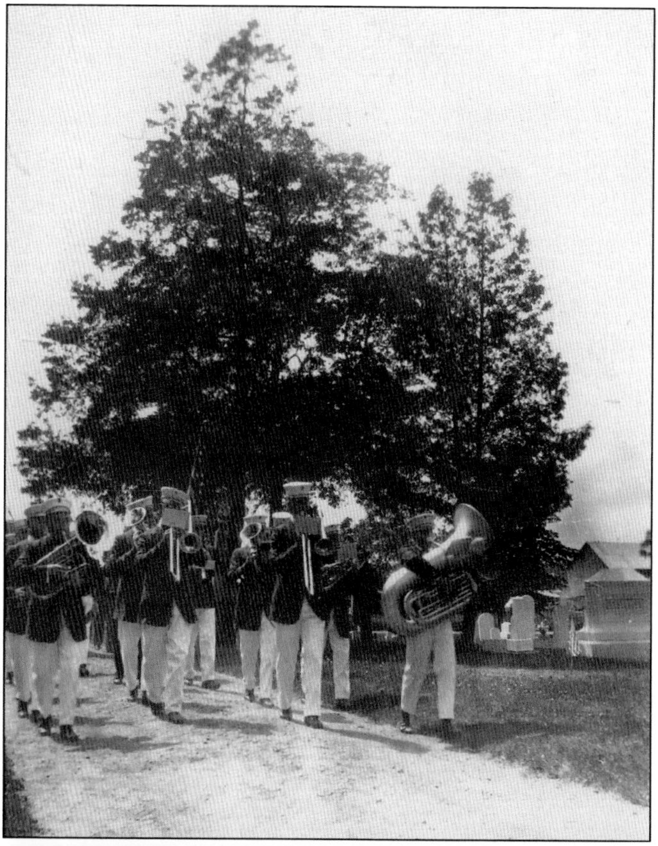

This is an unidentified band at the Oak Park Cemetery in Ligonier. The uniforms do not look like those used by any of the Ligonier bands. The men in the band appear to be adults. It is believed that this is for a Decoration Day or Memorial Day celebration.

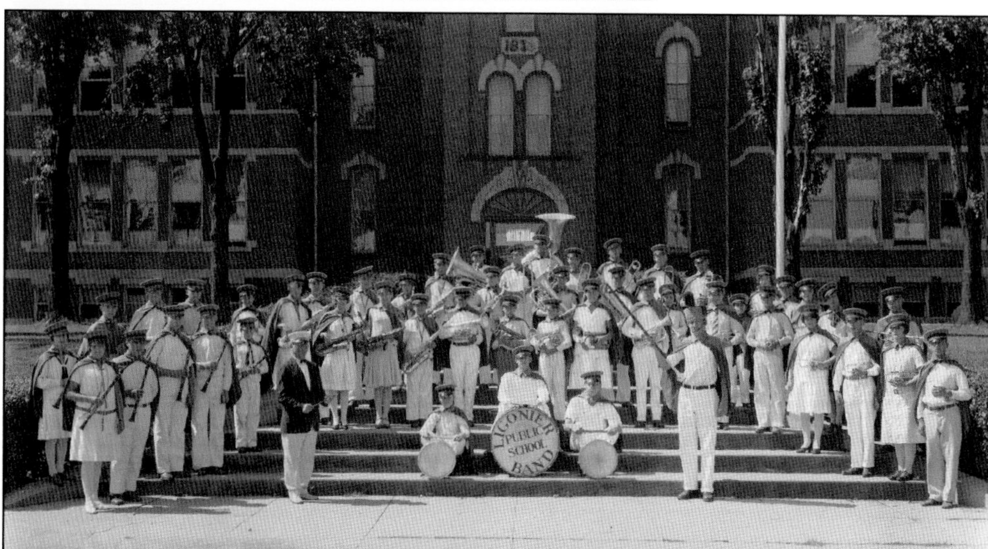


This is the Ligonier Public School Band in the 1924–1925 school year. Later, the name was changed to the Ligonier High School Band. The director, on the left, is Arthur Reed. The drum major, on the right, is Carroll Goshorn. Margaret Hite and John Leming are in the right corner. Baron Steller is in the back row to the left of the tuba.

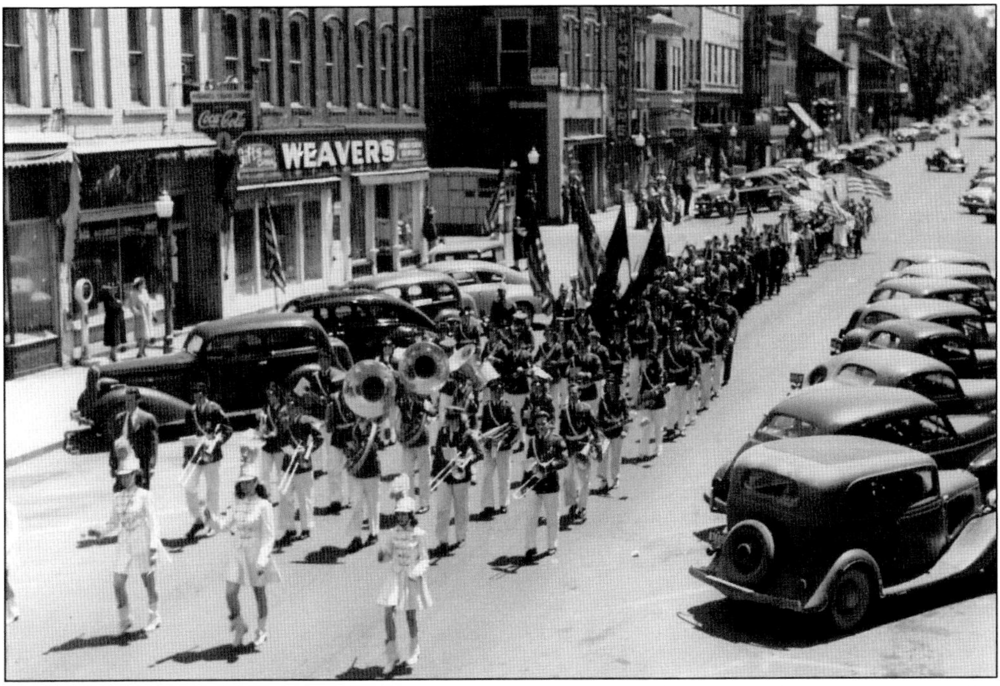


This 1941 photograph of Cavin Street in Ligonier is wonderful. The band looks very nice. On the left side of the street are some building the signs help call attention to. There is the Weaver's Hardware Store. It used to be King and Weaver's Hardware. There is the popcorn wagon on Third Street by Levy's Furniture Store. On south a bit is the Crystal Theatre.

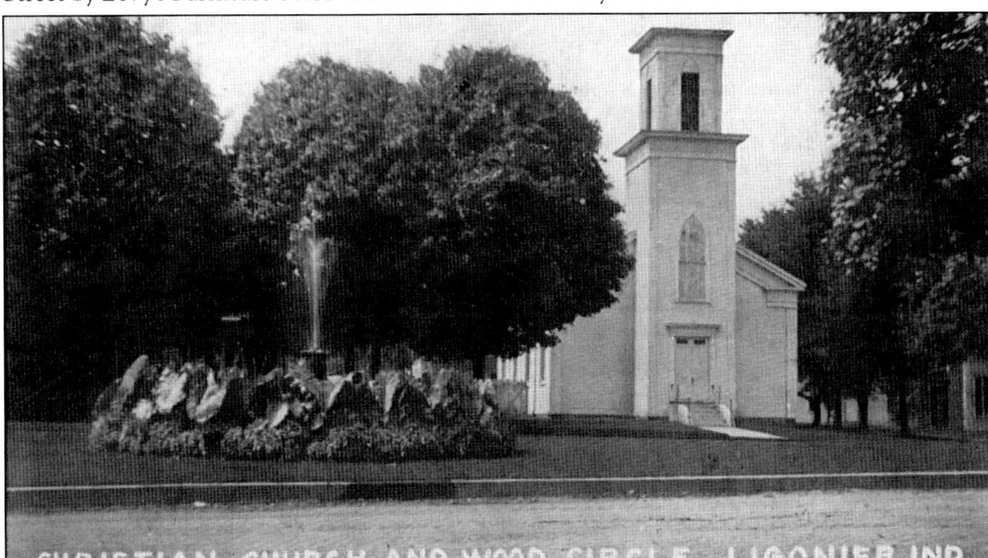


This is the Christian church at Wood Circle Park on South Cavin Street. The road forks at the northern edge of the park. Today, it is called Triangle Park. The Christian church had a bell tower with a pointed roof. A lightning strike took care of that. The church repaired the structure, chopped off the pointed steeple, and made other repairs while remodeling the building. The Christian church started out as the Universalist church but the name changed during its history. A similar transformation happened in other churches in Ligonier.

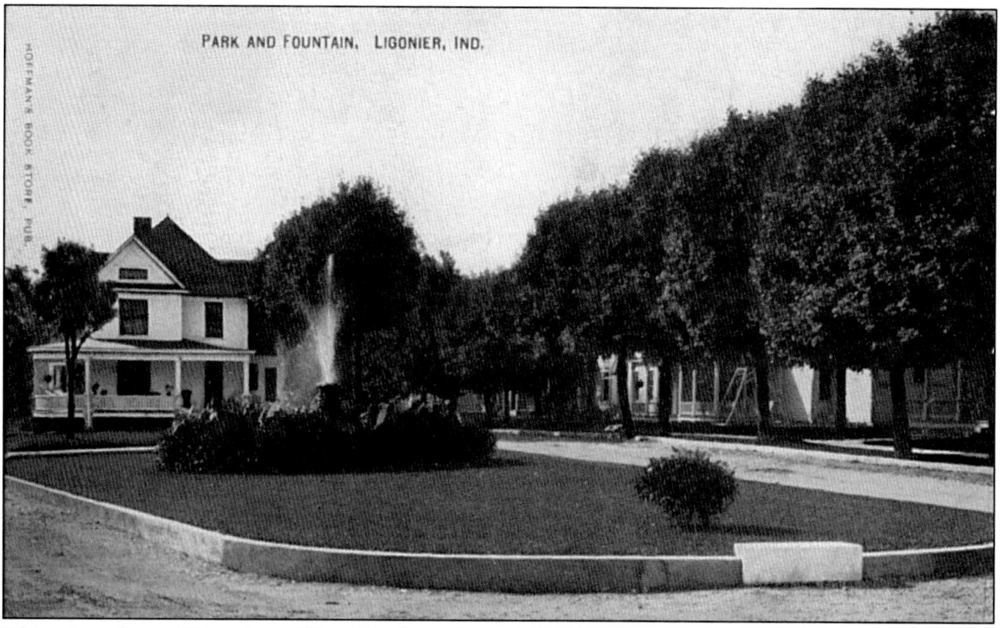


This view shows Triangle or Wood Park at the south end of Cavin Street, where the road forks. The house shown used to be a state police post. Today, Dr. Dragoo's Dentist Office sits about in the same area as the house seen in this photograph.

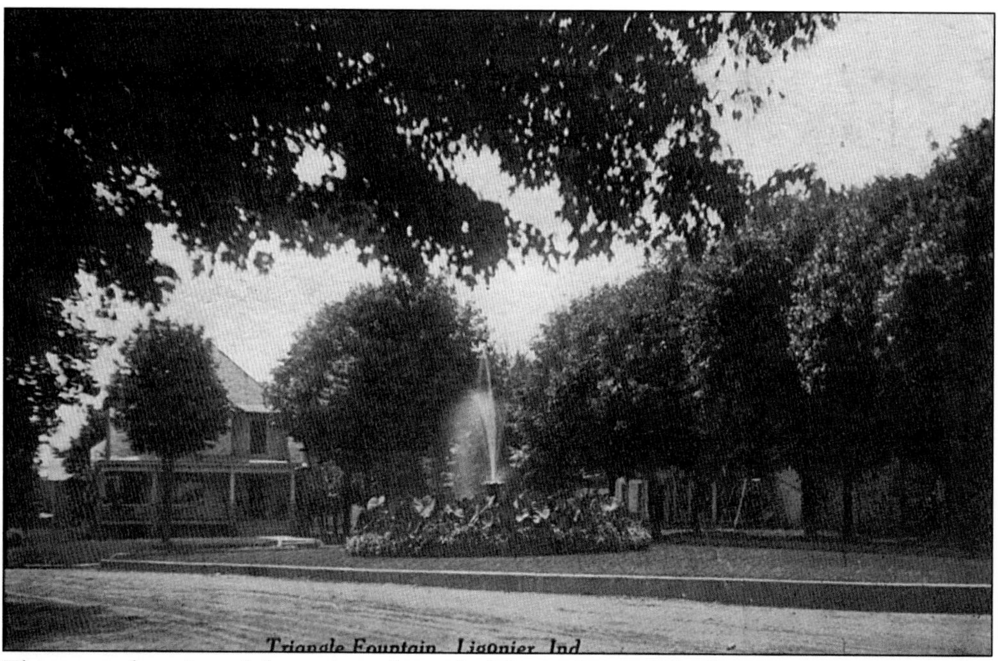


This is another view of the park at the end of Cavin Street. The fountain, according to this postcard, was called Triangle Fountain. The Indiana State Police post is seen in the photograph, though it looks like a house.

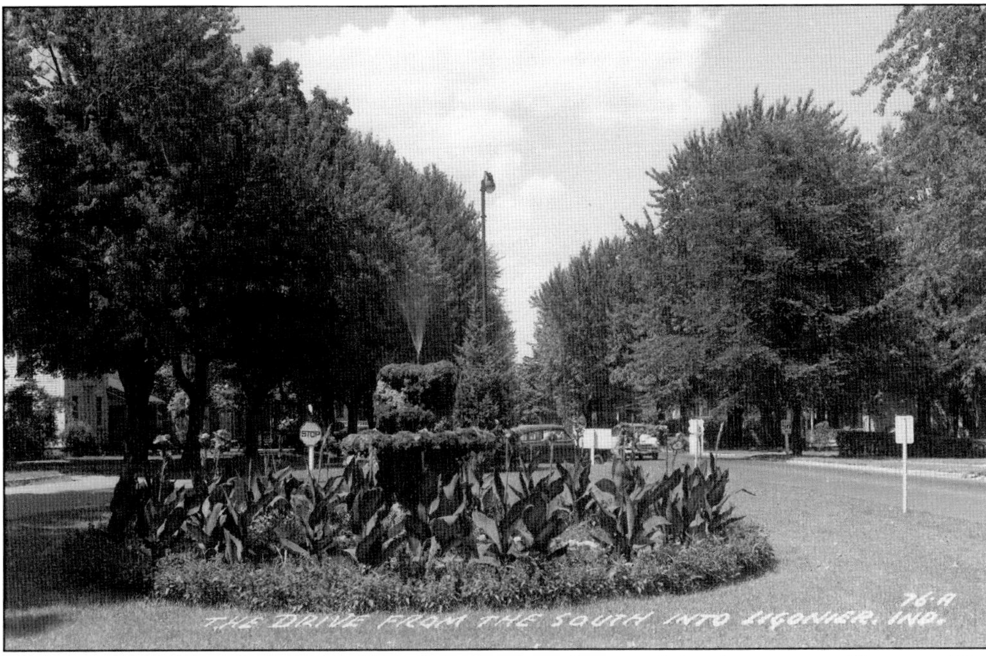


The view is inside Triangle or Wood Park looking north toward the downtown of Ligonier. The fountain is shown, but the clock is not there yet.

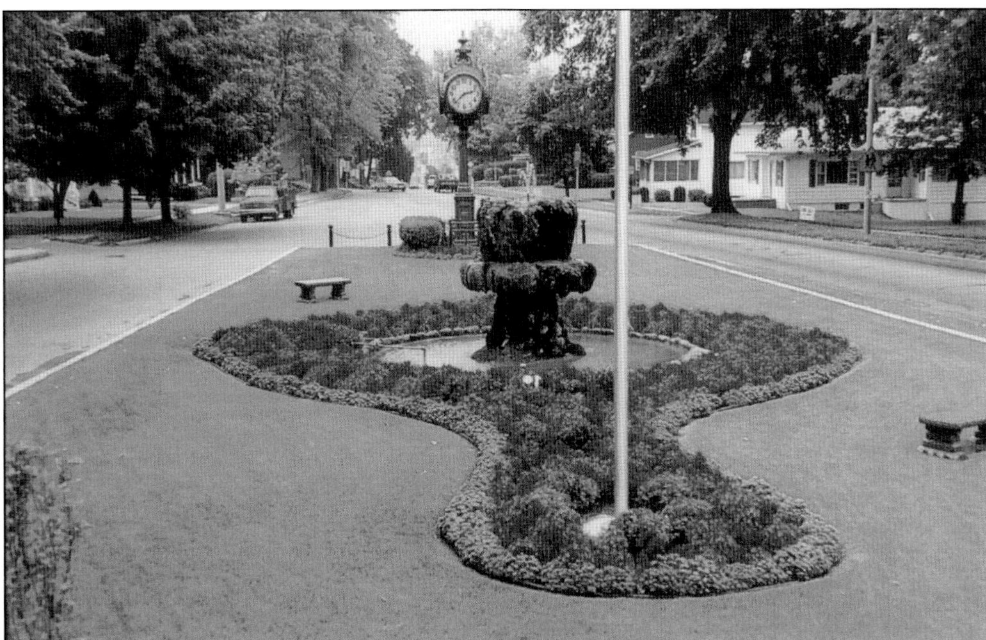

This modern view shows a view from the park looking north today. There is a fountain surrounded by a lagoon. And at the far northern end of the park is the Cavin Memorial Clock.

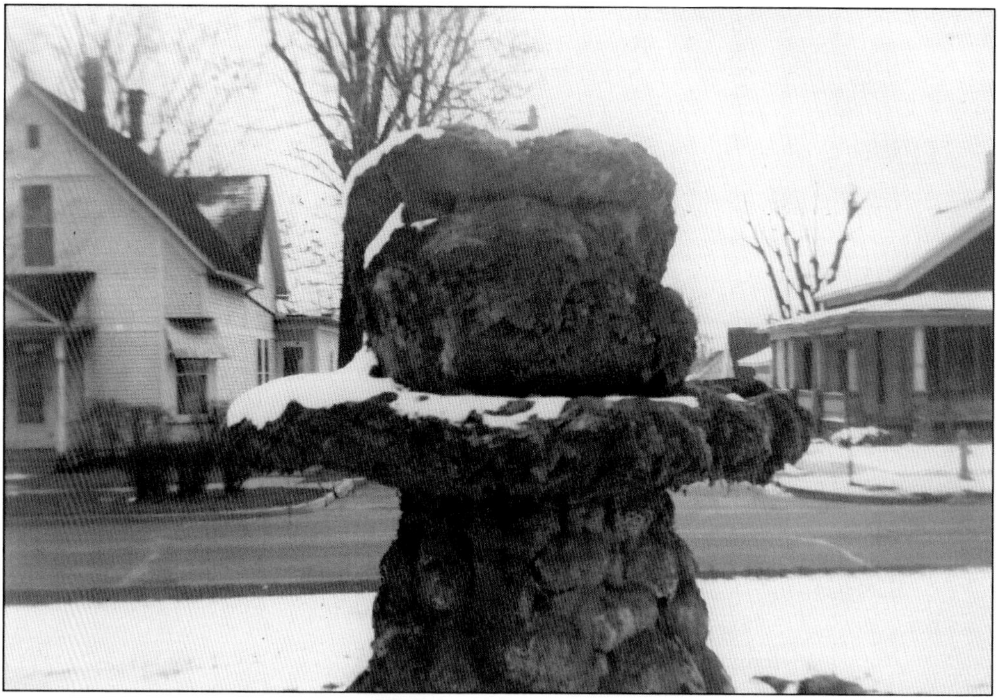

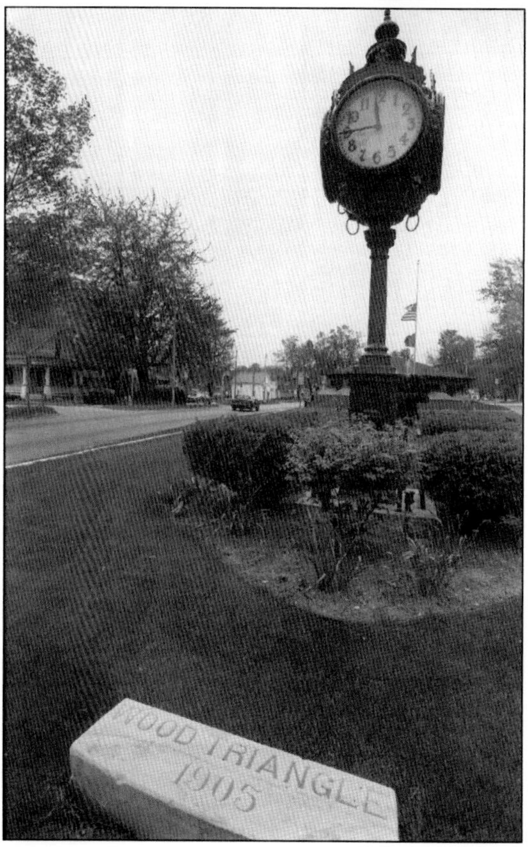


This photograph shows the old gnarled fountain with the moss or lichen growths that give it character and age. Made of cobblestone, the fountain has been in the park since 1894, and it is still working. The camera is pointing east.

This view of the park is looking to the south. The Cavin Memorial Clock is clearly seen, and the 1905 Wood Triangle monument is visible. The land for the park was deeded to the city in 1896 by the Christian church. The clock was bequeathed to Ligonier in 1924 by John L. Cavin.

# *Four*

# People in Ligonier Love Their Homes

This chapter takes a tour of some of the homes and other community buildings in Ligonier. Most of the photographs focus on Main Street. Submissions to the National Register for Historic Places provide descriptions of the homes and of the people who had the homes built.

Since much money is spent on homes and about a third the average person's day is spent in his or her home, it is only natural that homes would be so important. The home provides shelter from the mosquitos, the sun, the cold, the rain, the snow, and other threats.

This tour begins at the south end of South Main Street where it crosses Union Street. It then heads north on the west side of South Main Street. At the stone Straus mansion, it crosses over to the post office, then it heads south returning near where the tour began.

A home is often associated with a name of a person who lived there. That works if everyone knows that name and where that home is. For example, Sol Henoch's home probably means nothing to the reader. But if it is 706 South Main Street, one probably could find it. Therefore, 2016 addresses are used. Ligonier did not have postal delivery to homes until 1912; perhaps that is when the need for an address on each home began. Lots of historical documents identify a home by a person's name since Ligonier did not have street addresses until 1912.

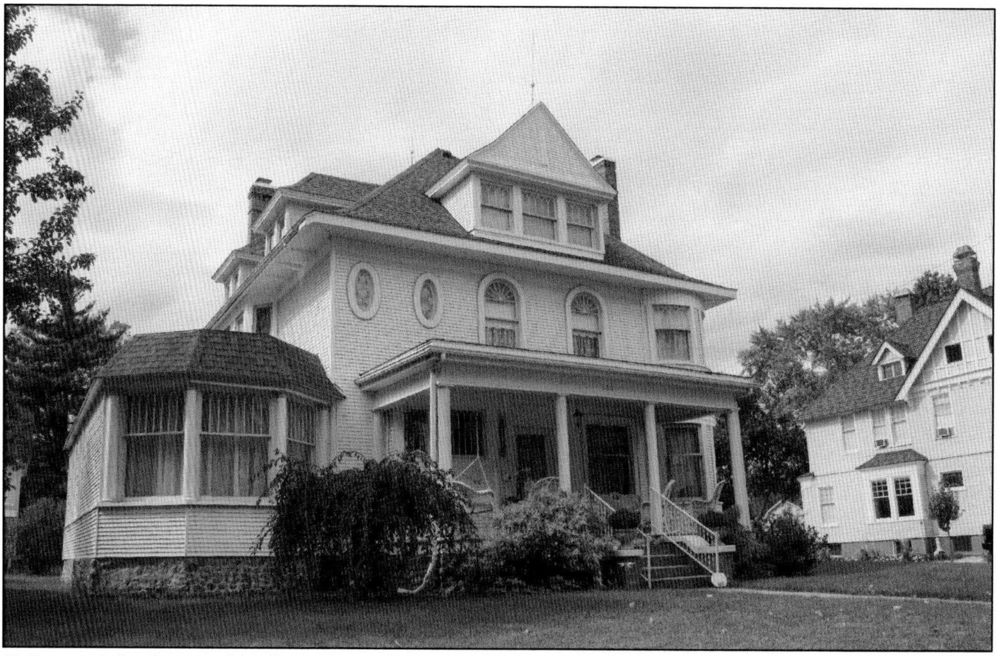

Solomon Mier's son, Abraham Mier, built this Queen Anne house in 1898. Abraham assumed leadership of the Mier Bank after his father's death in 1910. When the Mier and Straus banks were combined as the American State Bank in 1928, he was the first president. The two-story, yellow stucco, Spanish-style home was built originally as a Cape Cod. Later owner Daniel Green and one of his four wives were in Florida when Mrs. Green admired the Spanish-influenced style so prevalent there. Consequently, in 1927 or 1928, the home was redesigned. This house is also called the Abraham B. Mier home.

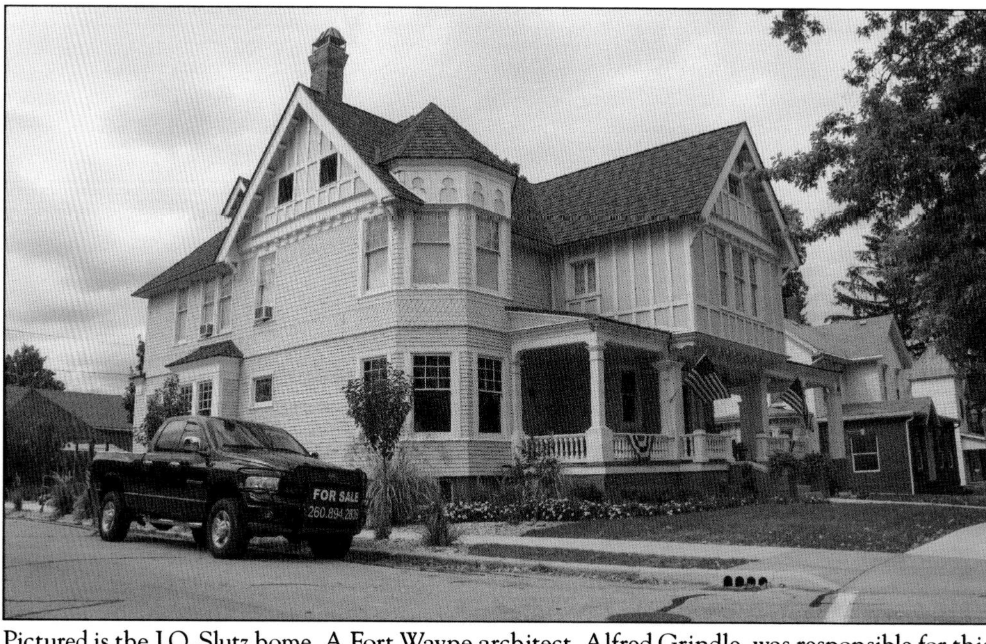


Pictured is the J.O. Slutz home. A Fort Wayne architect, Alfred Grindle, was responsible for this 1904 Tudor Revival design. Slutz was a salesman for a Fort Wayne drug company.

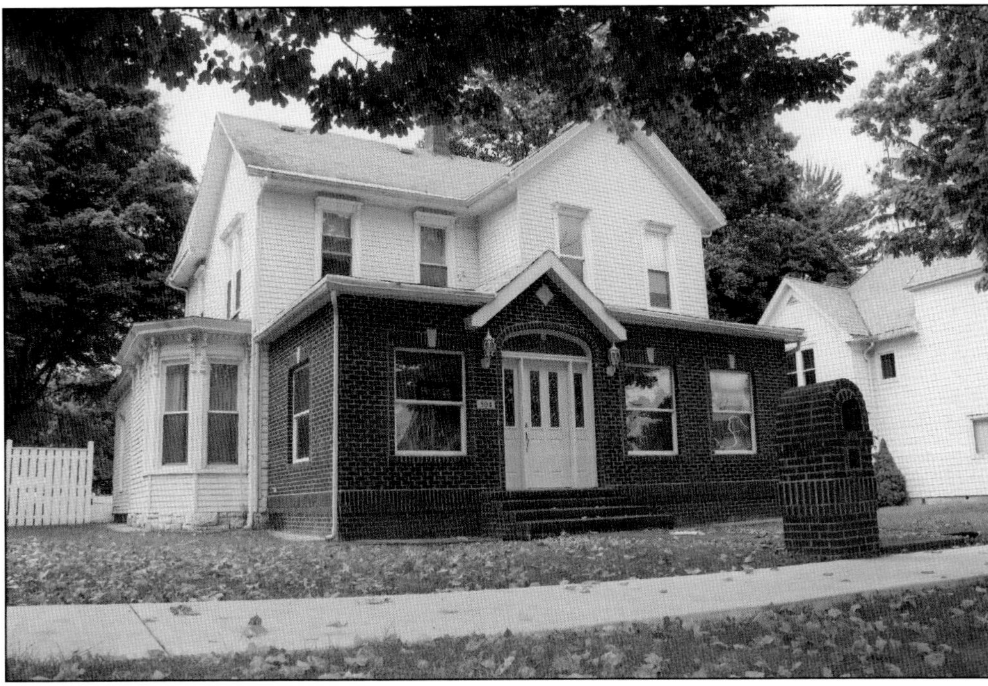

This two-story, wood-frame, Italianate-style home was built from 1877 to 1880 by George W. and Mina Best. This home sits on one of the original lots deeded to Isaac Cavin in 1834. All lots were to be a quarter acre. John Cavin, son of Isaac Cavin, assumed ownership in 1905 and lived in this home until his death in 1923.

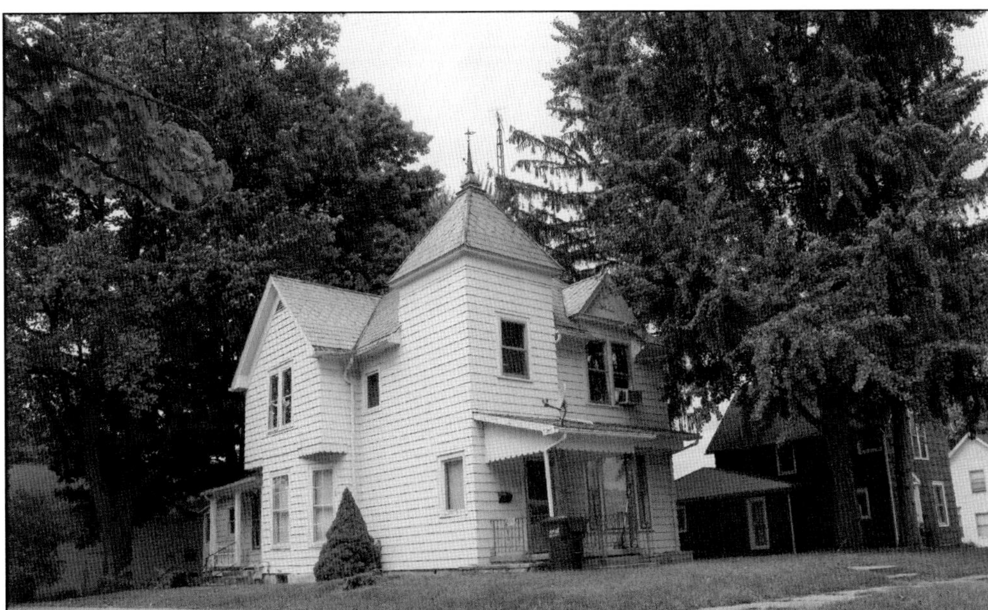

This home at 502 Main Street was once the home of Dr. William Alvin Shobe. Notice the unusual lightning rod on the roof. It is still there after 120 years. The house is featured in a June 6, 1895, special edition of the *Ligonier Leader* (vol. 16, no. 784).

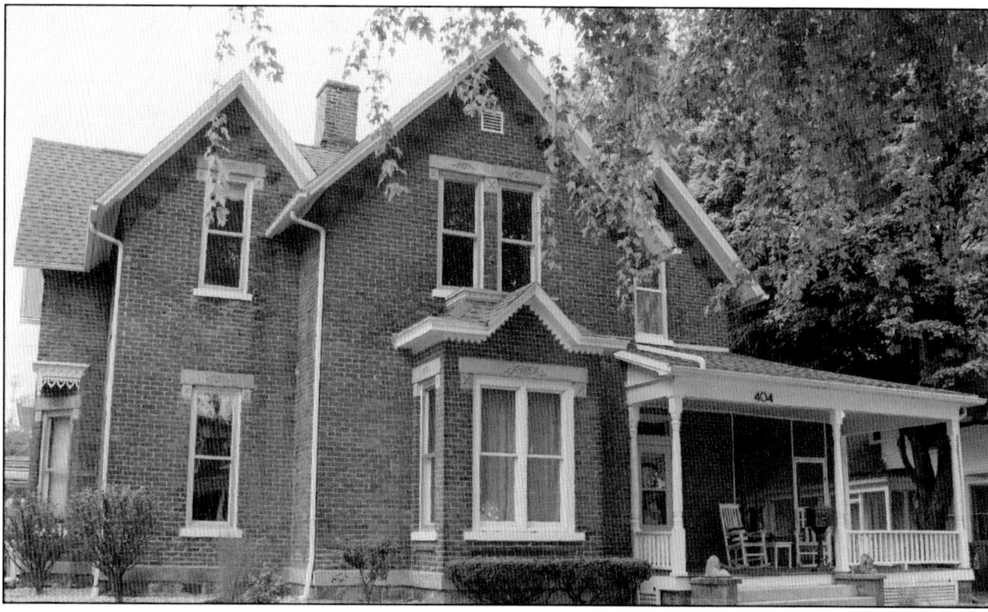

This two-story, brick Victorian Gothic home was built in 1880, as noted by an inscription on the facade. Frederick H. Green was a successful realtor who dealt extensively in farms and livestock before founding the Farmers and Merchants Trust Company in 1906. In public life, he served two terms as mayor, during which time the city waterworks was built. He was also the president of the library board at the time the public library was built.

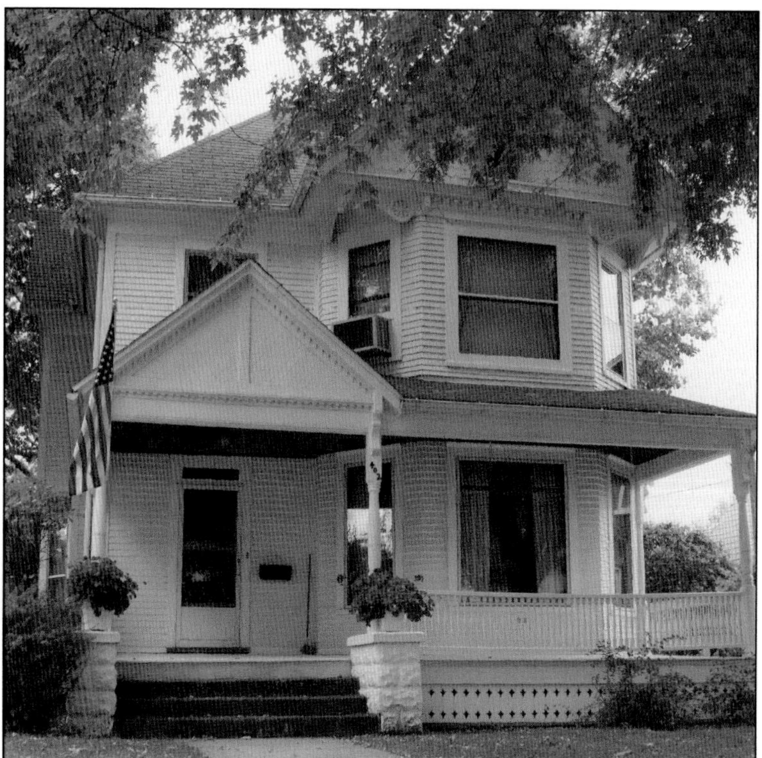

This comfortable eight-room Queen Anne home was built in 1895 by Eli Gerber for his newlywed daughter Minnie and her husband, Harry Green. Harry's two elder brothers, Fred and John, lived on either side of this construction. The next owner of the home was Dwight Green, son of Harry and Minnie Green, who was a special prosecutor for the trial of Al Capone and subsequently served two terms as governor of Illinois, from 1940 through 1948.

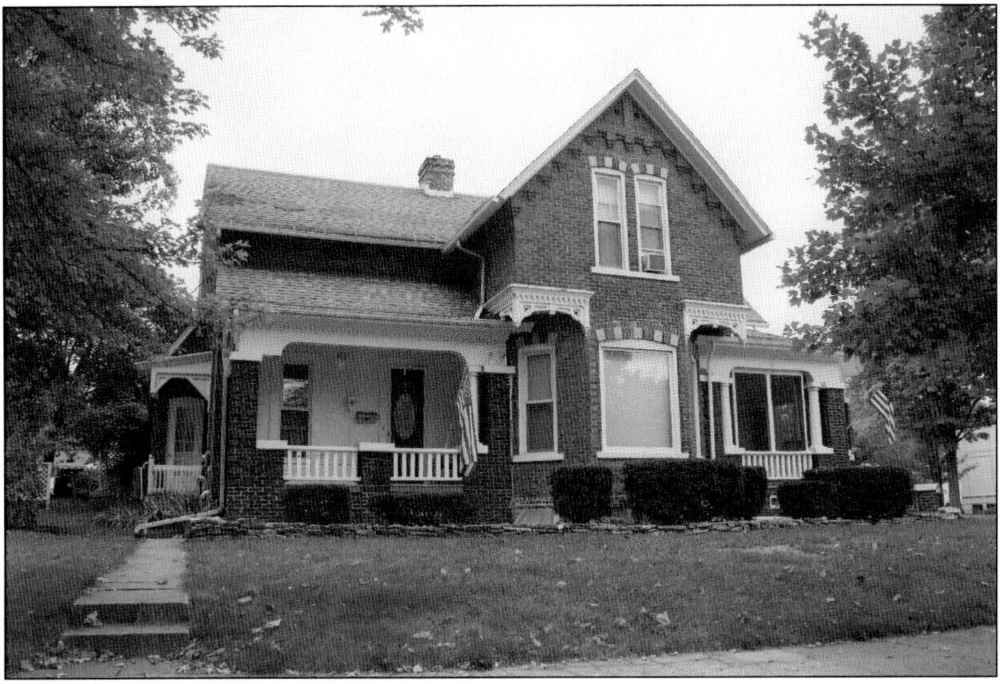

Bob Sedgwick, of Ulrey and Sedgwick funeral home, was the owner of this home in the 1950s.

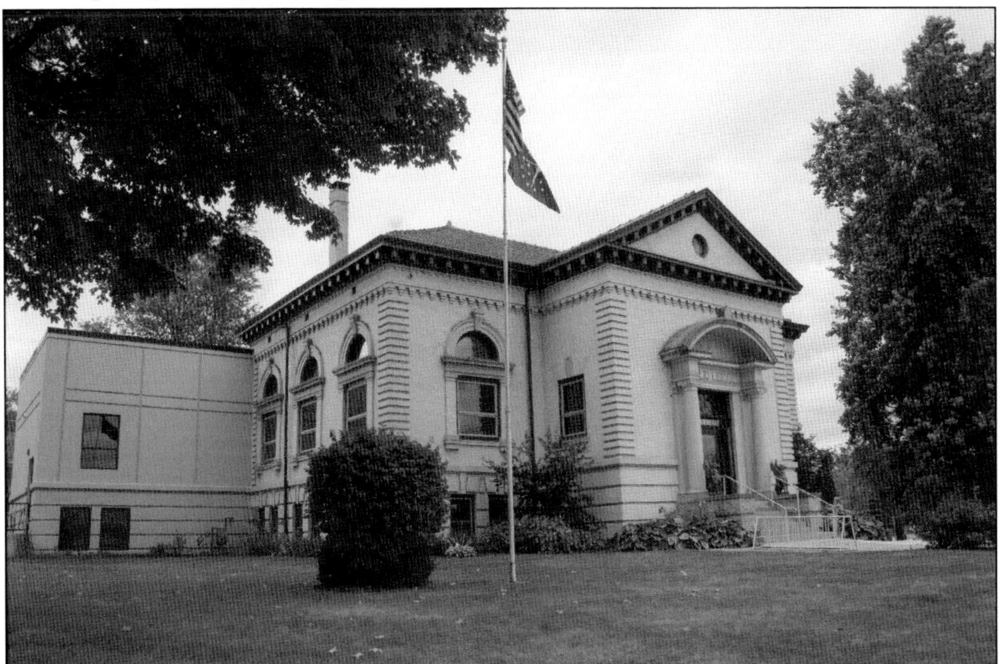

The Ligonier Library was constructed with a $10,000 grant from Andrew Carnegie in 1908. The site, originally intended as a part of the public square, had been occupied by a school until the construction of this Italian Renaissance Revival building. A semicircular rotunda addition was made to the rear of the library in the early 1970s to expand the stack area. In 2015, another addition enlarged the library and met user needs.

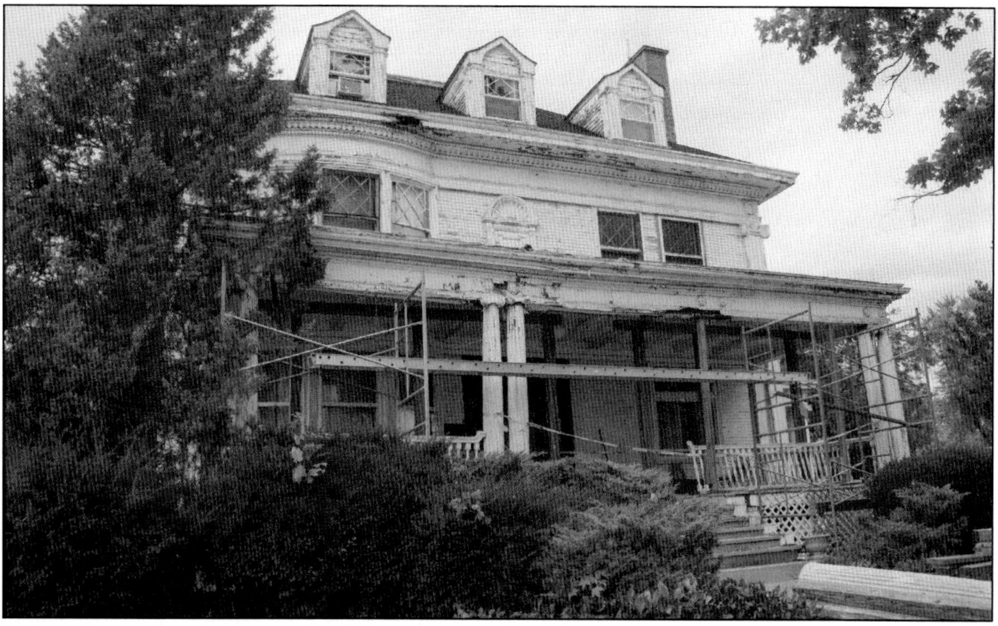

Jacob Straus, along with his brothers Frederick and Mathias, formed a merchandise business. In 1868, the brothers opened the Citizens Bank, and they formed a real estate firm in 1870 that had offices in 13 Midwestern states. Jacob was responsible for organizing the local school board, and he oversaw the construction of the first public school building in 1876. Jacob and his two sons, Isaac and Simon, were community business leaders. The family mausoleum is in the Jewish section of the Oak Park Cemetery.

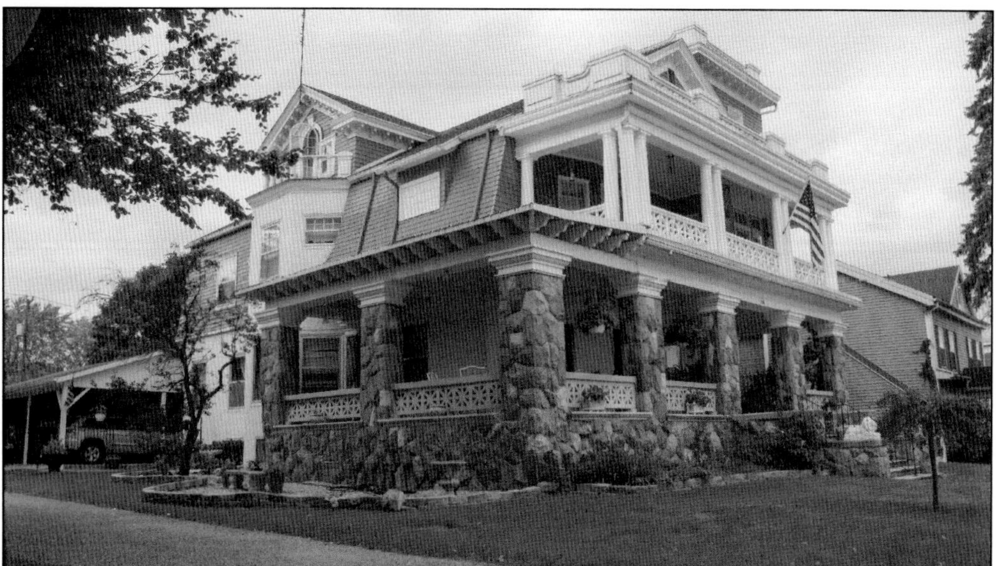

This home was built in 1900 by Isaac Straus, son on Frederick Straus, who was one of Ligonier's first Jews. The home burned in 1911, with the back part of the second and upper stories destroyed. It was rebuilt with the solid granite porch added. The home features lovely wood paneling in several rooms. Many of the original chandeliers remain. The third floor is a ballroom that was used for parties and card playing.

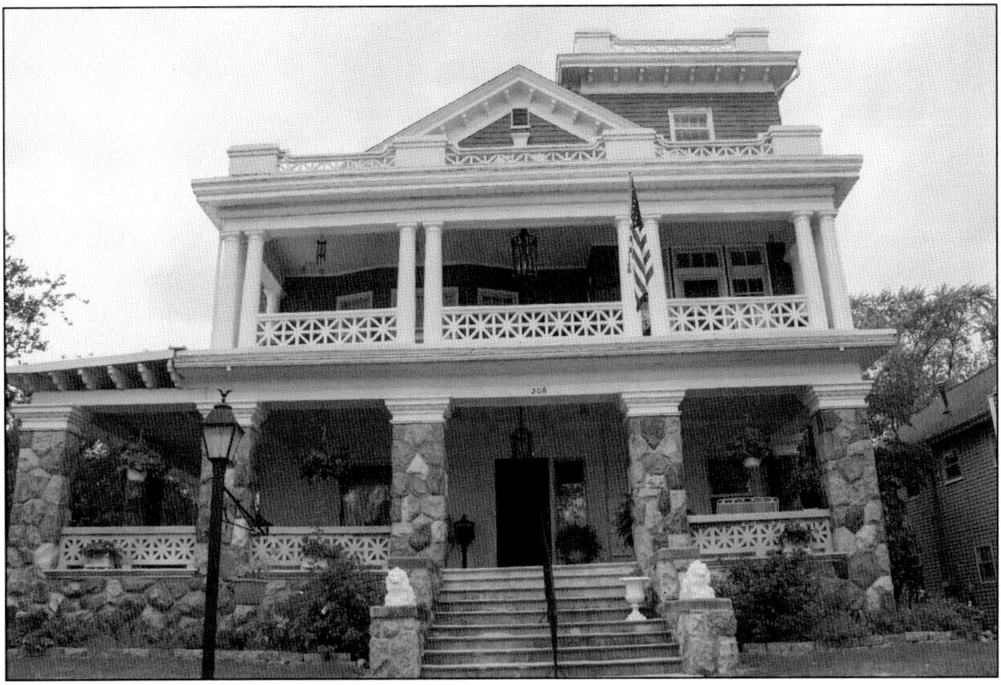

Isaac Straus was a member of one of the two most prominent Jewish families in Ligonier—along with the Miers. Both families appeared in Ligonier as peddlers. Both opened merchandise stores. Both opened banks. Both families were involved in land sales, primarily farms. Both started carriage and buggy companies. Both did well for their families and the town. Both were involved in the government of the town. And both contributed greatly to the development of Ligonier.

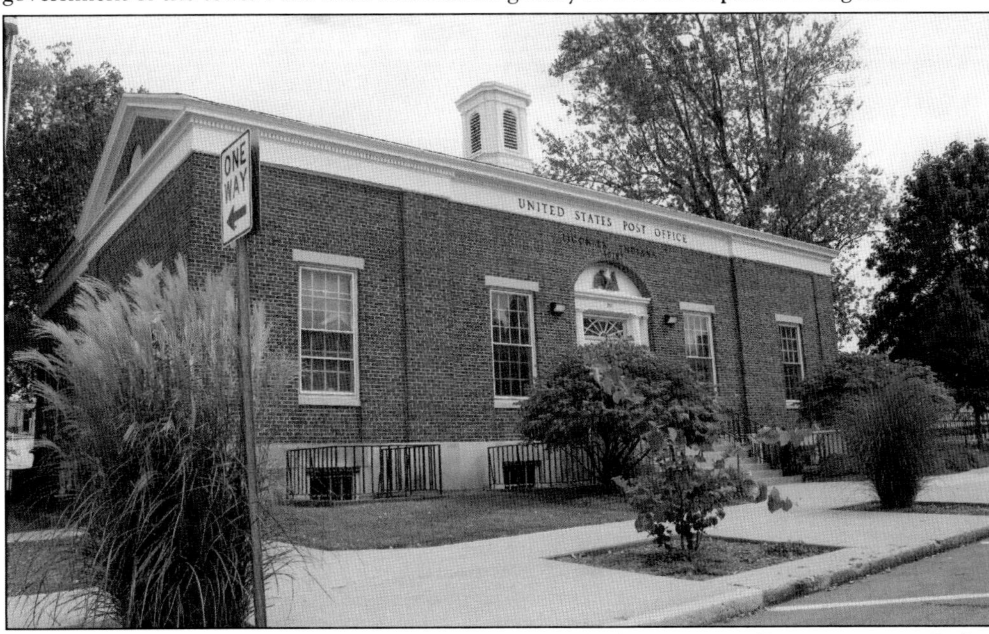


This 1935 Colonial Revival structure was the first one built as a post office in Ligonier. Before that time, post office service had been in various commercial buildings, such as the Gentry Hotel (212 South Cavin Street), which was the post office's home immediately before this site.

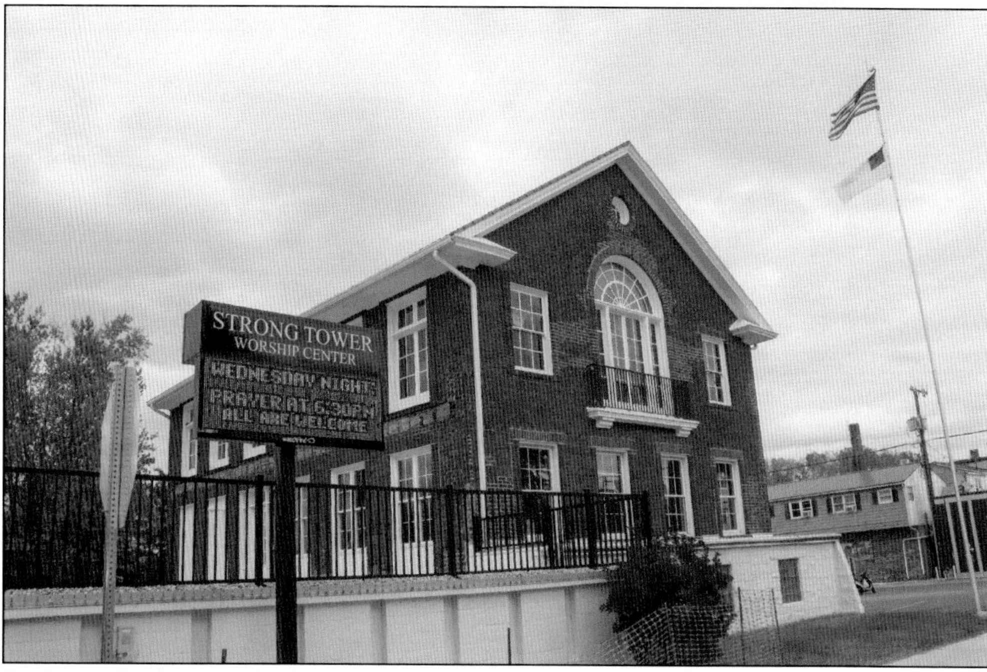


On West Third Street, the former Elks Lodge, which closed in 2008, was built in 1912. Before this structure was erected, a meeting place for B'nai B'rith was located here. Until 2015, this was the Strong Tower church (as pictured), but that too has closed. A 2015 *Ligonier Advance-Leader* reported that the owner has some idea of what to do with it but does not state a specific use.

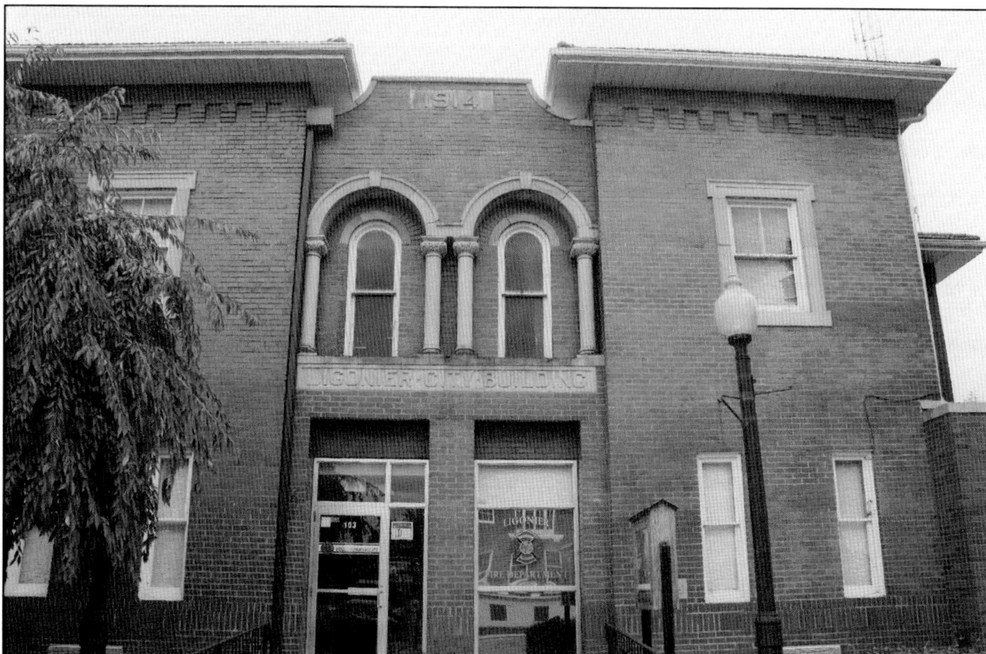


Ligonier's city hall was built in 1914 on what had originally been part of the public square on West Third Street. A city jail stood here until that time. Cosmo C. Elwood of Elkhart designed the building in the Italian Renaissance Revival style.

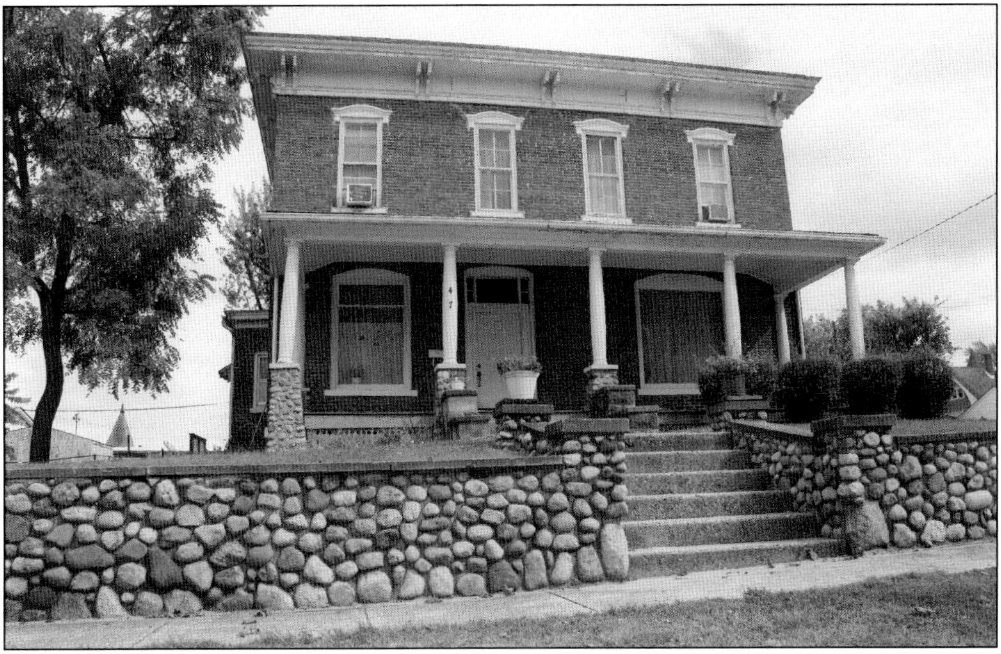

Pictured here is Charles Inks's home. The Italianate style can be seen in this two-story, four-bay brick house, which was built in 1875. Inks moved his granite and marble shop to Ligonier from nearby Wolf Lake in 1868. His trade was spread over a three-state area. When his son A.J. became the owner of the home in 1923, he replaced the original porch with the present one and built a cobblestone retaining wall around the base of the bank on which the house stands.

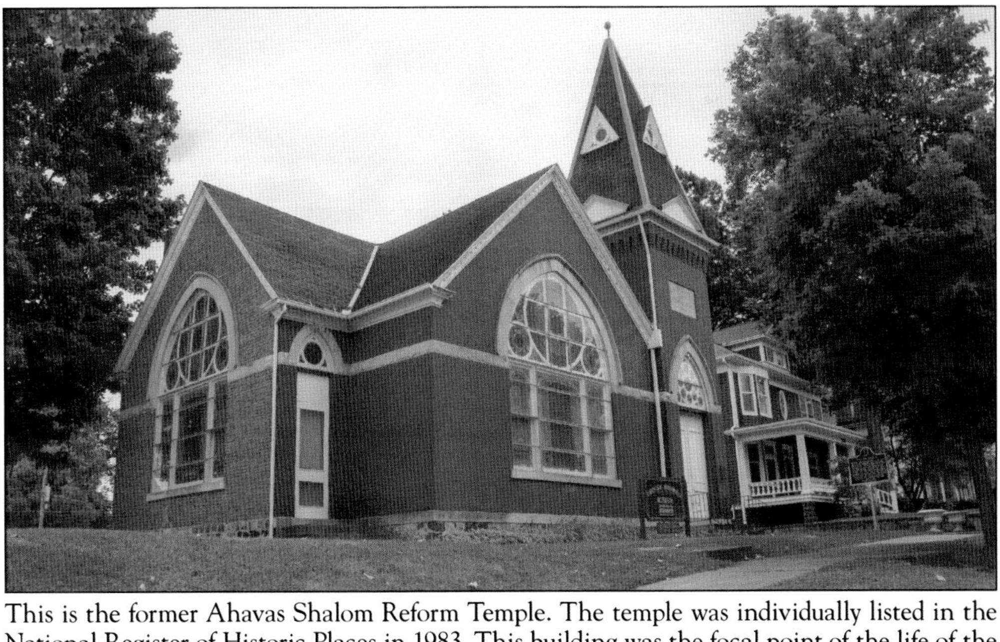

This is the former Ahavas Shalom Reform Temple. The temple was individually listed in the National Register of Historic Places in 1983. This building was the focal point of the life of the Jewish community in Ligonier. According to a local architect, the temple was built in 1889, and its Victorian Gothic design combines a cross-gable form otherwise used for Christian churches with decorative details, chiefly in the windows, of Jewish and Middle Eastern iconography.

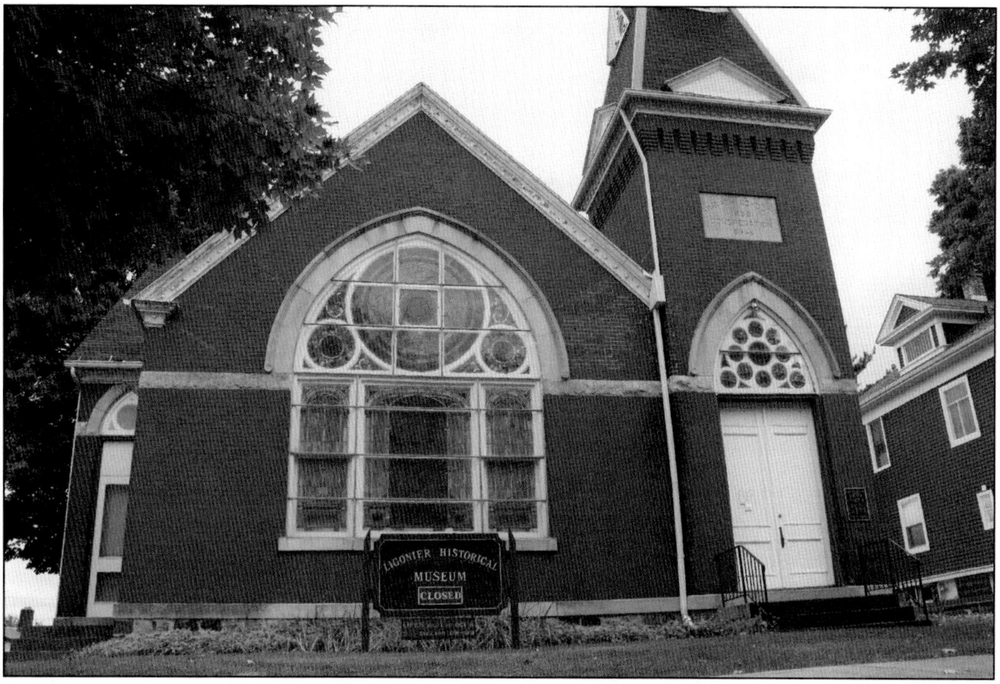


As the Jewish population dwindled, the temple saw increasingly sporadic use. In 1954, it was finally sold to the first of several Christian denominations that have since used it. It was owned by the Ligonier Library and is now offered for sale.

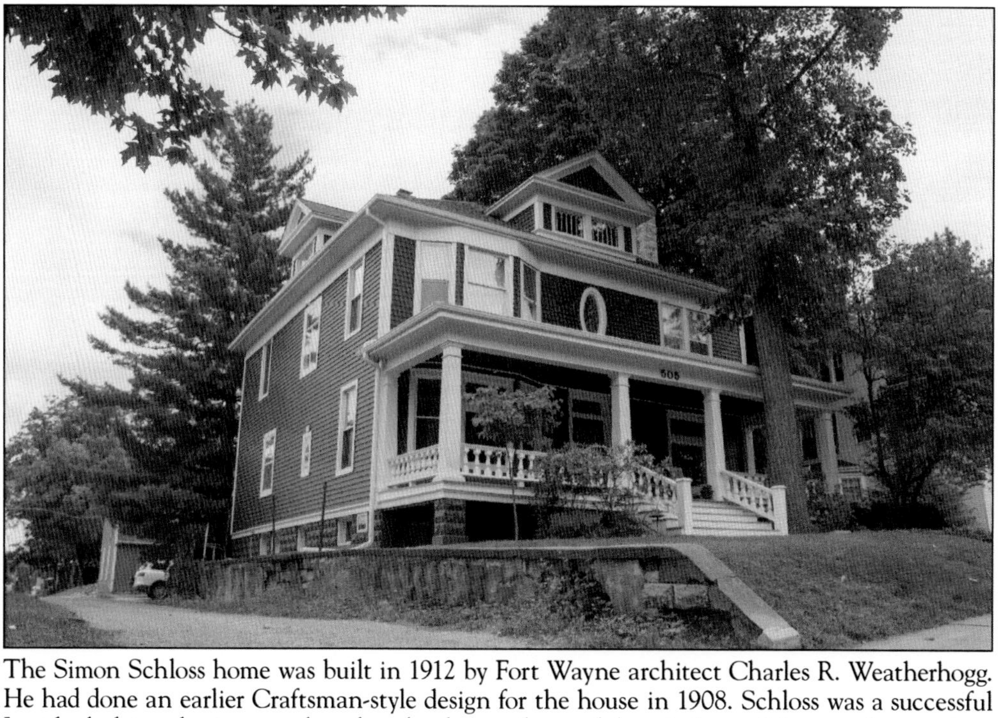

The Simon Schloss home was built in 1912 by Fort Wayne architect Charles R. Weatherhogg. He had done an earlier Craftsman-style design for the house in 1908. Schloss was a successful Jewish clothier who is remembered as the donor of one of the windows of the temple next door to this home.

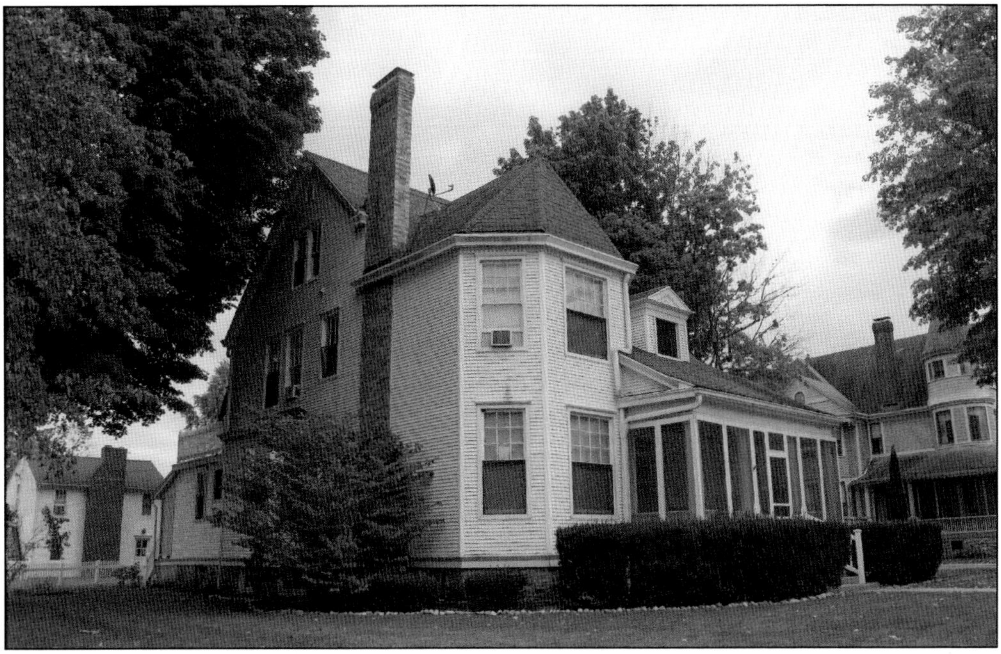

This is the second home of Eli Jacobs, which was built here in 1908. By the time Jacobs built this house, he was well established in Ligonier. His store was located in the south end of the Straus Block at 214 South Cavin Street.

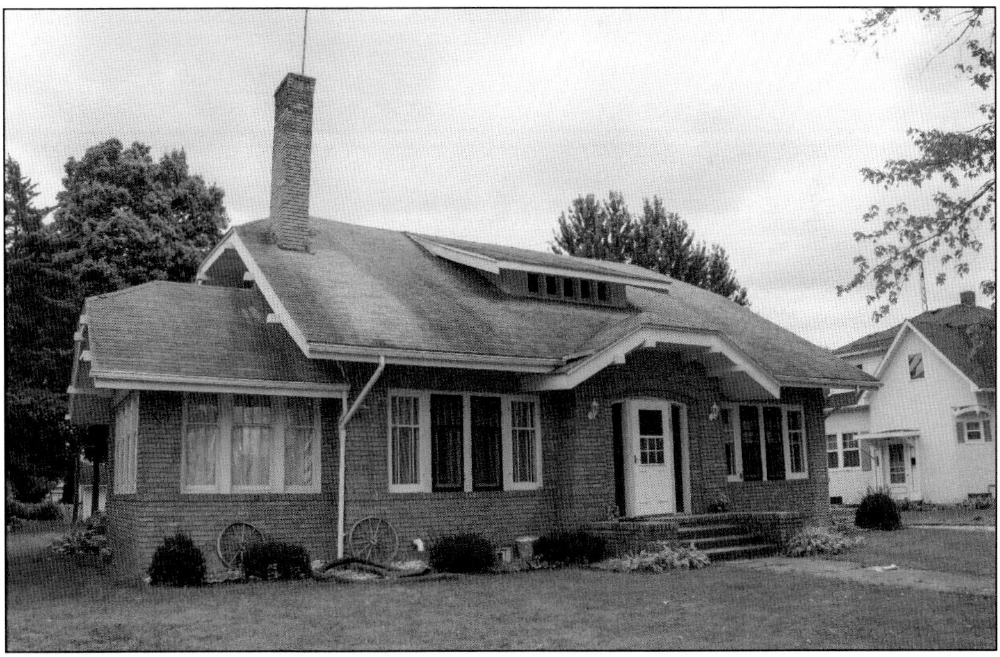

Harrison Wood was a Noble County pioneer. He came from New York via Michigan and had settled at Rochester. He served two terms as county sheriff, starting in 1844, then was probate judge until 1851, when he returned to farming. Wood owned the first threshing machine in the county. In 1858, he platted Wood's Addition to Ligonier, which is an area between McLean and Smith Streets from Fourth to Sixth Streets.

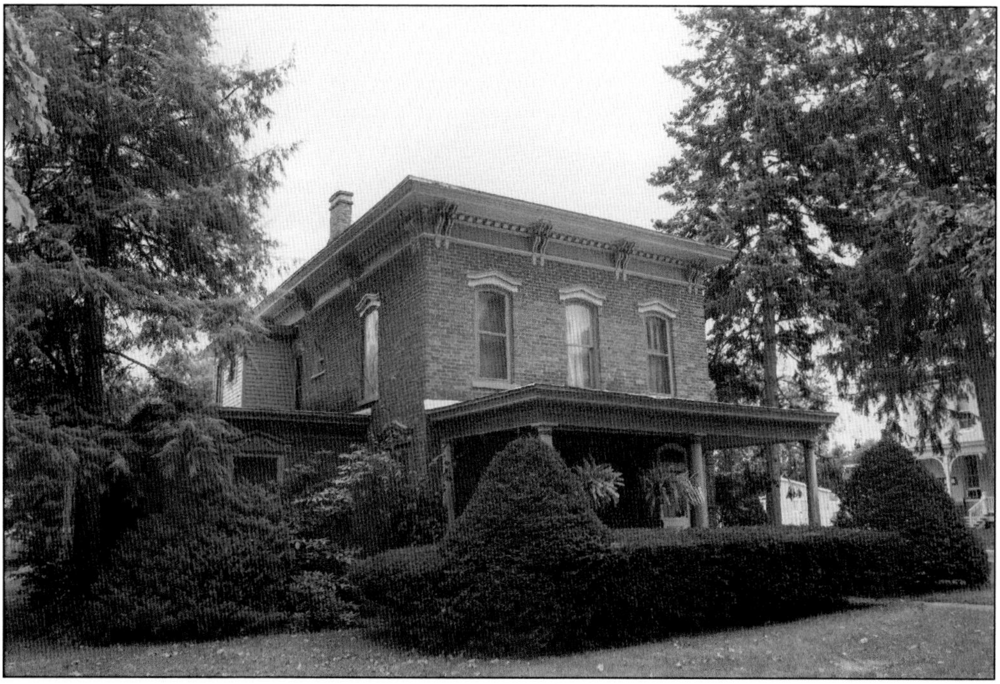

The Solomon Henoch home is a one-and-a-half-story tapestry brick bungalow. It was built in 1922, and its design represents the later development of the Craftsman bungalow. Henoch was one of the later leaders of the Jewish community. In 1915, he and Wilbur Wood took over the Ligonier Refrigerator Company and made it into one of the city's leading employers.

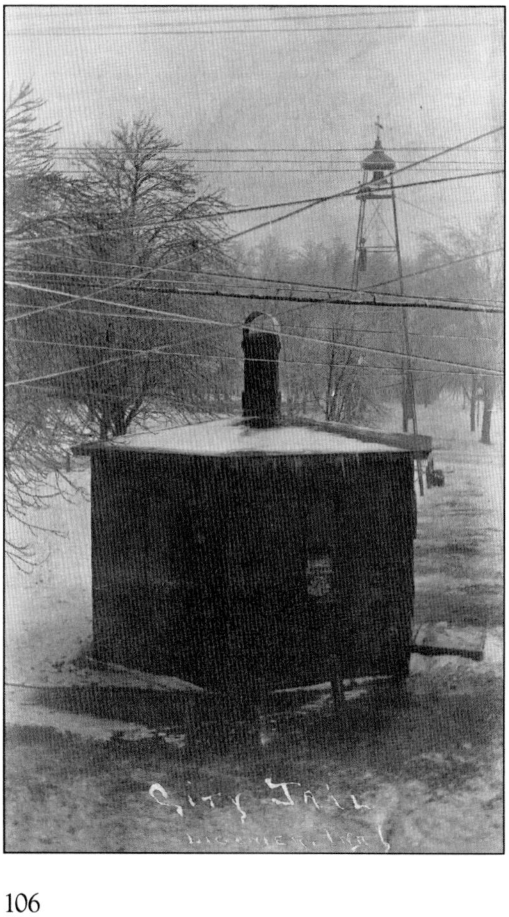


The infamous Ligonier Jail sat on the public square near Third Street, where the city hall would eventually sit in 1914. The 1886 Sanborn Map for Ligonier shows the jail as the only structure on the public square except for the fire bell, which is also shown in this photograph. This calaboose was the second one that existed in Ligonier. It was a hexagonal brick structure with almost solid oak flooring, with the boards laid on their edges and nailed together horizontally.

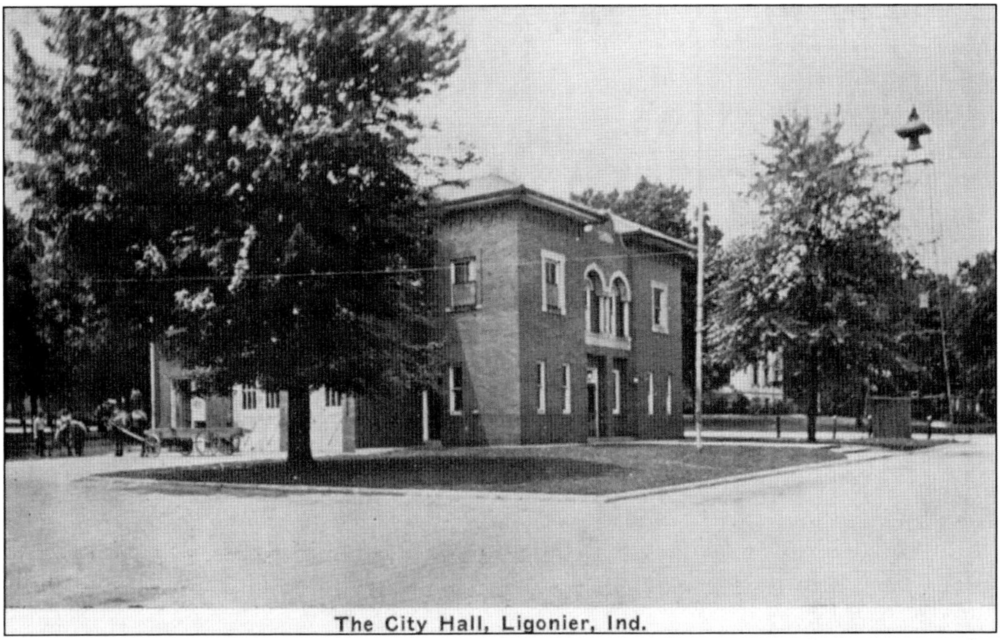


This c. 1915 picture shows the newly constructed 1914 city hall and the fire bell tower to its right. The calaboose is not shown, because it is either hidden behind the city hall building or it was eliminated when the new 1914 city hall was built. The jail is not shown on the 1914 Sanborn Map. Note the horse and wagon on the left side of city hall.

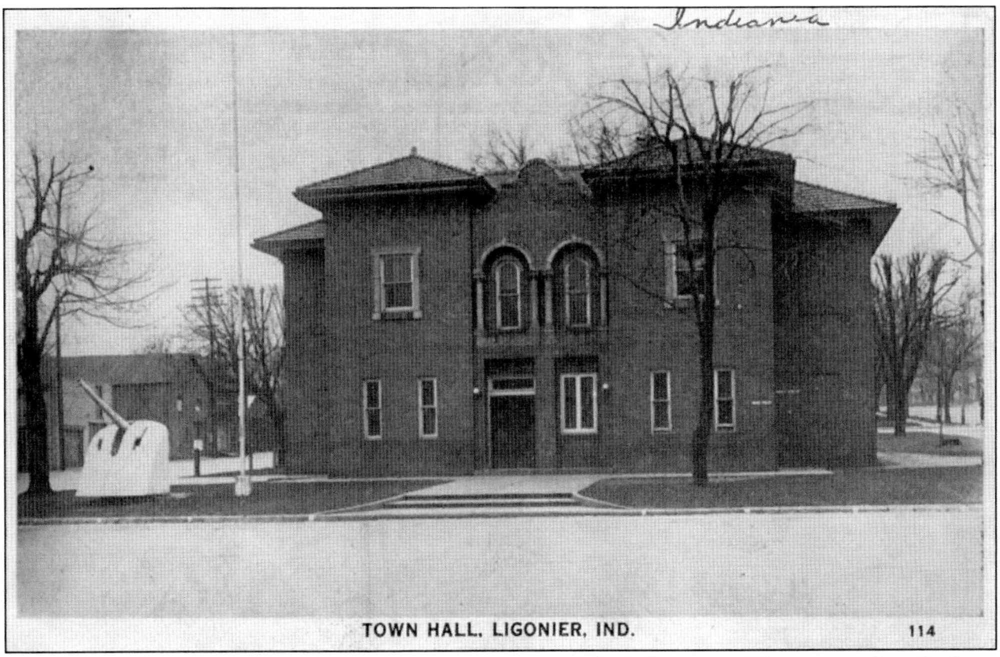


This c. 1920 picture of the 1914 city hall shows a gun in the left corner. The gun is placed where the memorial bell is sitting in 2016. The gun may have come from World War I.

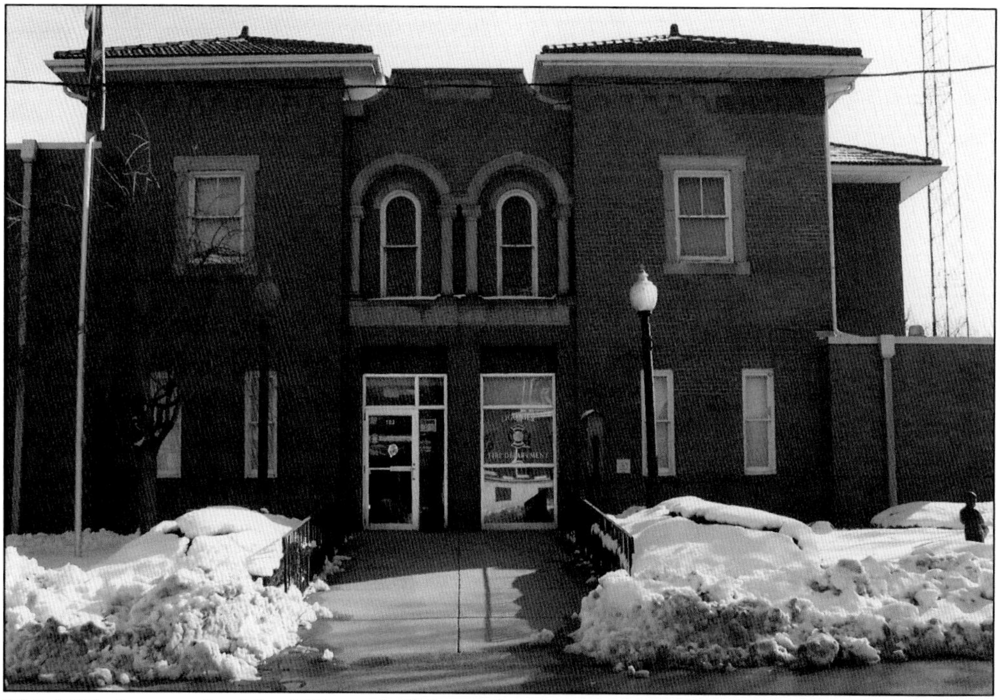

This 2015 photograph of the 1914 city hall shows the old structure still looking very well maintained and presentable. The building is now used as a fire station. There are also heated public restrooms on the northwestern corner of the building.

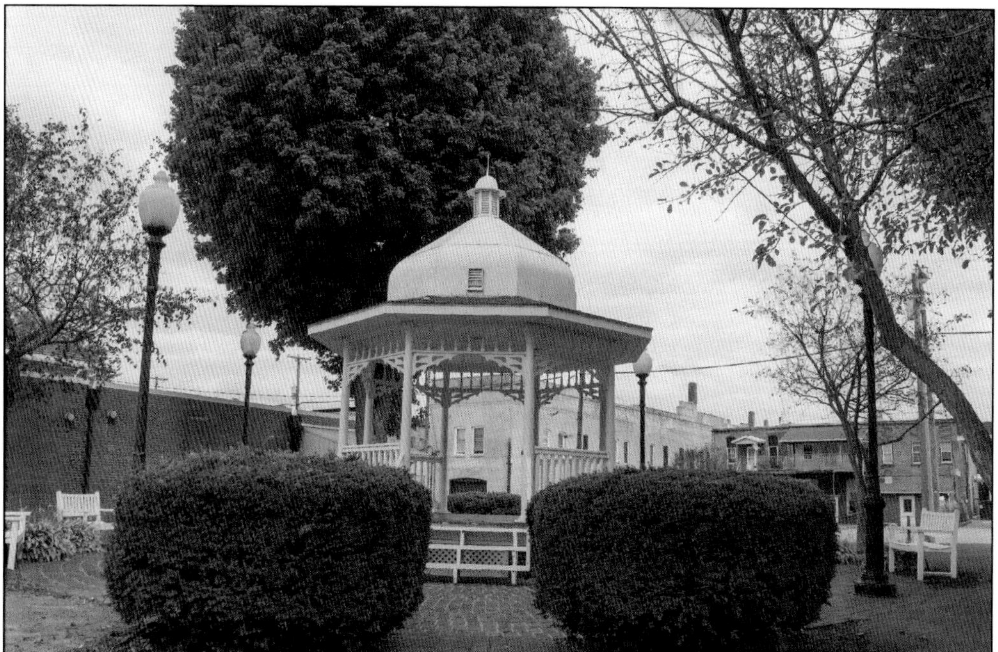

This lovely gazebo is just like one in Ligonier, Pennsylvania. A team went to the Pennsylvania town to measure its gazebo and retuned to Ligonier, Indiana, to build a replica here. They did an excellent job in 1983, and it still looks new and sound.

# *Five*

# THE END APPROACHES

Without the railroad, Ligonier might have never existed. The author prepared a presentation about Halle Goshorn and her career as a clerk on the railroad in Ligonier. The story of her involvement is not lost because she donated all of her photographs and memories to the museum.

Another character in Ligonier's history is William D. Cochran, who dedicated his life to maintaining the history of Ligonier by keeping a 50-volume scrapbook that he donated to the museum.

Ligonier was and still is a fantastic place, and there is not time or space here to illustrate everything. This book contains approximately 200 photographs from a collection of 1,300 covering Ligonier's history. It all comes back to the people, the early settlers who had a vision, who were willing to risk everything for something they believed in, and to the merchants who recognized the potential of a new town.

As the Jewish merchants like the Straus and Mier families began to migrate west to Ligonier, along with a host of other folks of other cultures, each with a talent of his or her own, prosperity followed and the town began to grow. Today as in yesteryear, Ligonier maintains a cultural diversity that allows the town to continue to expand the vision of its forefathers.

As industry made its way into Ligonier, the quality of life continued to increase. Following the jobs for a chance at a better life brings the story to today's mayor, Patty Fisel. As her family was making their way here, they became stuck at the bottom of Stone's Hill, at a time when there were no asphalt roads—only muck, mud, and mire. In the true pioneer spirit, someone came to the rescue and pulled them out and helped them up the hill. This gave them the start they needed and so impressed them that they declared Ligonier their home. There are so many more stories like this of the early days.

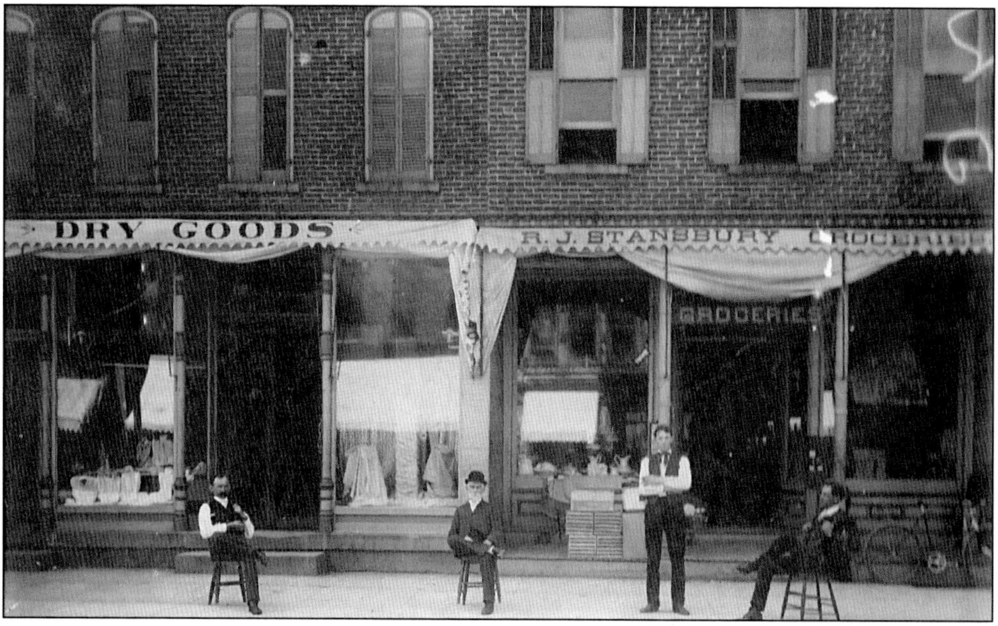


This c. 1900 photograph of the R.J. Stansbury stores on the west side of South Cavin Street includes the grocery store (on the right) at 112 South Cavin Street. The dry goods store (on the left) is located at 114 South Cavin Street. Four unidentified men, likely Stansbury employees or owners, accompany the buildings in this sharp photograph.

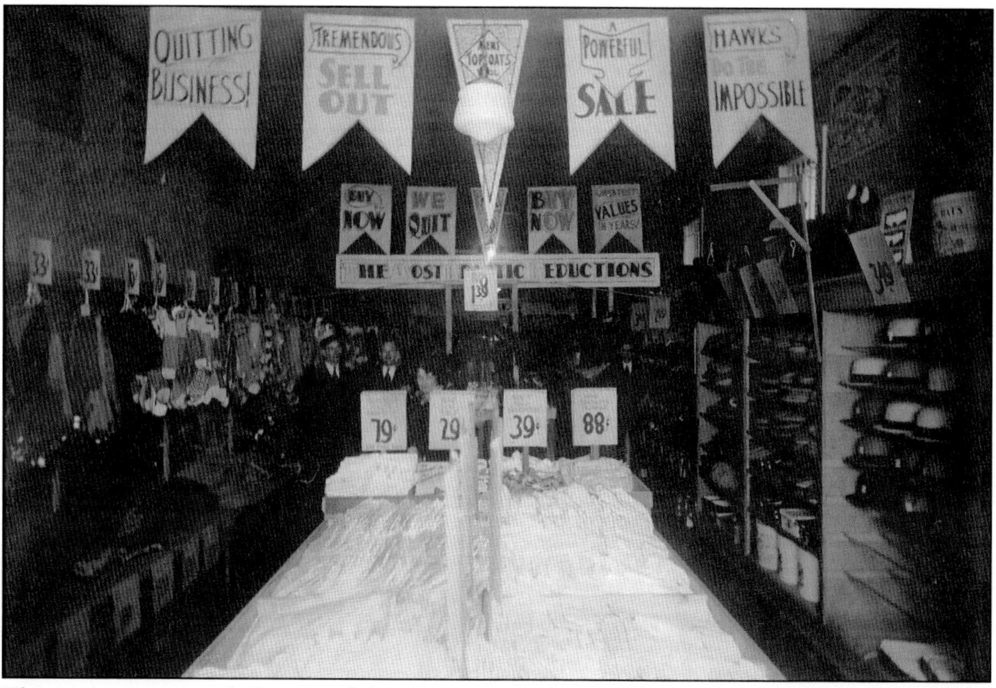


This is a more unusual photograph because it was taken inside a dark store. Pictured is Hawk's Men's Wear, which is going out of business because a new store is in town. Oscar Barch showed up in 1932, and Hawk's left the nest. This store was at 214 South Cavin Street, on the west side of the street. This is a 1932 photograph.

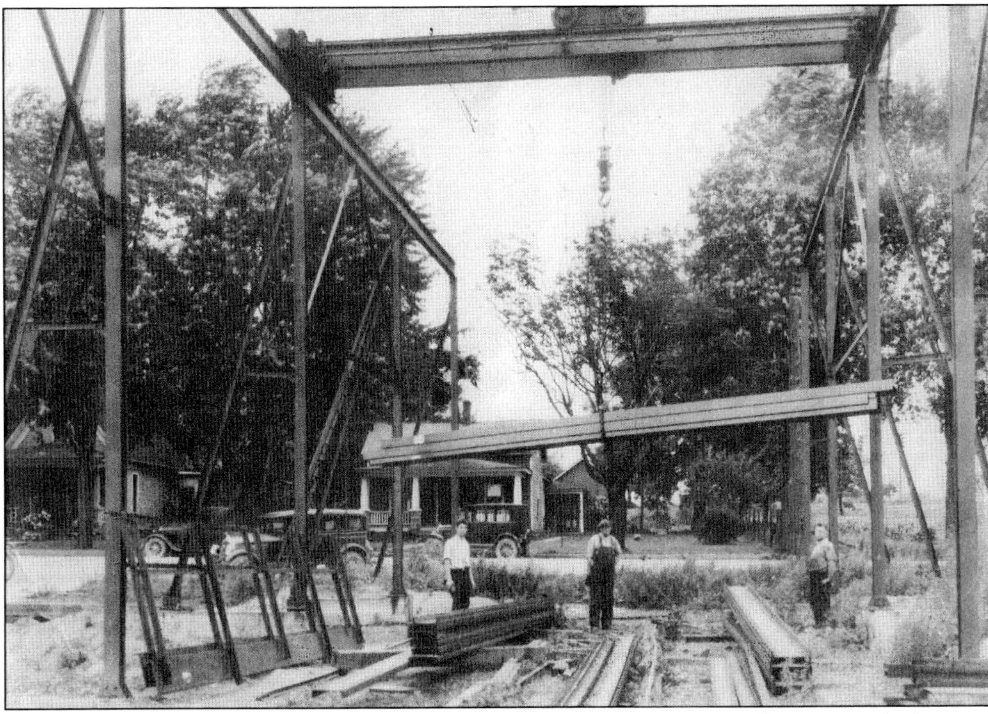

The Bridge and Culvert Company is pictured in Ligonier around 1918. This is near the home of Harley Fisher. The Loeser brothers and C.V. Joseph are some of the workers.

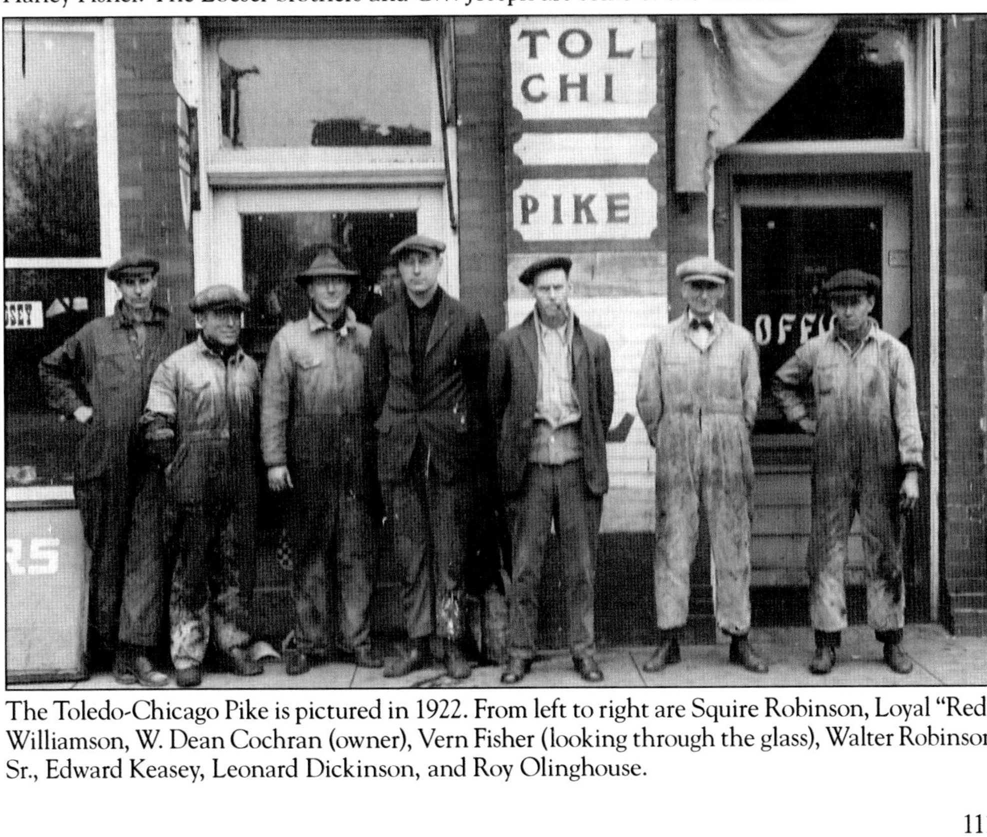


The Toledo-Chicago Pike is pictured in 1922. From left to right are Squire Robinson, Loyal "Red" Williamson, W. Dean Cochran (owner), Vern Fisher (looking through the glass), Walter Robinson Sr., Edward Keasey, Leonard Dickinson, and Roy Olinghouse.

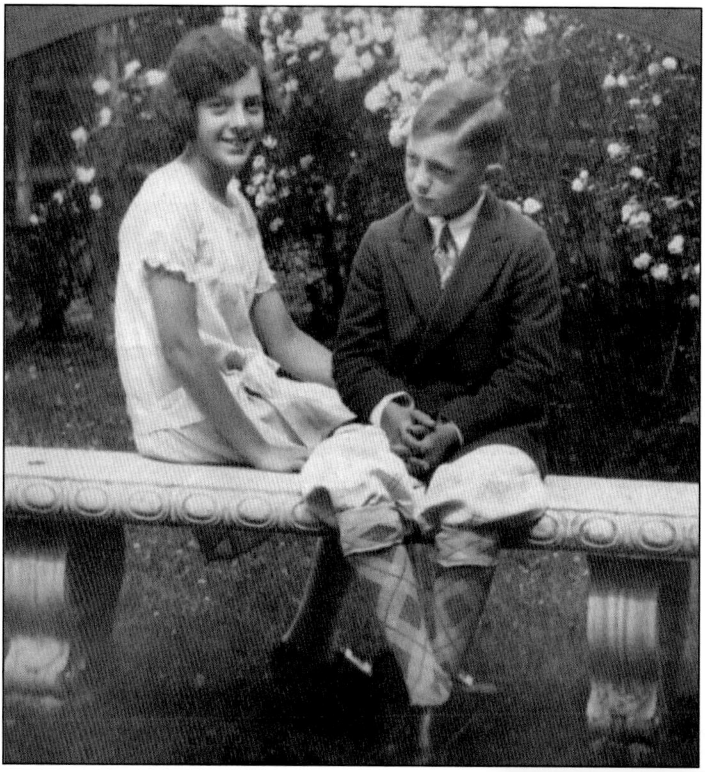

Pictured around 1930, Budd and Norma Levy are the children of Keith and Ruth Levy. They lived in the Jacob Straus home at 210 South Main Street, the first house to the north of the Ligonier Library. Budd's given name was Virgil L. He became an oral surgeon. He was born in 1918 and died in 1996.

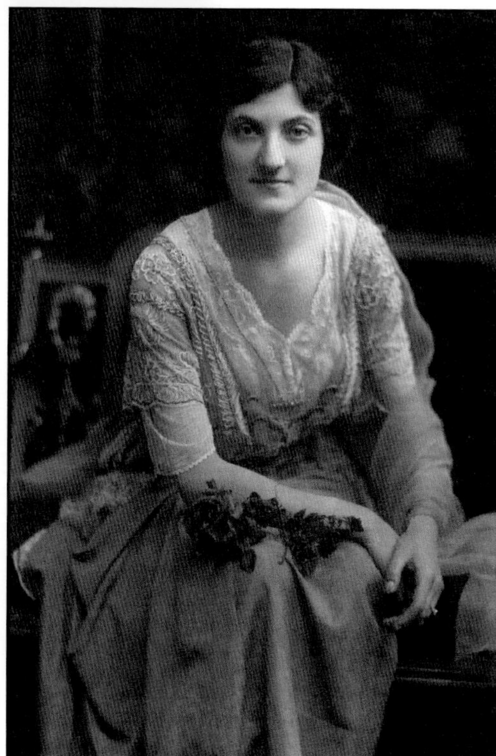

Mayme Miriam Loeser was born in 1866. Mayme married Chester Victor Joseph in 1914 in Noble County. She died in California in 1976. In this c. 1914 photograph, she looks well dressed.

This confirmation certificate for Mayme M. Loeser was issued in 1902 at the Ahavath Sholom Jewish Synagogue at 503 South Main Street.

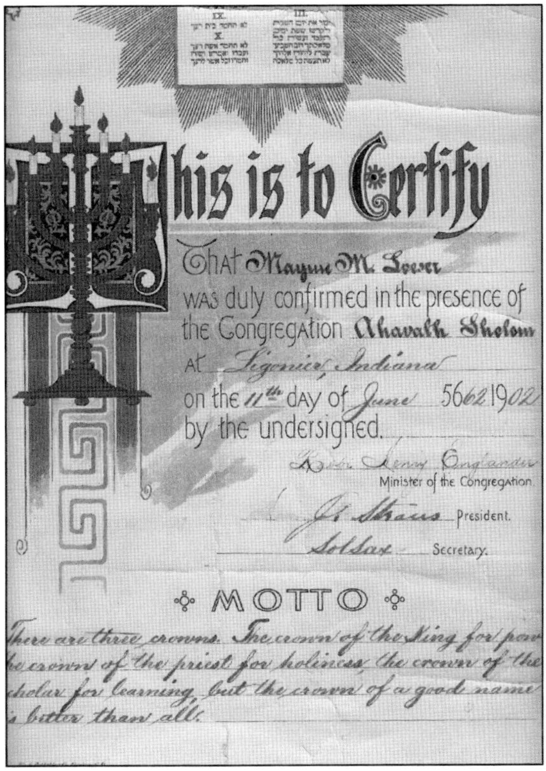

This is to Certify

That Mayme M. Loeser
was duly confirmed in the presence of
the Congregation Ahavath Sholom
At Ligonier, Indiana
on the 11th day of June 5662 1902
by the undersigned.

Rev. Henry Englander
Minister of the Congregation.

J. Straus President.

Sol Sax Secretary.

MOTTO

here are three crowns. The crown of the King for pow
he crown of the priest for holiness, the crown of the
cholar for learning, but the crown of a good name
is better than all.

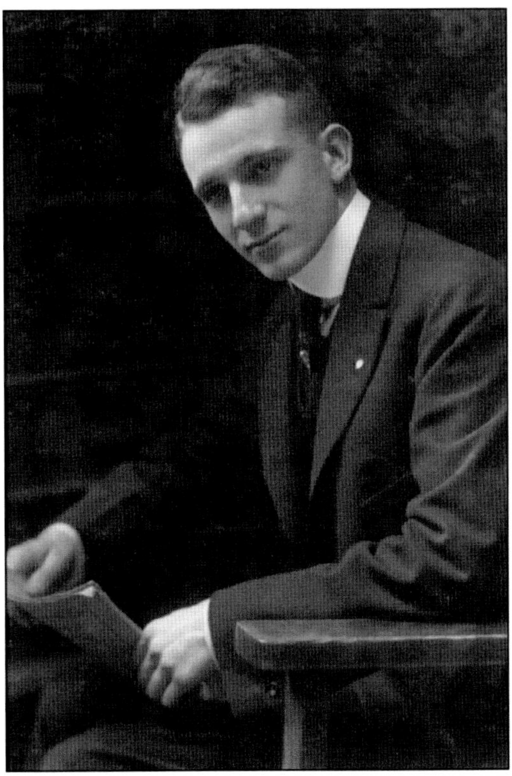

Chester Victor Joseph (pictured around 1914) married Mayme Miriam Loeser on January 27, 1914, in Noble County. They moved to California after their marriage. The Loesers were famous horse importers from Belgium. Their huge farm was on the western edge of Ligonier between US 6 and Union Street. The first county fairs were held on their property.

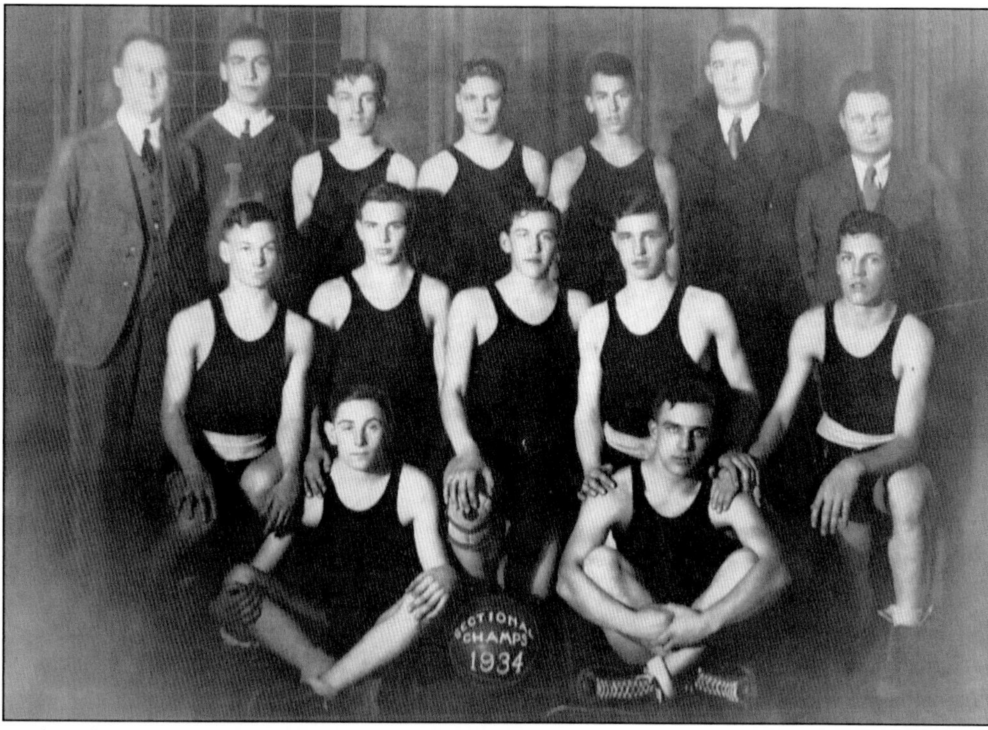


In this photograph of the 1934 Ligonier High School sectional basketball champs are, from left to right, (first row) Max Schlabach and Earl Pollard; (second row) Clair Lepird, Dewey Mayfield, Howard Chrisman, Clyde Mohler, and Jack Lough; (third row) superintendent O.R. Bangs, student manager Edwin Amelking, Richard Mathew, Robert Mayfield, Earnest Shell, coach Edward Fisher, and principal Fred G. Hendrickson.

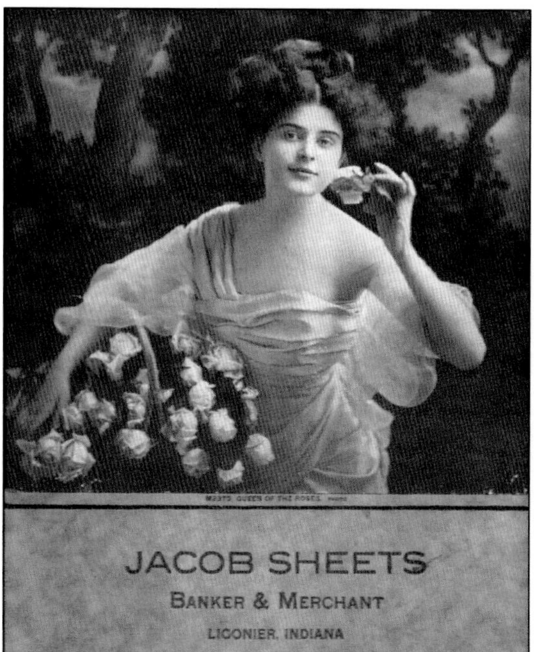


Jacob Sheets had a business at 301 Cavin Street, on the east side of the street where the new city hall sits. His business was also the site of Levy's Furniture. There are some photographs of the spot elsewhere in this book.

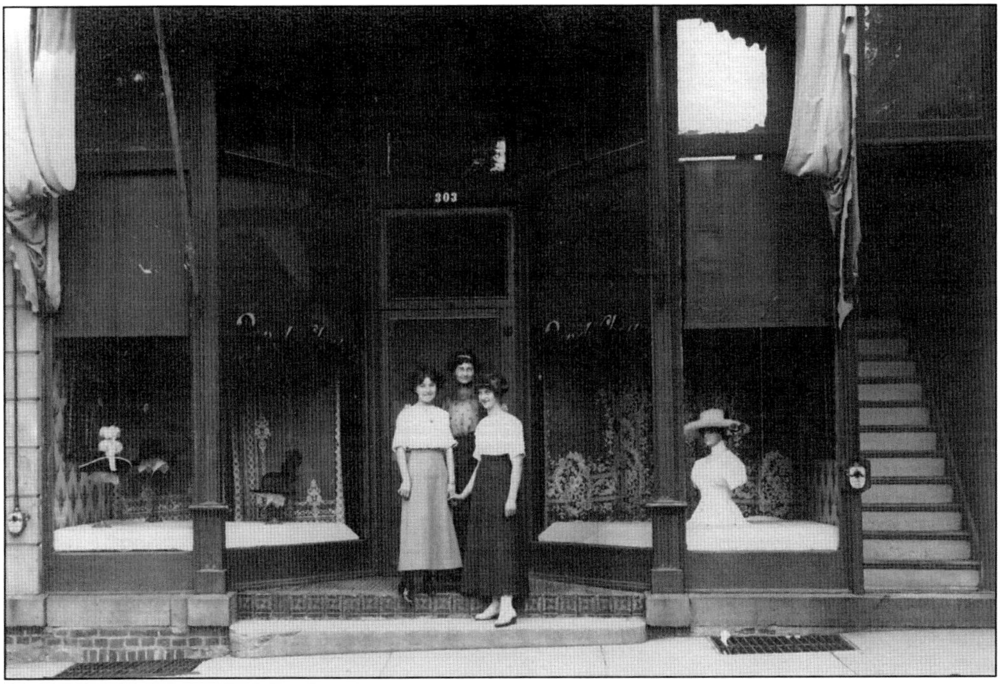


The Bon de Chea was a millinery shop at 303 Cavin Street (east side). Two owners, Wheeler and ? Wilcox, and the mother of one of them are said to be shown here at the entrance to the shop around 1924. Ladies' hats shops were very popular, and the presence of this one indicates that Ligonier was a wealthy town. A woman who worked at such a shop as a clerk remembered that her pay for the year was two hats—one for spring and one for fall.

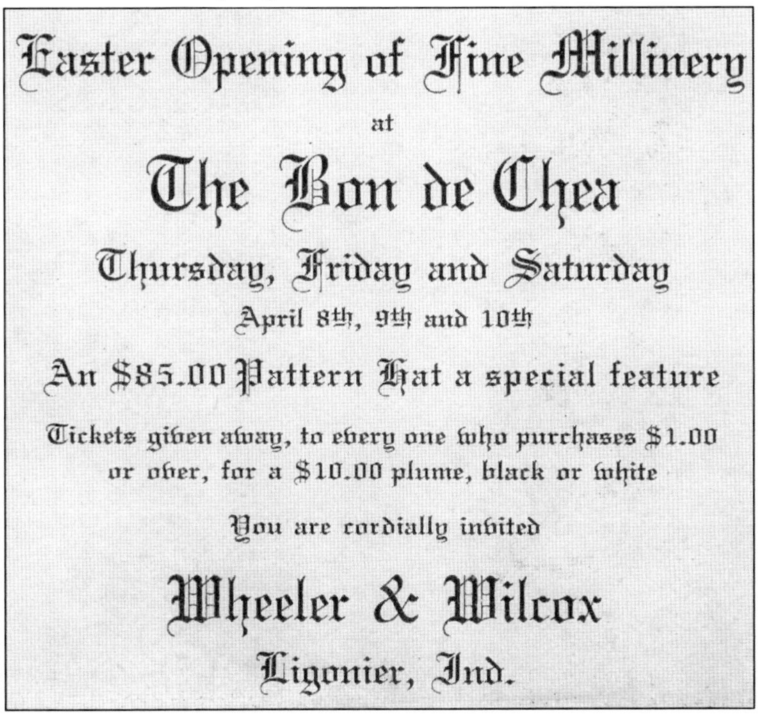


This 1924 advertisement ran to attract people to the Bon de Chea. The attraction might be the $85 hat featured.

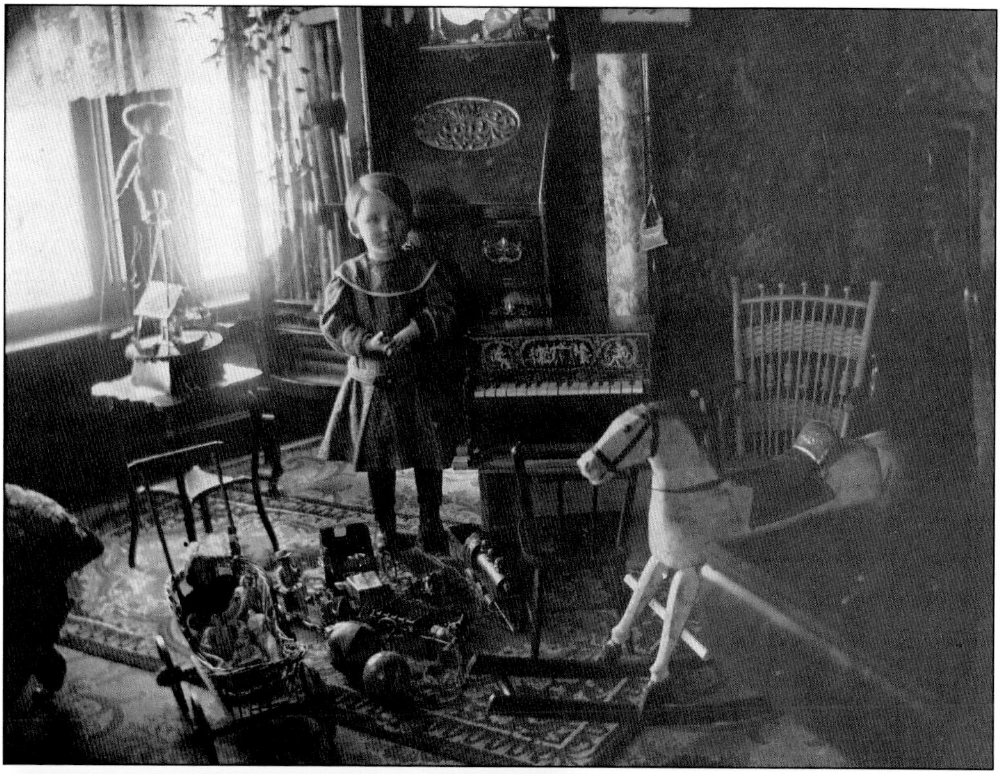

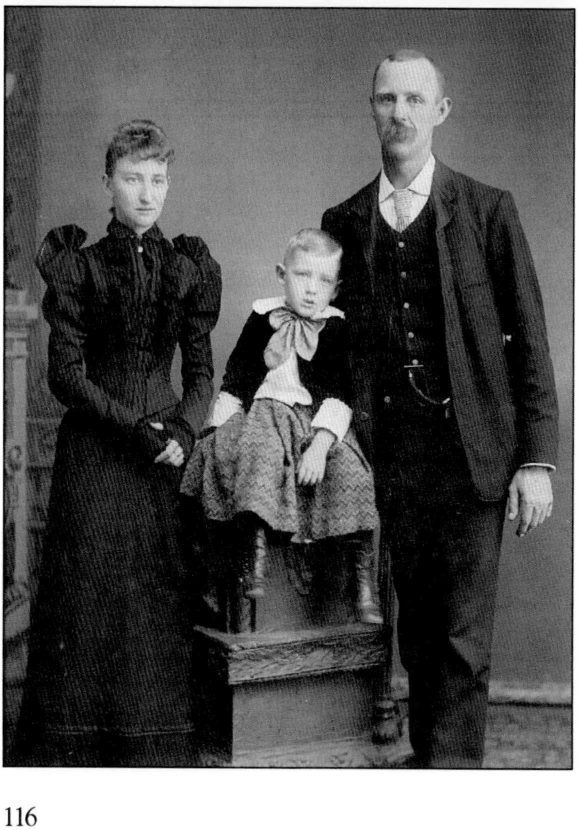

Pictured here is William D. Cochran (1905–1980) as a boy in 1909. He is shown at the Cochran Farm, one mile north of Ligonier on State Road 5. It looks like he had a wonderful set of toys. He is wearing a dress, since it was considered more convenient at that time for young boys to wear dresses.

Pictured are Tom and Minda Wagner and their son Earl Wagner. This family lived next door to the United Brethren church in Ligonier. Ligonier photographers Cornell & Wolf took this photograph. Note the dress Earl is wearing. He is estimated to be four years old, and based on that, the photograph was likely taken in 1893.

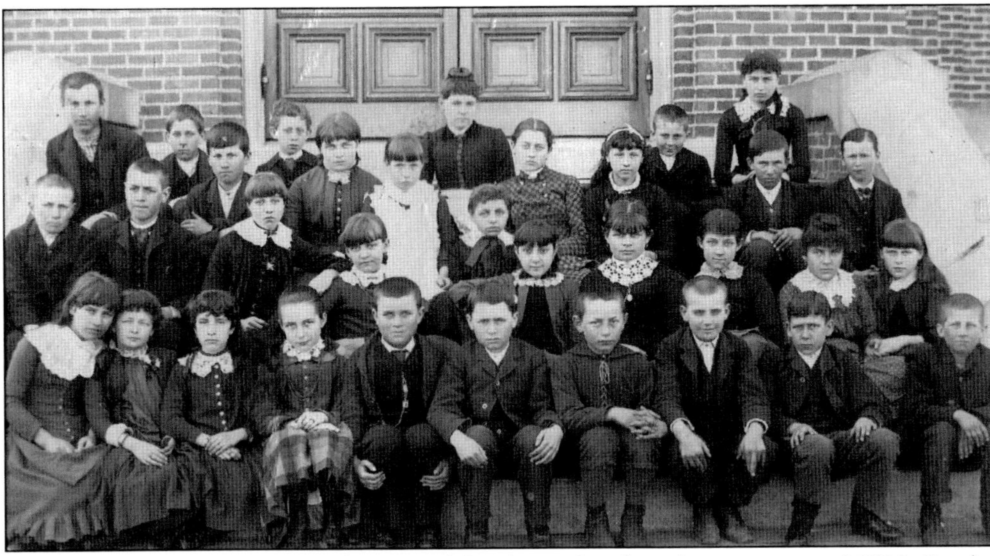

This photograph was taken at the United Brethren church in Ligonier around 1880. Sunday school students are in front of an impressive door. If one looks closely near the center, there are three girls who look like sisters.

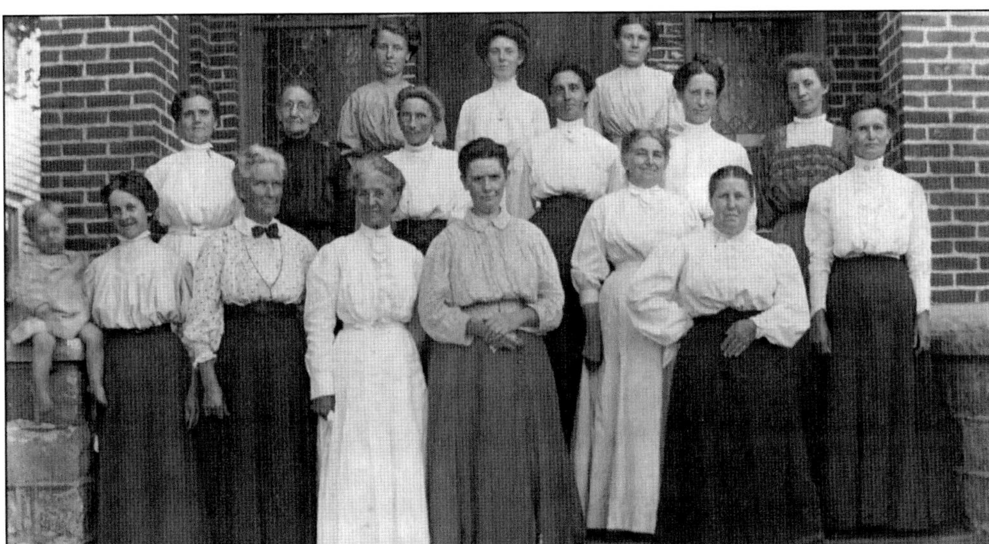

Pictured around 1885 is the United Brethren Ladies Group at Ligonier. Note the little boy on the stone pillar on the left side of the porch. The United Brethren church was at the corner of Miller and Cavin Streets. From left to right are (first row) Merle Chiddister; his mother, Maggie Chiddister; ? McDowell; ? Pancake; ? Yerger; Rachel Billman; ? McDaniel; and ? Karshner; (second row) unidentified; Samantha Stansbury; Mrs. Will Krane (?); unidentified; Erma Golden; and Blanche Bellman; (third row) Alta Yerger; unidentified; and Eva Cook.

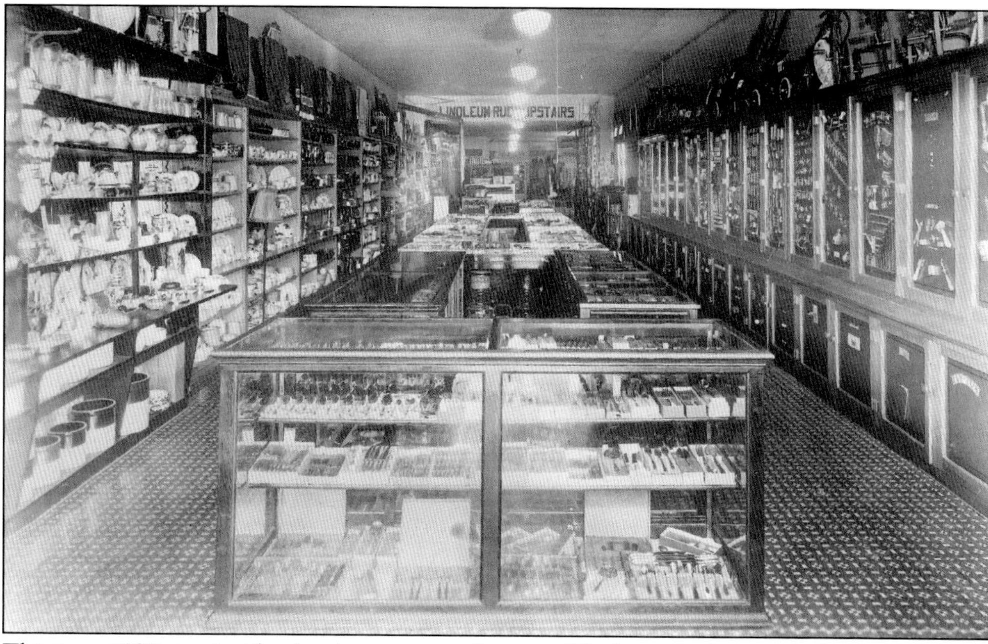

This is a c. 1930 view inside a hardware store in Ligonier. The kerosene heaters in the center and the stovepipe in the back left show this is an earlier photograph. The floor looks like inlaid tile.

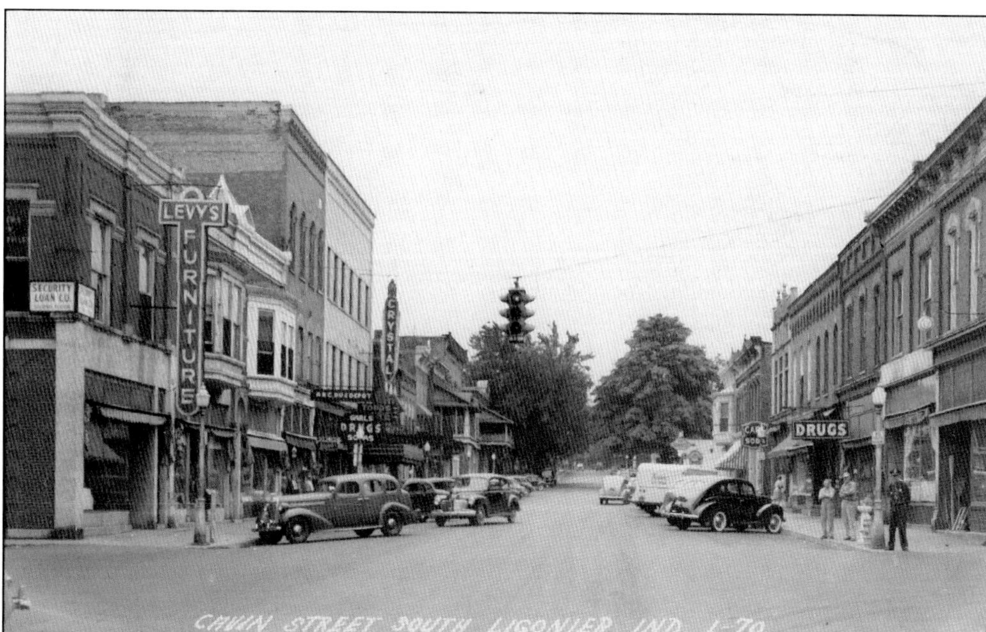

This is a view looking south along Cain Street from Third Street. The Bon de Chea is on the left near the second-floor bay windows. The Crystal Theatre sign is farther south on the left, and the Mier Bank is halfway down the right/west side. Today, most of the buildings in the first block on the left have been replaced with Ligonier City Hall.

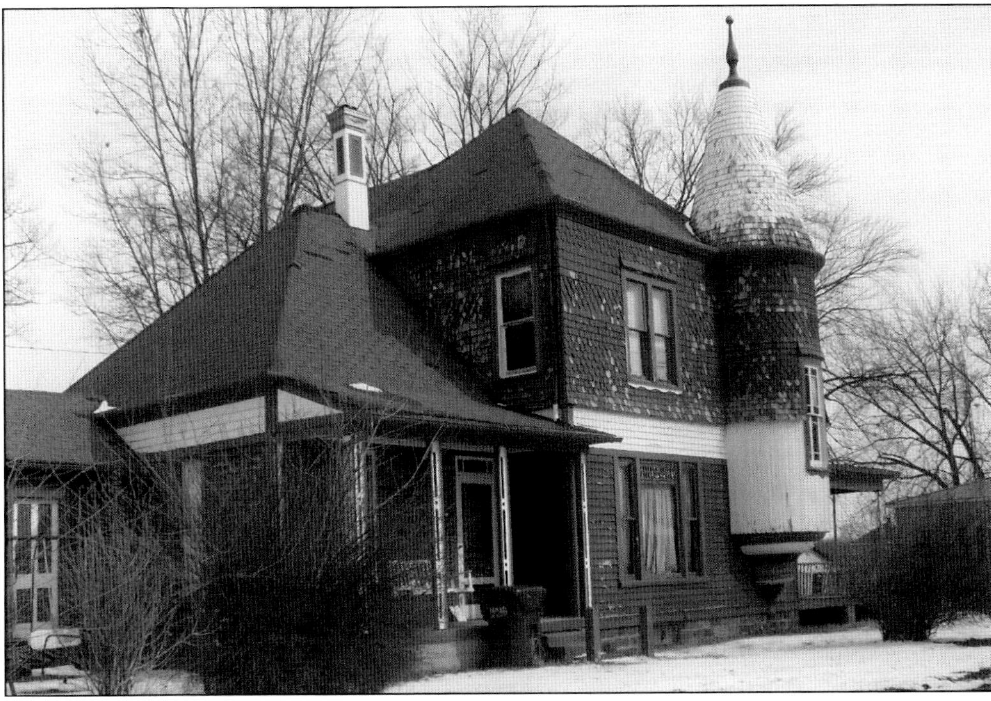

This unusual Queen Anne–style home built in 1895 is still standing in Ligonier in 2016 at 108 South Martin Street. It used to be the Methodist Episcopal parsonage. Sidney J. Osgood was the architect.

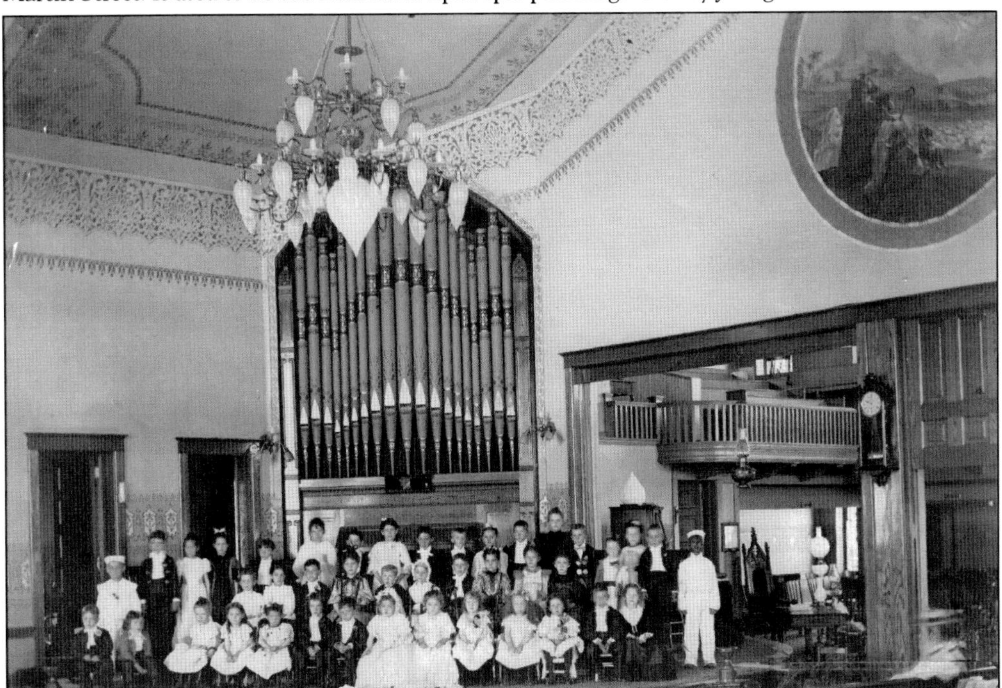

This c. 1930 photograph shows the inside of the Methodist church before a fire in 1933 destroyed it completely. A replacement built after the fire still stands at the corner of Fourth and Martin Streets. Look at the quality of the workmanship on the walls and ceiling. The church sat 1,000 people.

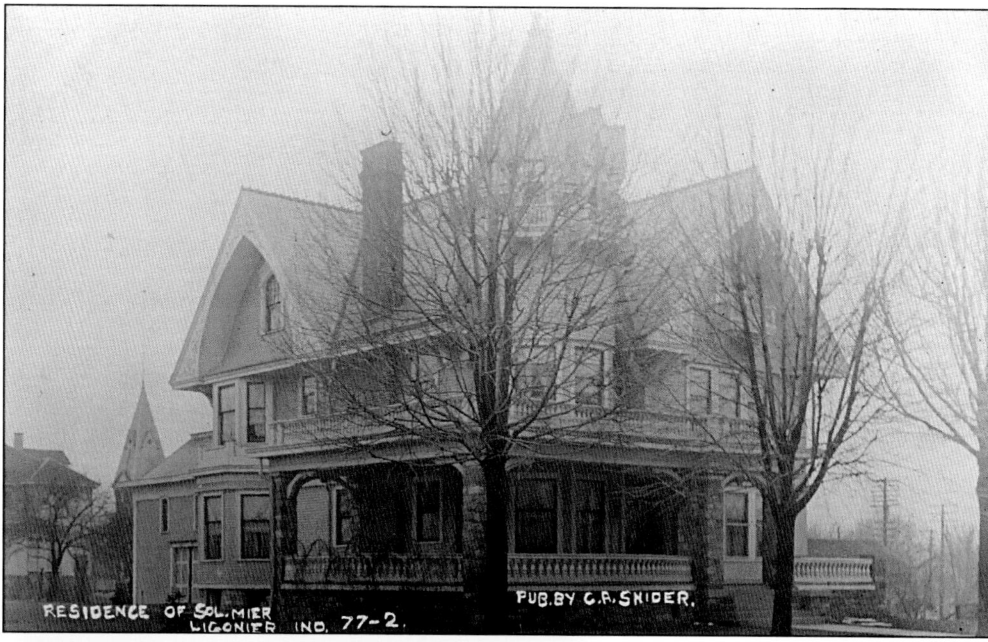


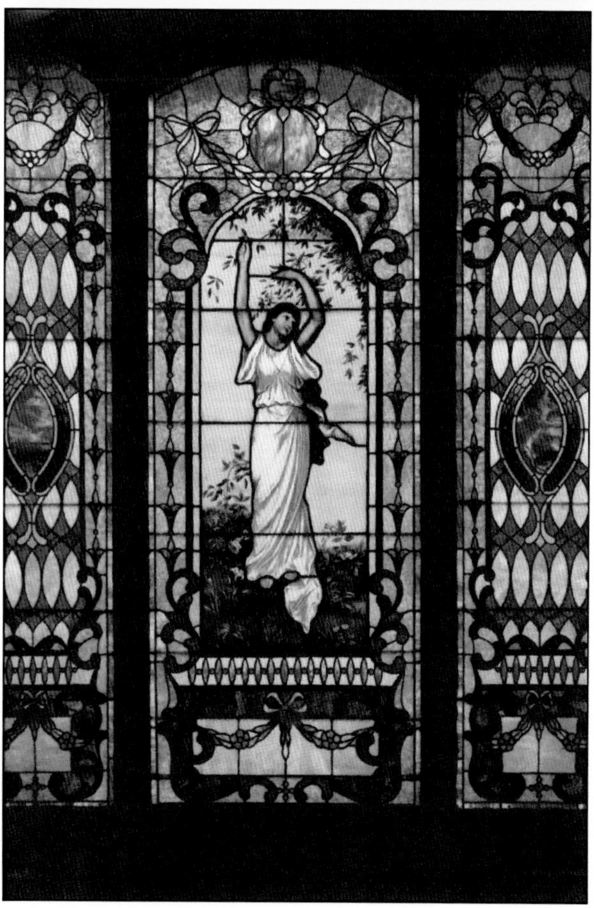

This photograph is of the Solomon Mier Manor (now a bed-and-breakfast) at 508 South Cavin Street. Built around 1898, the manor still looks great today, although the stained-glass windows were removed when a former owner sold the house. This home is one block east of the Jewish temple, seen on the left side of the photograph. (Courtesy of Amanda Smith, Solomon Mier Manor.)

The previous owner showed the windows in the home when he was selling the house. When the buyer took possession, the stained glass had been removed and replaced with ordinary glass. This building is listed in the National Register of Historic Places. (Courtesy of Amanda Smith, Solomon Mier Manor.)

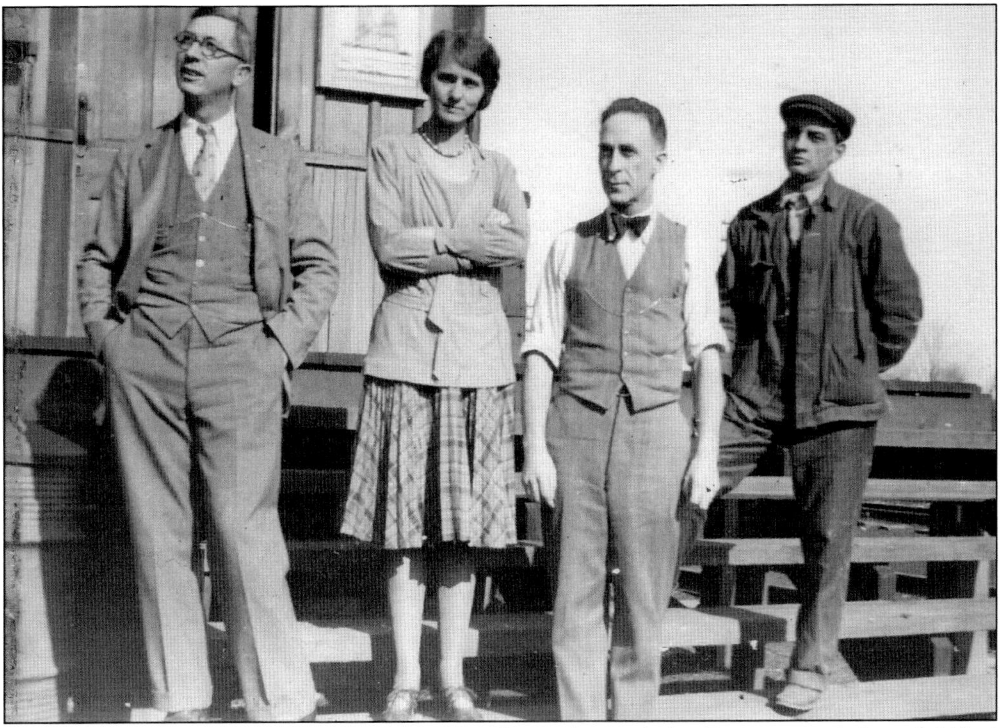

From left to right, G.C. Waffle, freight agent; Halle Goshorn, clerk; I.R. Stevens, clerk; and Alfred Jefferies, warehouseman, are on the steps of the Ligonier Freight House, located along the New York Central Railroad tracks in 1920. Goshorn knew William Cochran via the United Brethren church, so her memories were saved for history by Cochran at the Ligonier Historical Museum.

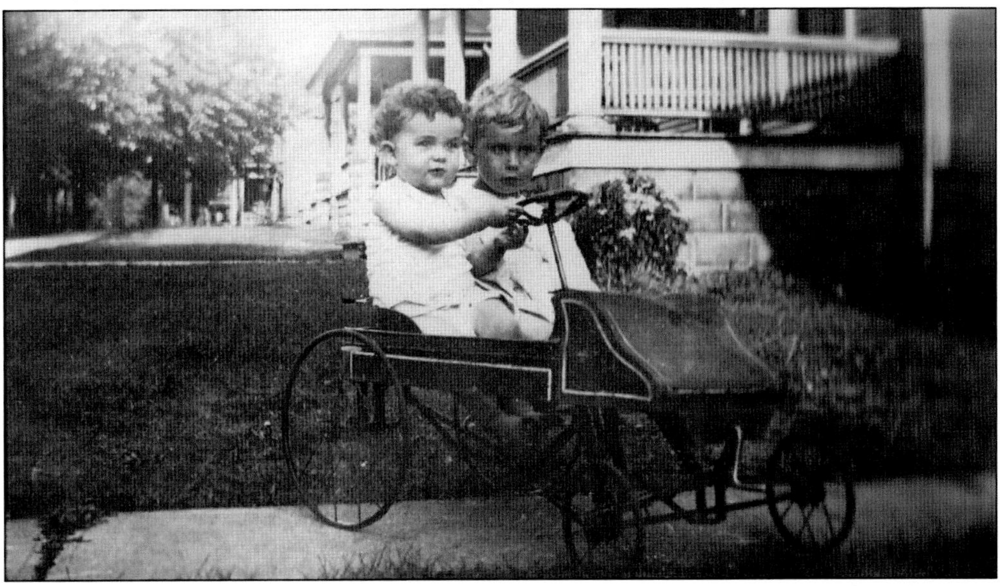

Merrill Hire Jr. (left) is taking his unidentified friend for a ride around 1922. The quality of toys can indicate the wealth of a family. The curls really helped identify this boy. An album was donated to the Ligonier Historical Museum so that the memories that brought so much joy to this family can now be observed. Hire died in a plane crash in Costa Rica at an early age.

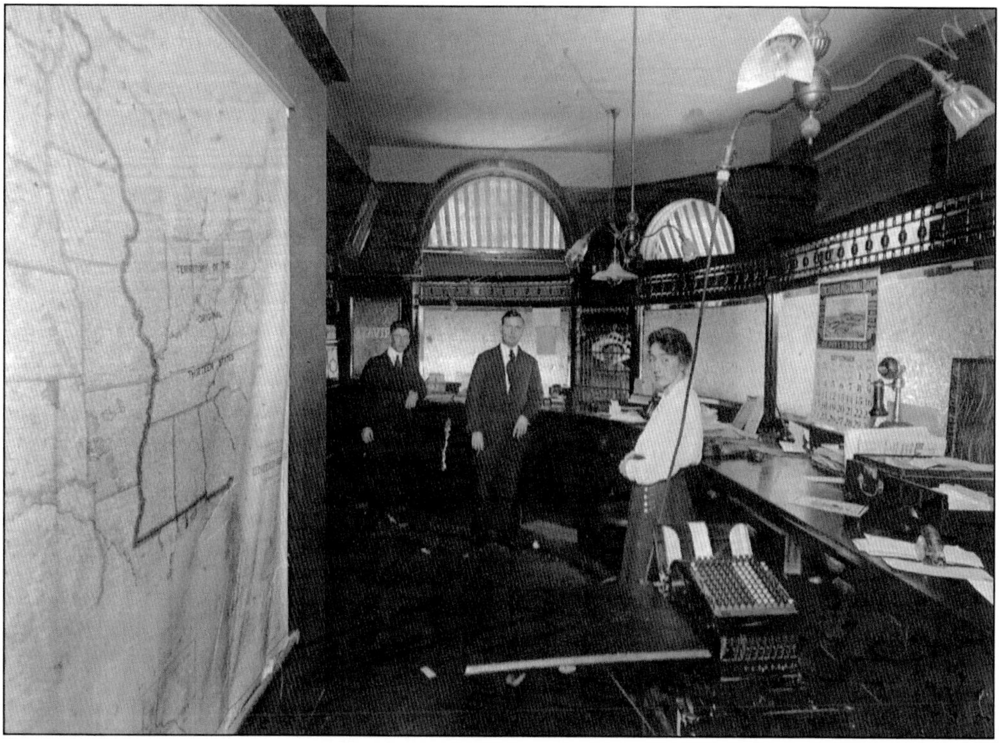

This photograph was taken inside the Citizens Bank at 222 South Cavin Street. One can see that electricity is available, but outlets are in short supply. A cord was run to an adapter in place of one of the lightbulbs.

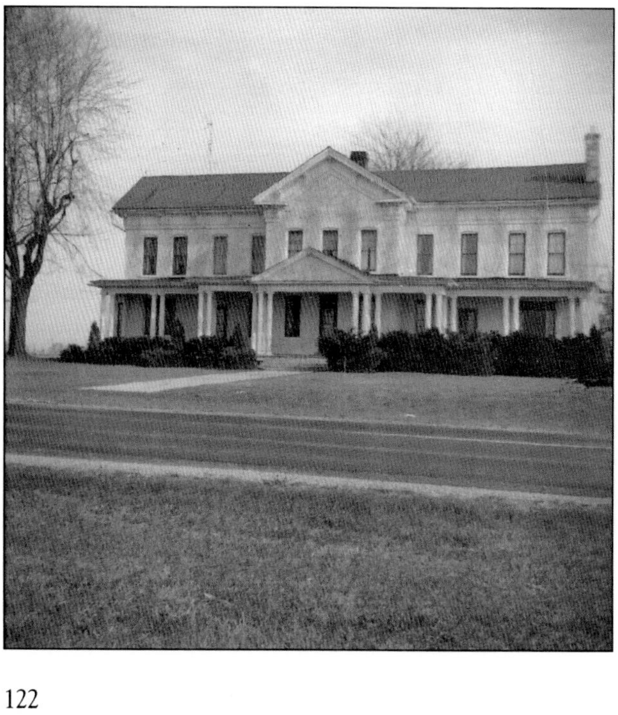

This "modest" home is the birthplace of William D. Cochran, about one mile north of Ligonier on State Road 5. The home has been in the family over 100 years and has 20 to 23 rooms. It stands today in the same place and is owned by a one of Cochran's relatives. William D. Cochran preserved many of these photographs in his 50 volumes of scrapbooks, which are now preserved at the Ligonier Historical Museum.

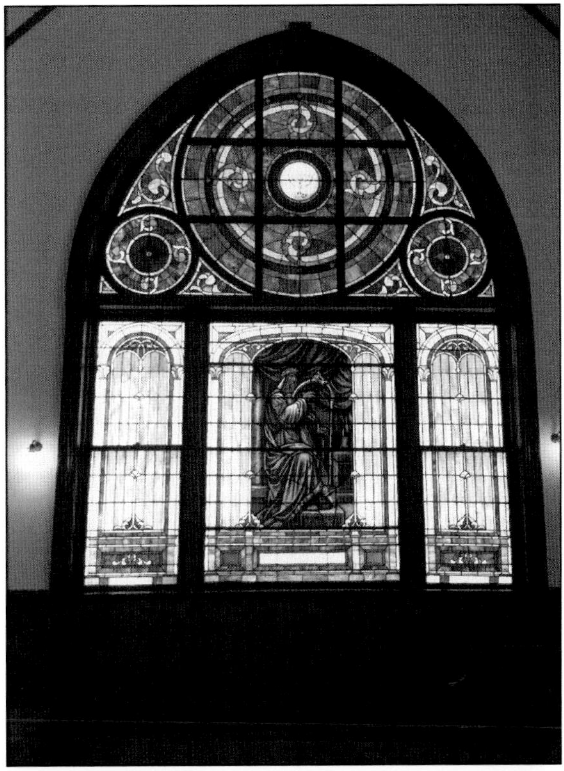

At right is the south window in the Ahavath Sholom Synagogue at 503 South Main Street, and below is the north one. Currently the home of the Ligonier Historical Museum, the building is for sale. The windows were donated in 1889 by members of the synagogue.

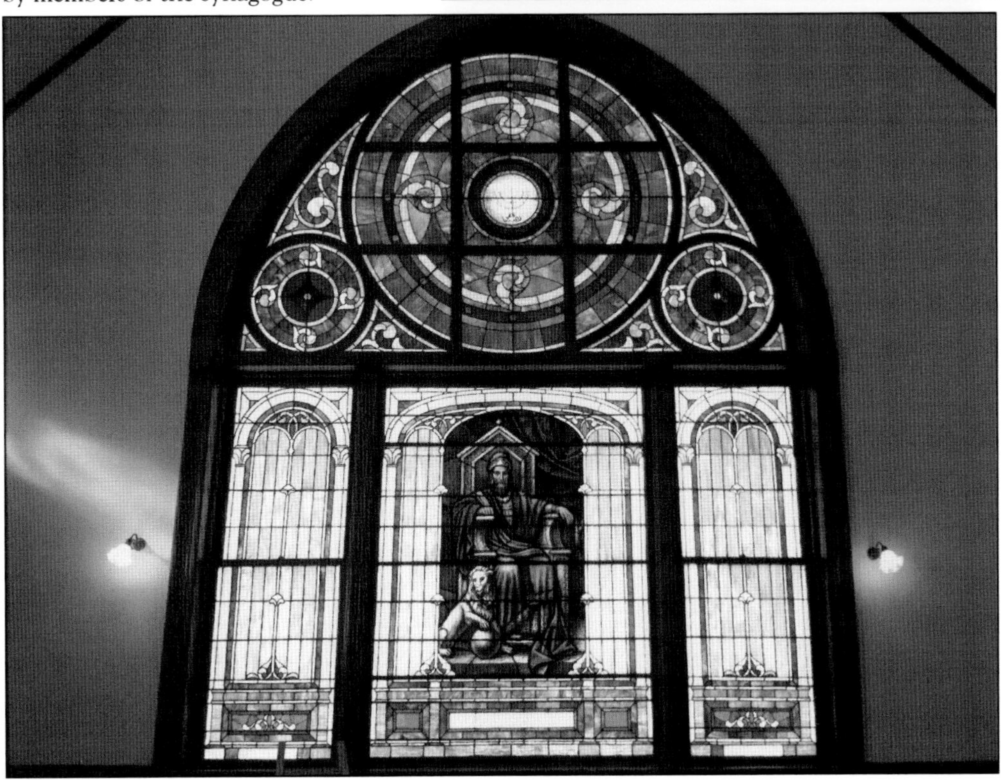

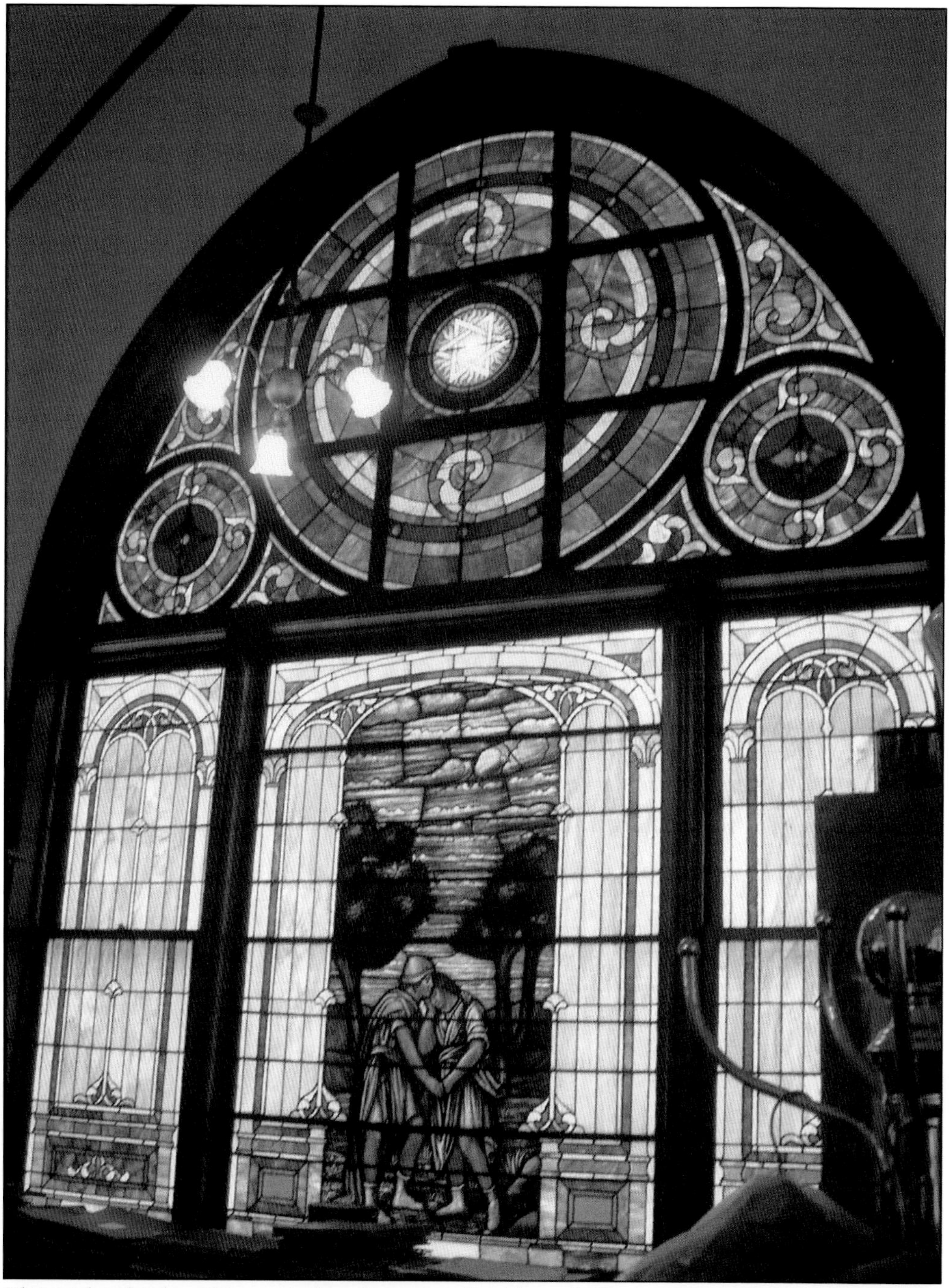

This is the third, and last, window shown in the Ahavath Sholom Synagogue at the Ligonier Historical Museum at 503 South Main Street in Ligonier.

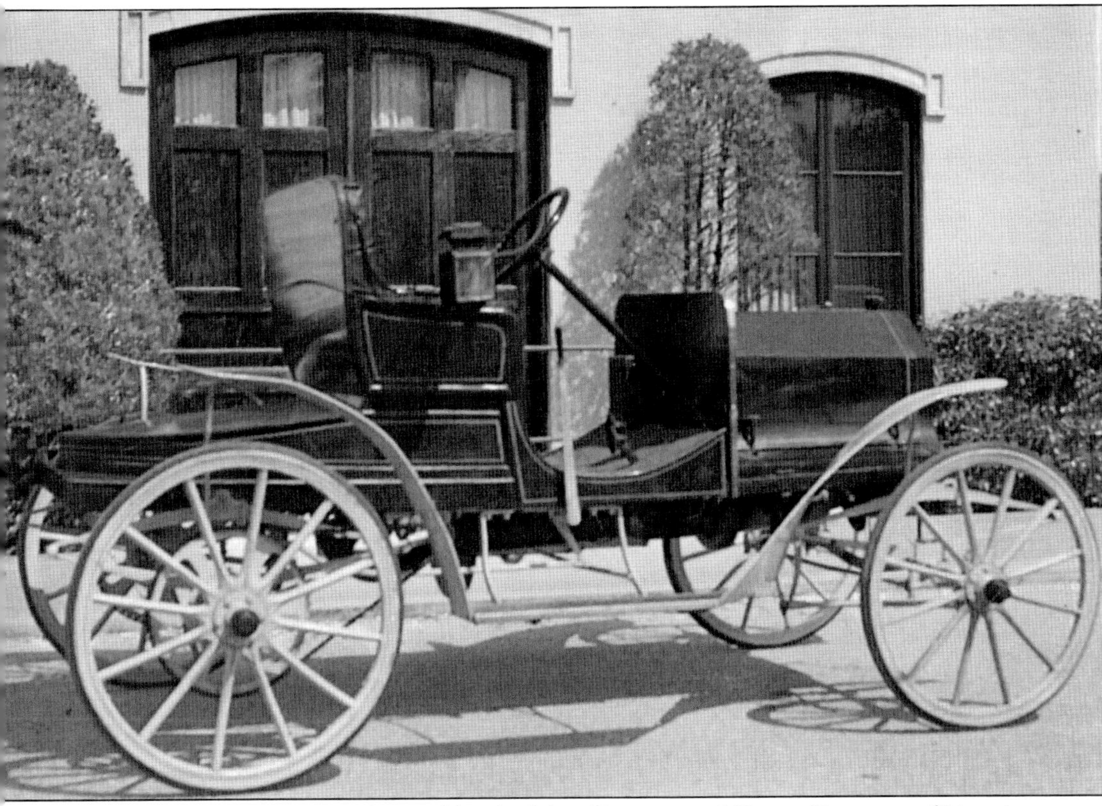

This is a Mier Carriage, manufactured by the Mier Carriage and Buggy Company of Ligonier, Indiana, around 1909. The car sold for $600 in 1910. It was probably not popular for winter driving, but it was a start on the new way of getting around town. Solomon Mier was the owner of the company.

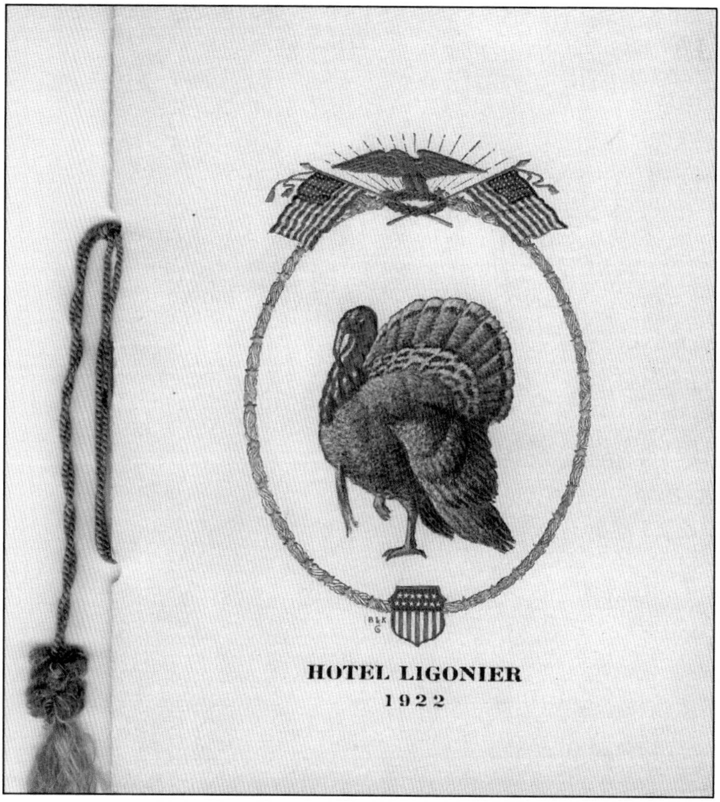


Owner/manager John Boyts of the Ligonier Hotel invited people staying at the hotel or anyone who just wanted a nice meal to come to the Thanksgiving dinner in 1922.

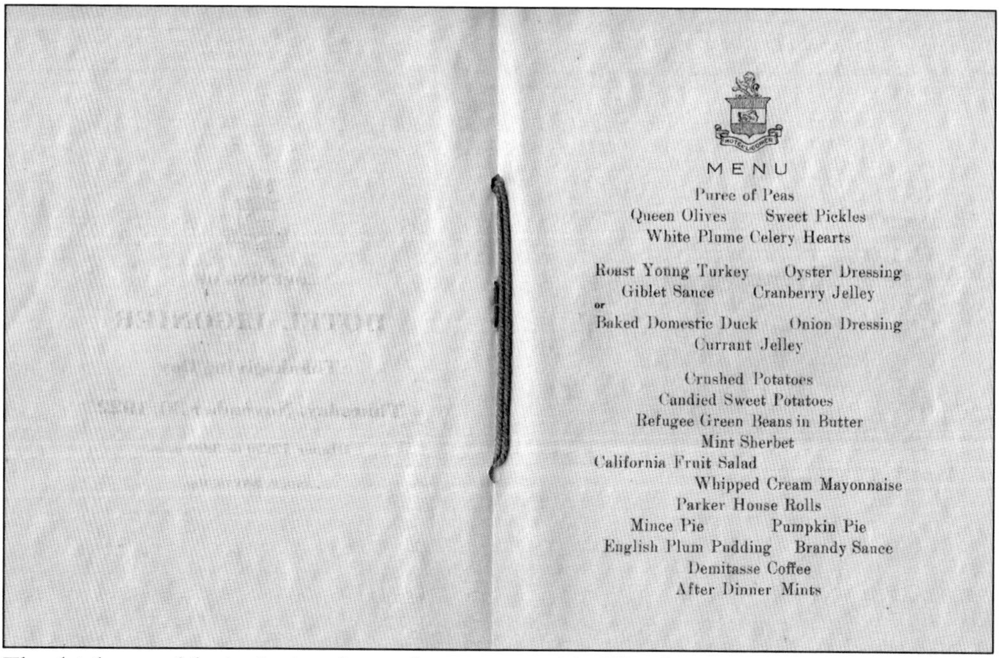

MENU

Puree of Peas
Queen Olives Sweet Pickles
White Plume Celery Hearts

Roast Young Turkey Oyster Dressing
Giblet Sauce Cranberry Jelley
or
Baked Domestic Duck Onion Dressing
Currant Jelley

Crushed Potatoes
Candied Sweet Potatoes
Refugee Green Beans in Butter
Mint Sherbet
California Fruit Salad
Whipped Cream Mayonnaise
Parker House Rolls
Mince Pie Pumpkin Pie
English Plum Pudding Brandy Sauce
Demitasse Coffee
After Dinner Mints

The third page of the invitation shows what was served for Thanksgiving. The menu looks pretty fancy. John Boyts also owned or managed the South Shore Inn on Lake Wawasee. John only had an eighth-grade education, but he accomplished a lot with what he had.

# Bibliography

Alvord, Samuel E. *Alvord's History of Noble County, Indiana*. Indianapolis: B.F. Bowen, 1902.

Beckley, Charles S. "Ligonier, Indiana." *Interurban Journal Supplement* (January 7, 1915): 1–16.

Goldman, Marilyn. *The Wilkinson Quilt Company—America's Original Maker of Fine Quilts—1908–1943*. Muncie, IN: Pengad Publishers, 2015.

Goldman, Marilyn and Marguerite Wiebusch. *Quilts of Indiana: Crossroads of Memories (Indiana Quilt Registry Project)*. Bloomington: Indiana University Press. 1991.

*Ligonier Centennial: 1835–1935*. Ligonier Historical Museum.

Ligonier Sesquicentennial Committee. *Ligonier, Indiana: Memories of the First 150 Years, 1835–1985*. Ligonier: Ligonier Sesquicentennial Committee, 1985.

Moerchen, Jeff. *Ligonier: A Photographic Essay*. Bloomington: Indiana University Press, 2011.

Schwartz, Lois Fields. *The Jews of Ligonier—an American Experience*. Fort Wayne: Indiana Jewish Historical Society, 1978.

Wertheimer, Leon. Transcribed notes of Leon Wertheimer's dictation, June 7, 1963.

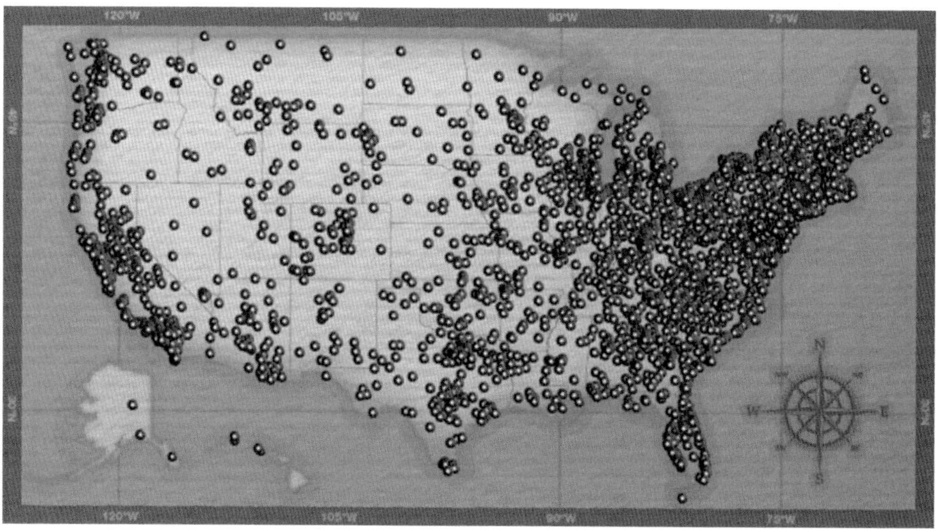